At the Helm

AN ARTIST'S FIGHT THAT EXPOSED FORECLOSURE BUILT ON FORGED DOCUMENTS

Leena Hannonen

Sisu Vision, San Diego, California

Copyright

At the Helm:
An Artist's Fight That Exposed Foreclosure Built On Forged Documents

The events described in this book are based on court records, certified government documents, expert testimony, and the author's personal recollection. All documents referenced are part of the public record or are included in the appendices available at www.leenadesign.com/mybook. Names have not been changed.

Published by

SISU VISION
4231 Balboa Ave, Suite 732
San Diego CA 92117

ISBN 978-0-9897003-9-9

First Edition, 2026
Printed in the United States of America

Table of Contents

A Note on the Record

Everything in this book happened. The documents are real. The court transcripts are real. The signatures, and the forgeries, are real. Names have not been changed. Cases are cited by number. The appeal referenced in these pages is pending before the California Court of Appeal, Fourth Appellate District (San Diego) as of the date of publication.

I couldn't have invented this even if I tried.

— L.H.

Foreword

I have spent years sitting across from homeowners who came to me with the same look. Not anger, not grief — something closer to disorientation. It is the look of someone who followed the rules, did what they were told, and still ended up in a courtroom they never expected to enter, facing an institution that seemed to have unlimited paperwork and unlimited patience.

Most of them had the same story in different variations. They called the servicer. They submitted the documents. They were told their loan modification was under review, then denied. They were told the foreclosure was proceeding because they had defaulted, as if the default had happened independently of everything that came before it.

What they rarely knew was why.

I knew Leena Hannonen's case before I knew Leena. The pattern she uncovered — forged notary signatures, fabricated assignments, documents created after the fact to create the appearance of legal authority that never actually existed — is not unique to Julian, California. It is not unique to U.S. Bank, Specialized Loan Servicing, or MERS. I have seen variations of it in case after case, state after state, courthouse after courthouse.

When I did meet her, I recognized immediately that she was not looking for someone to solve her problem. She was looking for a method. She took everything I had developed over years of working foreclosure cases, absorbed it completely, and applied it with a precision and persistence I rarely see. She mapped the forgery pattern across multiple counties, identified the notaries, obtained the state certifications, and built a case that most attorneys told her couldn't be won. She followed my methodology further than most people are willing to go — further, frankly, than I expected anyone to go alone. When her case finally reached trial, she had proved what I had seen in hundreds of cases but rarely seen documented so completely in open court.

After that, she came to me with a different question: how do we make this accessible to everyone else? That became David v. Goliath: The Homeowner's Guide to Fighting the Mortgage Machine — a course Leena conceived and outlined, built on the methodology she had used to fight her own case, and that we developed together. The goal was simple: give homeowners the tools before they need a miracle, not after.

What is unique about Leena's case is that she proved it. Not suspected it. Not merely alleged it. Proved it. With state-certified records, forensic handwriting analysis, and testimony from the notary herself, under oath, saying: that is not my signature. I did not sign that document. I was not there.

And the court acknowledged it. Called it compelling. Called it uncontroverted. Then issued what it called an equitable remedy that canceled nothing, specified nothing, and changed nothing. The property value it awarded was offset to zero. The instruments it claimed to cancel were never identified. The law that required voiding forged documents was acknowledged, cited, and quietly set aside. That is not a system that failed. That is a system that performed exactly as designed — absorbing proof of fraud, containing its consequences, and ensuring that the machinery kept moving. That sequence is not an accident. It is the system working exactly as designed.

I have watched homeowners lose everything trying to prove this in court. Most ran out of time, money, or will long before they got to trial. Leena did not. She showed up sixty-four times. She learned the language. She built the case.

At the Helm is the book I wish I could hand to every homeowner who has ever sat across from me with that look. Not because it will tell them how to win — the courts have made winning very difficult — but because it will tell them the truth about what they are up against. And the truth, even when it does not produce a remedy, is worth having.

If you have a mortgage, read this book. Not because your situation is necessarily like Leena's. But because understanding how this system actually works is the only real defense available. The system does not just tolerate forgery. It runs on it. Leena proved it. Now you can see it too.

Richard Mendez, Co-creator,
David v. Goliath: How to Fight the Mortgage Machine

How to Read This Book

This is a memoir about fighting foreclosure fraud for seven years while representing myself. It is also a legal record. Not a vibe, a paper trail.

If you're here for the story — how an artist ended up cross-examining notaries and reading bankruptcy rules at 2 a.m. — read it straight through. It unfolds the way it happened: slowly, then all at once.

If you're here because you're in foreclosure yourself, pay attention to what I filed, what the courts said, and what they avoided saying. The pattern matters more than any single ruling. The appendices are there for a reason.

If you're a lawyer, journalist, or skeptic with a highlighter, welcome. Everything can be checked. I made it easy.

The cover promises a courtroom. The book delivers one — but not until Part III. That's intentional.

The first hundred pages are about who I was before any of this happened. A Finnish girl who learned to steer a boat at eleven and carried that instinct across two continents. A graphic designer who built a career from nothing, learned to read systems, and trusted them — until one system failed her in a way she couldn't ignore.

That background isn't preamble. It's the argument. The person who spent years in court teaching herself civil procedure and tracking forged signatures across three states was built by everything that came before it. The catering truck. The Olympic Games. The mountains of Julian. The losses that compounded before the fraud ever began.

If you skip to Part III, you'll understand what happened. But you won't fully understand who it happened to — or why she didn't stop. Read it in order. The courtroom lands harder when you know what was at stake.

What This Book Is

It is a personal story about persistence and trauma and the strange skill set you develop when no one is coming to save you. It is a case study in foreclosure fraud and institutional resistance. It is documentation of systematic document forgery affecting far more than one house in the mountains. And it is a field guide for fighting the machine alone — not because you wanted to, but because you had to.

What This Book Is Not

This is a record, not a recommendation. It is not legal advice. I'm not a lawyer. I just learned to read very carefully.

It's not a conspiracy theory. Conspiracies hide. This is documented.

The evidence held. The outcome didn't. I won. A California judge canceled the instruments and put it in writing. I have the order.

I still lost the house.

I spent years believing the law was black and white. Evidence in, finding out, justice delivered. Turns out that is a charmingly naive reading of how courts actually function. The law, as I came to understand it, is a vast gray institution that can find forgery on the record, acknowledge it, praise its documentation, and then hand the property to the forging party anyway on equitable grounds. Perfectly legal. Happens all the time. You're welcome.

So. Not a victory lap. A record. Written by someone who followed the evidence all the way to the end, won the argument, lost the house, and decided that what she found was too important to leave in a filing cabinet.

It's not light reading. Some chapters are technical. Some are brutal.

About the Technical Sections

There are chapters that dive into bankruptcy procedure, notary law, and chain-of-title analysis. If legal language makes your eyes cross, here's the short version: Forgery happened. The courts acknowledged the evidence was "compelling" and "uncontroverted." Foreclosure proceeded anyway.

You don't need to understand every rule to understand the outcome. Evidence does not enforce itself.

Terms You'll See

MERS — a private mortgage database created by banks to track transfers without recording them publicly. It calls itself a "nominee." It owns nothing. It appears everywhere.

Assignment of Mortgage — the document that transfers a mortgage from one party to another.

Substitution of Trustee — the document that substitutes the trustee. Mine was notarized by someone who swore she never signed it. Details matter.

Standing — the legal right to sue. You're supposed to prove you own what you're trying to foreclose on. "Supposed to" does a lot of work here.

Lis Pendens — a public notice at the county recorder's office that property is in litigation. Translation: your house is frozen in place while the fight drags on. There's a full glossary at the back, page 293.

Content Warning

This book includes violence. I was stabbed during the years I was fighting this case. It includes financial trauma and housing instability, institutional betrayal and judicial indifference, and the kind of sustained stress that eventually lands you in medical emergencies. The legal system does not pause because your life implodes. Deadlines remain deadlines. Motions remain due. You keep filing or you lose.

Why I Wrote This

The evidence exists and almost no one wants to look at it. Millions lost homes after 2008 and were told they had no case. I brought proof of systematic forgery into court and watched procedure outrank truth. If documented evidence doesn't matter in a court of law, that is not a niche problem.

This book is proof of something simple: I wasn't imagining it. The documents were forged. The system knew. It moved forward anyway.

But before any of that — before the courtrooms and the forged signatures and the sixty-four hearings — there was a life. A Finnish girl who learned to steer early and never quite stopped. That's where this begins.

Prologue

A forensic handwriting expert testified at trial that one notary's signature on the foreclosure documents was not authentic. The second notary testified under oath that she had not signed the documents bearing her name. The trial judge described the evidence as "compelling and uncontroverted" and stated in open court that she could not let what had happened stand.

I lost the house anyway.

Under California law, a forged deed is void from inception — legally as if it never existed. It cannot transfer ownership. It cannot confer the right to foreclose. Courts have said this plainly. *(Wutzke v. Bill Reid Painting Service; OC Interior Services LLC v. Nationstar Mortgage.)* If that rule is applied, the foreclosure cannot stand.

The rule was not applied.

This is a book about what I found when I followed the evidence — through seven years of litigation, sixty-four court appearances, and a paper trail that did not stop at my property line. The forgery on my documents was not an isolated mistake. It was a method. Documented. Repeatable. Scalable.

The judge's words are in the transcript. The transcript is in the appendix. The documents are in the public record. I did not write this book because I am angry, though I am. I wrote it because the record exists and someone should say plainly what it shows.

Not because the evidence was weak, or the law unclear, but because the system that processed that evidence did not require it to change the outcome. This book is the record of how that happens.

Once the machinery begins to move, it continues. Deadlines do not pause. Filings do not wait. Outcomes, once set in motion, do not easily reverse.

I believed that facts mattered. That documents meant what they said.

That fraud, once proven, stopped proceedings rather than coexisted with them. I believed courts existed to resolve contradictions, not formalize them. That belief did not survive contact with the system.

I grew up in Finland, in a culture where systems were expected to function because accountability was built into them. Silence meant consideration, not avoidance. A handshake carried weight. Rules were not decorative — they were followed, and when they failed, they were corrected quietly, without theater. I carried those assumptions with me into adulthood — into contracts, into business, into homeownership — believing that if something could be proven, it would matter. It does not necessarily matter.

In court, procedure can outweigh evidence, and timing can outweigh accuracy. A document does not have to be authentic to be enforced; it only has to be accepted. Once a narrative is filed and processed, it acquires weight independent of whether it is true. I did not understand that at the beginning.

I followed instructions. I contacted the loan servicer. I was told to stop making payments in order to qualify for a modification. I did what I was told, and that decision placed me into default — the one condition the system is built to act on.

From there, the process advanced step by step.

Years later, when I began examining the documents used to justify that process, I found signatures that did not belong to the people whose names were attached to them. I tracked the notaries, obtained their certifications, hired a forensic handwriting expert, and built a record.

The evidence held. The outcome did not change. The legal system did not ignore the contradiction. It acknowledged it. It described the evidence in clear terms and then, through procedural mechanisms and equitable reasoning, allowed the result to stand.

This is not a story about a misunderstanding or a clerical error. It is about what happens when facts, law, and outcome diverge — and the system proceeds anyway.

Everything that follows is documented. The filings exist. The transcripts exist. The testimony exists. The signatures — and the forgeries — exist.

This is not a reconstruction. It is a record.

I did not set out to write a book. I set out to keep my home. What I found instead was a system that can absorb proof of defect, contain its consequences, and continue forward without correcting it — not because it failed, but because that is how it functions.

The system did not require the documents to be valid. It required the process to continue.

That is not a gray area in the law. If the deed is forged, the chain of title collapses. There is nothing to enforce.

I was made captain at eleven — handed the tiller of a small boat on a Finnish archipelago and told to bring it back.

What the system does to homeowners is paper terrorism — forged documents filed in sequence, each one generating deadlines, costs, and legal exposure that a single person cannot outrun. Cheap to deploy, expensive to survive. The storm did not pass. The course did not stabilize. The filings kept coming while I navigated a criminal court I never expected to see the inside of, while I rebuilt a life across the border, while the violence reshaped everything except the docket schedule. None of it mattered to the machine. But I learned how to steer anyway. I'm still here. And this is what happened.

PART I

LEARNING TO STEER

Before I Knew I'd Have To

Life can only be understood backwards;
but it must be lived forwards.
— Søren Kierkegaard

CHAPTER 1

Born North

I didn't grow up questioning systems. I grew up inside one that worked. People in Finland assumed things functioned the way they claimed. Silence meant consideration, not avoidance. A handshake meant something — you could trust it, and people expected you to. Rules existed for a reason, and when they failed, someone fixed them. Quietly. Without theater. The weather didn't negotiate, and that alone teaches you respect for reality early. You prepare, or you suffer. Complaining is optional. Competence is not.

***

My father was a builder — not the Pinterest kind, the kind that looked a challenge in the eye and kept going. He built boats, windmills, and an ultra-light aircraft that he somehow managed to fly without ending up in a tree. In winter it grew skis, because of course it did. One afternoon a local news crew arrived to film him landing on a frozen lake — a perfectly reasonable assignment, given that Finland has roughly 800,000 of them, you'd think they'd planned it out a bit better. He landed on the wrong one. The crew stood at their designated lake. He stood at his. Neither group could see the other. He became briefly infamous, which is its own kind of Finnish achievement.

I didn't know it then, but I'd inherit that same energy — the willingness to land on the wrong lake and keep going anyway.

***

Fishing was our shared language. I learned to put a worm on a hook before I learned how to tie my shoes. Growing up in Helsinki, the ocean was always close. It wasn't scenery; it was part of daily life—complete with a side of seaweed.

Summers unfolded at my godparents' remote retreat — no electricity, an outhouse, a sauna obviously. I climbed the tallest pines, swam long stretches of open water, learned to fish and clean fish and row boats and forage for mushrooms and berries and build things that didn't come with instructions. Each night ended the same way: sauna, then cannonball into the ocean. A ritual that left me feeling both invincible and slightly uncivilized, which was the point.

I joined the Girl Scouts young and went all in — badges, leadership roles. I even earned a Mannerheim medal — named after Carl Gustaf Emil Mannerheim, Finland's most celebrated military commander and statesman, awarded to scouts for exceptional achievement. It sounds impressive because it was. I made lifelong friends. Frankly, this should be required for every human being, but somehow we collectively settled for TikTok instead. Those years grounded me in nature and taught me actual survival skills. Not inspiration. Skills. There's a difference, and I've been grateful for it ever since.

My dad used to say that other people do what they know how to do — but Leena does what she wants. It wasn't praise exactly. It was an observation that explained a lot about my future.

As a kid I was painfully shy, thrived in solitude, always had something to do. Art was a steadfast companion who never judged.

The Witch on the Mountain

I was three the first time I skied. The family lore insists I climbed my mountain, skied straight down, and flopped into the snow like a disoriented penguin. My father helped me up and said: "Do it again. You have to kill the witch, or it will follow you your whole life." So down I went, over and over, until fear gave up.

The mountain was about two feet tall. It still counts.

The lesson stuck anyway: if you don't face it down, it follows you. Years later, after something happened in Mexico that should have sent me running in the opposite direction, I went back to the house. Not because I was brave. Because I knew that if I didn't, I'd spend the rest of my life looking over my shoulder. The witch doesn't die from distance. It dies from walking back through the door. Later still, I'd apply that same logic to forged documents and lying attorneys. The mountain just got taller.

The Triptych

Art became my escape at twelve. "Dad, I need a giant roll of craft paper and a six-inch brush." A blink, then a trip to the store.

Dead of winter. Bleak and cold. Wind howling like it had a complaint the whole neighborhood needed to hear. I popped open the window anyway. My mother thought I'd lost my mind. *Leena, you'll freeze.* But I needed the cold. Needed the air moving. Needed to feel something sharp while I worked.

I pulled on my hand-knitted wool sweater — thick, uneven stitches, the kind you make when you're twelve and still learning. In Finland, knitting isn't a hobby. It's survival. I turned on the record player. Vivaldi's Four Seasons. Always Vivaldi.

The music started with Winter — sharp, urgent, strings like wind cutting through trees. It matched the scene outside: snow piled high, sky the color of old metal, everything muted and held in place by cold. But I didn't paint winter first. I started with sunset.

The first panel: a mountain at dusk, snow-covered, pine trees impossibly green against the white. The sky, deep saturated pink — the kind that only happens when the sun is low and the air is frozen and the light has to fight through layers of cold to reach you. I mixed cadmium red with white, then more white, then a whisper of yellow. Too orange. I scraped it off. Started again. The pink had to glow.

The snow wasn't white. It never is. Pale blue in the shadows, deep indigo where the mountain sloped away from the light. The pine trees were vertical, dark, anchoring the composition, keeping the sky from floating away.

Winter ended. Spring began. The tempo shifted — lighter, quicker, hopeful. I moved to the second panel: a frozen lake, deep translucent blue, the kind you see when a lake freezes thick and clear and the light goes all the way down. Rocks jutting through the surface, casting long cold shadows. At the edge, golden reeds, dead but still standing. And ducks — small, deliberate, walking along the frozen reeds like they had somewhere to be. Quick strokes. No detail. Just shapes and movement. The ducks made the scene alive. Without them it was a landscape. With them it was a moment.

I worked for hours. Time disappeared. The light outside changed. My hands went numb. My back ached. I stepped back.

Three panels. Connected but distinct. A journey.

It wasn't perfect. The proportions were off. The ducks were too small. The shadows didn't quite match the light source. But it was mine. Start to finish, no instruction, no permission. I chose the colors. I decided the composition. I held the course from the first brushstroke to the last.

My father saw it the next day. He stood in front of it a long time, hands in his pockets, saying nothing. Then: "You stayed with it, impressive." Not *good job*. You stayed with it. That's what mattered — not talent, not the result. The fact that I'd started something difficult and finished it. That I'd made decisions and lived with them. That I hadn't waited for someone else to tell me what to do.

My mother stood beside him, silent. Then I saw it — a tear at the corner of her eye. She didn't say anything. She didn't need to.

Sixty years later, I still paint to Vivaldi. Still open the window even when it's cold. The triptych is long gone — thrown out, or painted over. But the lesson stayed: you don't wait for permission. You don't assume someone else is steering. You make the first mark. Then the next. Then the next. And you stay with it.

What Competence Costs

School was an afterthought. I blended into the back like a chameleon. Talking in front of people — that was the witch I couldn't slay. Public speaking turned my chest into a vice. That fear lingered far longer than my skiing anxiety ever did, until life decided to replace it with problems on a grander scale. Honestly, an upgrade.

One teacher made a lasting impression. At the end of school, I told her I was planning to go to America. She looked at me and said: "What do you think you're going to do there? You'll never succeed." That comment might have crushed someone else. For me, it landed as a dare.

Five years later, I mailed her a glossy catalog — the first major client I'd landed, a national catalog for Dell Computer — with a short note: *You were wrong.* That was the whole letter. Petty? Maybe. Educational? Absolutely.

Early independence feels good in the body. There's a specific satisfaction in finishing something yourself—carrying the groceries in one trip, fixing the broken thing, not waiting for someone else to notice. You feel competent.

What no one mentions is how quickly competence becomes obligation. Once people know you can handle something, they stop offering to help. They assume. And if you drop it once, you're unreliable. The bar only moves one way. I thought adulthood would reward this. That someone, somewhere, would notice and say: you've earned a break.

Adorable.

What actually happens is you get very good at carrying weight. And the better you get, the more you're given. Not maliciously. Just… efficiently.

People start bringing you problems already half-decided. Not asking what you think—asking you to fix what's already broken. You become the person things get handed to when they're inconvenient, complicated, or slightly uncomfortable.

And because you can handle it, you do.

That's how it builds. Not in one moment, but in a series of small handoffs. One responsibility becomes two. Two becomes a pattern. Eventually it's not something you notice—it's just the structure of your life.

The Finnish word sisu gets translated as grit or perseverance. What it really means is simpler: you're going to do the hard thing anyway. So you do.

You stop waiting for conditions to be right. You stop expecting help to arrive. You stop asking whether something is fair before you take it on. You just assess what needs to be done and start. That looks like strength from the outside. From the inside, it's quieter than that.

I learned early that competence means being the one who carries it. I painted that triptych at twelve to prove I could finish something difficult on my own. I did. What I didn't understand was that finishing it set the expectation. From then on: you're good at this, figure it out.

No instruction manual. No backup plan. Just repetition.

The captain doesn't get shore leave. The captain gets the next problem. The next decision. The next moment where something has to be handled and no one else steps forward. So you do.

And eventually you stop asking whether it's yours to carry. You just notice that it's already in your hands.

Early independence feels good—until you realize it doesn't let go.

CHAPTER 2

Captain at Eleven

At eleven, I was made captain. Real authority. Real responsibility. Leadership arrived before childhood was finished—and it never really left. This wasn't a surprise promotion. It was a natural progression.

My father had been building me a boat in secret. It was supposed to be my tenth birthday present, but boats — like life — run late. I spent that entire year trying not to notice the tarp in the corner of the garage, trying not to ask questions, trying to be the kind of child who could wait. By the time it was finished the following summer I had sprouted nearly a foot and barely fit inside it. I didn't care. I sat in it anyway, knees up, motor idling, and felt something I didn't have a word for yet — the specific satisfaction of a thing that was made for you, that exists because someone thought you were worth the trouble. Minor detail. Still my ship. It came equipped with a small Evinrude motor. That was enough. I was free.

***

I became the undisputed captain of the local waters. Queen bee. Commander of my little domain, ready to cross the Atlantic—if snacks were provided, of course.

I understood responsibility immediately: fuel, direction, weather, and the fundamental rule of not dying. No manuals. No hovering supervision. Just trust.

My first excursion was so exhilarating I couldn't believe what I was doing. All grown up now. Kind of.

The motor was loud—at least to my ears. I was safe. I was alone. So I did what any newly liberated eleven-year-old would do. I let loose.

I was giggling out loud, howling like a wolf, singing at full blast — arms wide, face up, the motor loud enough to drown out every version of myself that knew better. My chest felt enormous. Like I'd been breathing shallowly my whole life and someone had finally told me the lungs could go further than I'd ever let them. The everyday constrained version of me would never do that, not even in the shower. But this was new life. Freedom on water. It deserved celebration.

I came back to shore feeling renewed, like I'd discovered a secret the adults didn't know about.

That night in the sauna, Dad had a smirk on his face. "What are you smiling about?" "It was very interesting to listen to you today. New sounds I've never heard before." I was mortified.

My safe place wasn't safe. I hadn't taken into account that even though the motor was loud to my ears, the still waters of a Finnish lake carried sound for miles across the surface. The whole neighborhood — every dock, every sauna, every porch — had heard me.

My dignity was gone. Finnish dignity, no less — the kind that doesn't recover quickly. Restraint snapped back into place like a rubber band. Never again would I let go like that in public — not on a lake, not anywhere, not even when every cell in my body was begging to. The universe doesn't always protect you when you think you're alone. Sometimes it has excellent acoustics. Lesson learned: privacy is an illusion, especially on open water.

***

I was supposed to stay within sight of shore. I didn't.

There were islands farther out — ones I'd only seen from the mainland, and I wanted to know what was there. So one day, I just went. Took extra fuel. Told no one. Spent three exhilarating hours exploring channels between rocks, watching seals, and feeling like Magellan on a miniature adventure.

When I got back, my dad was standing on the dock. Arms crossed. The look. "Where were you?" I told him. I didn't lie. I wasn't sorry. I'd been safe. I'd been smart. I'd just expanded my jurisdiction.

He was quiet for a long time. Then: "Next time, tell me first. Not for permission. So I know where to look if you don't come back."

That was it. No punishment. No taking away the boat. Trust wasn't unconditional. But it was renewable. That kind of trust does something to a kid. It teaches you that freedom and accountability aren't opposites—they're the same bargain, negotiated in good faith. Being made captain at eleven came with one dangerous side effect: I started believing I was right about everything. Most of the time, I was. I could read the weather, navigate the channels, handle the boat in rough water. I'd earned the trust, and I knew it. But trust without oversight is just rope. Eventually, you hang yourself with it.

The Wake

The adults had a bigger boat, and when they'd take it out I'd follow in mine, riding the wake like dolphins surfing the current — way better than any amusement park ride. I'd circle them, cut through the chop, feel the spray, push the limits of what my little Evinrude could handle. The motor would whine, the hull would bounce, and I'd laugh like a maniac because this was freedom and speed and control all wrapped into one perfect afternoon.

One day I was making a particularly aggressive turn through their wake when the steering cable snapped. No warning — just gone. I slammed straight into their boat, no time to think, no time to correct, just impact and adrenaline and the sudden understanding that mechanical things fail without announcement, and when they do, physics takes over. It scared the shit out of me. But no one got hurt, the boats were fine, and my pride took the worst of it. I had to be towed back home.

Once I was over the shock, I dangled my feet over the side of the boat, let the water splash against my legs, and enjoyed the tow. Sometimes being rescued isn't defeat. Sometimes it's just part of the deal. Don't trust blindly: not equipment, not assumptions, not the comfortable idea that everything will keep working smoothly just because it always has.

The sea was never symbolic to me. It was practical. It moved, it pushed back, and it didn't care how confident you felt. At eleven, I learned that if you're at the helm, you pay attention. You don't daydream. You don't assume someone else is steering. I just knew how to start the motor, read the water, and come back under my own power.

Years later, when lawyers would tell me I had no standing, I'd think about that day on open water.

CHAPTER 3

Systems and Switchboards

As a teenager in Helsinki in the 1970s, I worked summer vacations as an international telephone switchboard operator. Long shifts. Long calls. Voices traveling farther than bodies were allowed to. The headset left a groove across the top of my head by the end of a shift. My neck learned to hold still for hours. You developed a kind of professional stillness — outwardly calm while inside you were tracking six conversations at once, deciding which one needed you most.

You learn quickly how systems sound when you're not inside them. You hear hesitation, privilege and urgency. You hear who gets routed through, and who stays waiting.

Every international call passed through us. We were *sentraali santra* — party-line operators. Each call was logged on a small card and handed off by language, sometimes creating stacks inches high. Three- to five-hour waits were not uncommon; sometimes, the calls had to wait until the next day. You learned fast who mattered. Certain names moved to the top. Others never did.

The Russian table was always busy, and I sat there often, partly because of my grandmother's language living somewhere in the back of my memory, half-understood, like a song you know but can't quite sing. I'd catch a word here and there and feel the strange vertigo of almost-fluency, close enough to follow the tone but not quite close enough to trust it.

I spoke a little Russian — but I never learned the language properly, and in 1960s Finland that was complicated. Embarrassing, even. The war was still close. Until 1955, Porkkala — a peninsula jutting into the Gulf of Finland, less than thirty kilometers west of Helsinki — had been occupied by the Soviets as a naval base, and that proximity hadn't faded from memory the way geography suggests it should.

My father spoke fluent Russian. As a railroad engineer he traveled frequently as an interpreter, mostly to Kyiv where the factories were, and because no Finnish-Russian dictionary existed yet, he made his own — a handwritten pocket edition with immaculate, almost printed lettering. Some entries had nothing to do with machinery. More about human relationships than technical terminology. Little did he know that if he'd stuck with it, we might have ended up on the right side of history's money.

He always came back from Russia with a "gift" — always in quotes. At one point we had half a dozen accordions under the bed, and none of us could play. Russia apparently had a surplus. One Christmas I decided to learn Silent Night on one of them. A full month of auditory terrorism was unleashed on the household. By the end it was recognizable. Barely.

Samovars were another favorite — the large ornate Russian urns used for heating water and brewing tea. Those we actually used. The others sat on top of the bookcase, collecting dust and ideology. Then there were the endless floral scarves, which we got thoroughly sick of. Ironically, I'd love one now. That's how time works.

I wish I'd been more curious. Asked better questions. Paid more attention. But when history is unfolding in your living room, it just melds into furniture, and by the time you realize what you missed, it's too late.

***

My father often hosted factory delegations visiting Finland, and sometimes I tagged along. They arrived by train with their wives — always together, always polite, always watchful. Driving through Helsinki, the reactions were predictable: "Ooh." "Aah." At grocery stores they'd marvel at the fresh produce and warn us to come early before it ran out. We tried to explain that it wouldn't run out, ever. This was not convincing.

What confused me most were the wives. Many were physicists, doctors, scientists — highly educated women with brilliant minds, carefully shelved.

Sometimes we'd have dinner plans and a family simply wouldn't show up.

No explanation, no goodbye, just gone. There was a lot happening behind the curtain, and we weren't allowed to ask about it. Even if we did, no one answered. The system was already built. Only the top knew the truth. The rest were useful — pawns, really, keeping the machinery humming. Sixty years later, it doesn't feel like much has changed.

At the switchboard we became familiar with the corporate world in a different way. With business travel came relationships — girlfriends, affairs — and we knew who was hot, who was desperate, and which party lines "had to be monitored." We lived vicariously through calls we weren't supposed to listen to, but did. So many "I love yous" while the gifts poured in, but when the color wasn't right or the gift wasn't expensive enough, the love evaporated accordingly. We also knew what to bring across the border. Pantyhose. Chewing gum. Always.

***

Once, we tracked a violinist defecting from Moscow. Finland wasn't safe — we had a treaty requiring defectors be returned. She had to cross quietly, reach Sweden, and apply for asylum there.

We followed her entire journey through intercepted calls — south to north, through Lapland, then across the border. When we knew she was safe, we celebrated at our desks. She later became world-renowned.

Years later, I'd track another kind of paper trail—assignments moving from bank to bank, notaries who never notarized, a chain of custody that existed only on forged documents. Same principle. Follow the evidence. See where it breaks.

But not every call we monitored ended in celebration. Some revealed darker patterns.

The phone company sat next to the post office, which meant we also ran public payphones. You made the call first and paid afterward. Very trusting. Very Finnish. What could possibly go wrong.

Over the course of several months an Indonesian man brought in young women to make long overseas calls. Always blond. Always pretty. Never the same one twice.

On the other end, someone was selling a dream. Beautiful houses. Amazing food. Paradise.

One problem. Finns don't talk to Finns in English. Especially not when they're emotional. That alone earned a raised eyebrow and a mental note. So yes, the calls had to be "monitored."

I listened — purely by accident, officially speaking — and realized it was human trafficking. Not subtle. Just dressed up as opportunity. I couldn't report it. Listening was forbidden. Knowing was allowed. Acting was... complicated.

I started following the girls. Felt like a stalker. I'd wait until the Indonesian man had left, then fall into step beside whichever girl was still on the street. My heart was going faster than the situation called for. I wasn't in danger — I was eighteen and Finnish and about to ruin someone's afternoon. That felt almost as bad. There's a specific discomfort in delivering unwelcome truth to someone who is genuinely happy. She was glowing. I was about to hand her a reason not to be. Once they were alone, I'd ask if they knew what they were getting into.

"Oh yes, he wants me to be a model for their fashion label. It sounds so wonderful. I'm so excited. The girl on the phone is so happy to get company."

I asked if she wondered why they had to speak English. Why the guy stood in the booth with her. Monitoring.

"Just be careful. It might not be what it sounds like. Check him out more carefully." She looked disappointed. I was raining on her parade, dampening her "big break."

So I did what I could. I warned the girls quietly, with no speeches — just enough doubt to crack the fantasy. Some time later, the news reported an international sex trafficking ring dismantled. Around the same time, my Indonesian "friend" stopped bringing girls to the payphones. Coincidence, I'm sure.

One girl came by afterward and said, "Thank you." Two words. I never knew whether I had actually stopped anything or just created enough doubt for her to make a different choice. That's the thing about small interventions: you rarely get to know if they worked. You do what you can with what you have, and live with the not-knowing.I worked constantly — summers, after graduation, extra shifts. I wasn't saving for anything romantic. I was saving for distance. Work was my exit strategy. They always welcomed me back. I was reliable. I moved a few friends onto the privileged list, and funded my own travels.The First System That Didn't Care

The first time I noticed systems don't care who you are, I was sixteen and working at Helsinki's telephone directory assistance. Everything was manual. Massive physical directories, phone books and yellow pages organized by region, human memory doing the heavy lifting. Five inquiries per call. Not six. Supervisors walked the floor checking speed. Efficiency wasn't optional.

I was good at it. Fast. I knew the quirks, which agencies hid under unexpected headings, how to navigate the chaos.

One afternoon a woman asked for a number. Not there. I checked the supplement. Not there. Neighboring district. Still nothing. She insisted it existed. I checked again. Nothing.

She got angry. Said the last operator found it in ten seconds. I stayed polite, apologized, suggested she double-check the spelling. She hung up.

The supervisor appeared. I explained. She checked herself. Not there. "Then why did you keep looking?" "Because she said it existed." She looked at me like I'd confessed to a crime. Thoroughness wasn't the job. Speed was the job.

"If it's not in the book, it doesn't exist. You don't waste time proving it doesn't exist. You move on."

I thought about that moment a lot in the years that followed. When I'd be standing in immigration lines having done everything right — and they'd still say no because the system said no. When I'd be in courtrooms, presenting evidence called compelling and uncontroverted, watching judges rule against me anyway because procedure said they could.

You adjust. You comply. You move on. Or you spend your life arguing with a phone book that can't hear you.

At sixteen I didn't have language for that yet. I just knew it felt unfair. By sixty I'd have language, evidence, expert testimony, and court transcripts proving the unfairness. And the system still wouldn't care. Turns out some things don't change. They just get more expensive.

But knowing the system doesn't care and accepting it are two different things. I stayed at the directory assistance job for a while longer—long enough to get good at disconnecting before the caller's frustration became mine. Long enough to understand that efficiency was the only metric that mattered. Long enough to realize I didn't want to spend my life as the polite voice telling people no.

I wanted more than two-week vacations. I wanted out. Not forever. Just long enough to see what else existed beyond Helsinki winters and predictable summers and the same small circle of people I'd known my entire life.

I put a plan in motion. I applied for a six-month tourist visa to America.

The consulate officer looked at my application. Looked at me. "How are you going to support yourself?" I explained I had savings. I had a job to return to. I just wanted to travel.

"Denied." No explanation. Just: denied. I walked out of the consulate and stood on the street for a moment, the stamp still ringing in my ears like a physical thing. Not disappointment exactly. More like the first time you push a door marked pull — the brief, stupid shock of a system that doesn't bend toward you just because you need it to.

I tried again. Different approach. My godparents had a distant relative in Florida—someone they'd never met but whose name existed in the family address book. Maybe they would sponsor me. I wrote a letter. Formal. Polite. Desperate.

Dear Paul, You don't know me, but we are distantly related through Ethel Hannonen. I am hoping to visit America for six months and would be honored if you would consider sponsoring my visit. I am responsible, employed, and will return to Finland at the end of my stay. Please let me know if this is possible.

I mailed it, months went by. Nothing. I gave up. Started filling out paperwork to go to a kibbutz in Israel instead. At least that was an option.

***

Then serendipity kicked in.

Late 1970s, still working at the Helsinki phone directory assistance office. Everything still manual. Operators. Switchboards. Handwritten logs.

One afternoon, my co-worker picked up a call. "International operator. Requesting phone number for Leena Hannonen in Helsinki, Finland." My co-worker's head snapped up.

"Leena Hannonen?" I looked up from my desk. She pointed at the phone. Mouthed: It's for you.

I jumped up. She jumped up. The entire office jumped up. The excitement went through the roof.

I grabbed the phone with both hands, heart going completely sideways, trying to sound like a professional while every nerve ending I had was doing something else entirely. The fluorescent lights. The smell of paper. The whole mundane office suddenly electric with the specific energy of a thing that was about to change. "This is Leena."

The American operator paused. "I didn't ask you to connect the call. I just wanted the phone number." "Too late. I'm right here."

Silence. Then a man's voice came on the line. The distant cousin. His boss was interested in hiring an au pair. Would I be interested?

Is the pope Catholic? "When do I fly?"

I still had to go a few rounds with Bo at the American consulate. He wasn't easily convinced that I was "just a tourist." He kept asking why I wanted to stay six months. What my real plans were. Whether I intended to work.

I told him the truth: I wanted to see America. I had a sponsor. I had a return ticket. I had a job waiting for me in Helsinki. He stamped the visa.

February 22, 1981 was the day I was ready to fly out.

When I finally quit, people said I was insane. A secure, lifelong job with the government. Pension. Stability. Why would anyone walk away from that?

I couldn't imagine spending my life routing other people's futures. I remember the last day. Walking out of that building for the final time, headset handed in, locker cleared. The feeling wasn't triumph. It was lighter than that. More like putting down something you'd been carrying so long you'd stopped noticing the weight. Helsinki winter outside. Cold and clear and entirely mine.

Years later around 1990, at a Finnish consulate party in Bel Air, I met the CEO of the phone company. I told him my story.

He laughed. "I'm glad you left," he said. "Tomorrow the whole place closes. Technology made operators obsolete." Four hundred jobs gone.

Job security was always a lie. So was procedural fairness. I just didn't know it yet.

CHAPTER 4

Red Pants Economics

In 1978-79, I took classes in handloom weaving. I loved it immediately and completely — the way the shuttle moved through warp and weft with a rhythmic click that got into your body after a while, the way a pattern emerged from nothing but repetition and tension, the way your hands learned the logic before your mind did. I tried sculpting next. Clay yielding under my palms felt like a different kind of conversation — slower, more forgiving, less precise. I wasn't good yet. I didn't care. I was twenty and learning what my hands were capable of, which turned out to be more than I'd expected.

Then a flyer caught my eye: an artist-led bus trip to Leningrad. Led by a famous sculptor. I wanted to find out if I could get to know him.

Challenge accepted.

***

I bought red corduroy Levi's. Statement pants. The kind that demanded attention before you'd said a word. In Helsinki in 1979, wearing something that loud was a small act of defiance — Finnish culture doesn't reward drawing attention to yourself, and I'd spent enough years being quiet and capable and overlooked. The red pants were a declaration. I'm here. I'm not sorry about it. Paired with a white sweater I'd knitted myself, I felt unstoppable.

We arrived in Leningrad — St. Petersburg in today's world, but back then it was still Soviet, still strange, still worth the gamble. We got situated at the hotel. The first round of bubblegum and pantyhose got sold to the cleaning crew before we'd even unpacked. Common currency those days.

That evening, the whole group gathered for dinner at the hotel restaurant.

Champagne flowed. I felt bold and secure in my red pants. So I walked up to the sculptor and asked him to dance. We danced all night — the kind of dancing that happens when champagne and adrenaline and being twenty-one in a Soviet hotel all combine into something that feels historically significant at the time. The chandeliers were elaborate. The music was too loud. The whole thing was slightly absurd and completely perfect.

The next day at the Hermitage, my red pants led the way through a world filled with history and grandeur. More dancing followed. More champagne. More laughter in a country that felt both familiar and impossible.

I got to know the sculptor *really well.* The next morning, we took separate elevators down to breakfast. As the doors slid closed, he leaned closer and whispered, "*You're the kind of woman I could marry.*" Sweet words that lingered like a melody that wouldn't fade.

Then there was the manager with the dark mustache and bushy eyebrows who'd been staring at me all night. I'd misread the situation, thinking I'd enchanted him with my youthful exuberance. But no. He didn't want me. He wanted my pants.

He bought them. I walked back to my room in my second-best outfit, carrying rubles I couldn't spend and the faint satisfaction of a transaction completed on my terms. The pants had traveled from a Helsinki store to a Soviet hotel manager's wardrobe in seventy-two hours. Value, I was beginning to understand, was entirely a matter of location. And my Finnish–Russian dictionary—prime currency in a world ruled by scarcity. Rather than pocketing the rubles, I bought champagne and a lavish dinner for the entire group that night. The tourist-hotel abundance was surreal: roast meats, solyanka, borscht, caviar, pierogi, and of course, champagne.

Outside, I noticed the stark contrast—people lined up for bread, faces locked in resignation, their hope extinguished by the weight of rationing.

Even after the feast, I was left with a plastic bag filled with rubles, the weight of those bills heavy in my hands. You can't take rubles across the border. And there was nothing to buy.

The next day on the way back to Finland, at a rest stop, an old *babushka* was cleaning toilets. I handed her the bag — a plastic bag full of rubles, more than she probably saw in a month — and watched something complicated move across her face. Not gratitude. Not surprise. Fear. The specific fear of someone who has learned that unexpected things carry unexpected costs. She looked left. Looked right. Whispered no and walked away fast, and I stood there with the bag still in my hands feeling the particular helplessness of generosity that can't be received.

I understood then—taking money from a foreigner could lead to interrogation. Questions she couldn't afford to answer. Kindness felt dangerous when the wrong people were watching. Big Brother was everywhere. Either you were inside the system—or very much not.

In a system built on fear, evidence is dangerous. Even kindness has to be hidden. So, I did the only thing I could think of. I started tossing handfuls of money out the bus window, leaning out as far as the frame allowed, watching bills scatter in the slipstream. People emerged from the treeline — I don't know where they came from or how they knew — and grabbed what they could before the bus was gone. Their faces in those seconds were the most alive things I'd seen the entire trip. Not joy exactly. More like the expression of someone who has been given permission, briefly, to want something. Those pants made a bigger difference than I had intended.

After the trip, I dated the sculptor, Kari Ovaska, for a couple of years. He was patient in the way that good people are patient — genuinely, without resentment, waiting for me to settle into something he could keep pace with. I was restless in the way that restless people are restless — not unhappy, just always aware of a door somewhere that I hadn't opened yet. He deserved someone who wasn't always half-listening for that door. I wasn't that person yet. Maybe I never became her. Curiosity kept knocking louder than commitment.

In 1981, I decided to take a leave for six months as an au pair in Florida. I returned, and we rekindled our relationship. Still, the restlessness persisted. It was a constant hum in the background, a calling I could never quite shake off.

Money as Movement

I never thought of money as stability. I thought of it as momentum — the difference between "I'd like to" and "I'm going." Growing up Finnish meant growing up practical: you didn't waste, you didn't show off, you fixed things instead of replacing them. Sensible, efficient, and very boring. But it also meant that money, when you had it, was meant to be used strategically. And the most strategic use I could think of was: get out.

The red pants were a lesson in value. I'd bought them in Finland for normal money — corduroy, nothing fancy. But to the Russians they were worth serious rubles, hard currency, because you simply couldn't buy them in Russia. Same pants. Different world. The fabric was ordinary, but scarcity made them worth whatever I asked. I sold them, and the transaction lodged something in my head that took years to fully name: value isn't inherent. It's assigned. It's what someone pays when they can't get it anywhere else.

What scarcity really trained me to see was the design of the system itself. You're supposed to save for emergencies, build a safety net, defer gratification. All of which sounds reasonable until you notice that the people telling you to be cautious are usually the people who already have enough that caution costs them nothing. I didn't save for retirement. I spent money on plane tickets, student visas, a Mac I couldn't afford, businesses with no safety net. Reckless, sure — but "reckless" is just what people call it when you use resources for movement instead of security.

The irony is that all that momentum didn't protect me when the system decided I was in the way. I had spent forty years moving toward something. It turned out the system was moving too — in the opposite direction, faster, with better lawyers. None of it mattered, because the system wasn't designed to reward responsibility. It was designed to extract value. And once extraction became more profitable than keeping me housed, everything I'd built just became a target.

CHAPTER 5

Leaving Without Drama

Coming to America in 1981 wasn't a dream. It was logistics. After the long battle of getting the visa squared away, I finally arrived in New York. I had a three-hour layover to go through customs and catch my flight to St. Petersburg, Florida, where my host family was supposed to meet me.

Customs had different plans. I was flagged right at the gate. Not pulled aside politely — flagged. Someone handed me a big yellow cardboard sign that routed me to an immigration checkpoint. Interrogation room. They'd already decided I was a criminal before I'd said a word.

For what? A twenty-year-old Finnish girl could not possibly have enough means to survive for six months in America, they'd decided. I was going to work illegally. They were certain. It took me five hours to convince them otherwise. I had a return ticket, fully paid for. I had my host family's information. I had documentation from my sponsor. I had everything required by law. Didn't matter.

They grilled me. Five hours is a long time to be treated like a criminal for having a return ticket. My Finnish held up better than my English — I kept my face neutral, my voice even, my paperwork organized in my lap like armor. Inside I was doing the math on whether stubbornness or politeness was more likely to get me through. I chose polite stubbornness. A hybrid. Very Finnish. Where would I be staying? How much money did I have? What was I really planning to do? Why would anyone come to America for six months without working? I wore them out with politeness and paperwork. Finally, they stamped my passport. I was secured for six months. I was free to go. By then, my connecting flight was long gone. The next one would put me into St. Pete at 11 p.m. Not 3 p.m. as agreed. Well, I'd deal with the next problem when I got there.

Midnight in St. Petersburg

St. Pete was a sleepy little airport at midnight, midweek. There I stood, alone with my two suitcases. Hardly anybody around. Another surreal moment in a day full of them. I walked around for fifteen minutes, looking for anyone who might be looking for me. And then I saw this couple walking towards me. Tuxedo and a pink boa. "Are you Leena?"

Whaaat?

"We are so sorry we're a little late." Nine hours late. Yes, a little late, I'd say. But for some reason it worked out, because I was nine hours late too. The couple had come straight from a party, and their car had broken down on the way to the airport. By the time they got there, they figured I'd already left or given up.

But there I was. Serendipity at work again. I laughed out loud in that empty airport at midnight — the kind of laugh that comes when a day has been so relentlessly absurd that your nervous system gives up on dignity and just releases. Nine hours late, standing under fluorescent lights with two suitcases and a pink boa in my face. Perfect.

Thomas asked if I was hungry. "Yes, I'm starving." We went to McDonald's. My first American meal. "What do you want?" I had no clue. There were no McDonald's in Finland back then. I stared at the menu like it was written in hieroglyphics. I saw "cheeseburger." That would do.

And I saw "beer" on the menu. After a rough day and an exhausting trip, I deserved one. When I took a sip of my "beer," I found out that root beer is not actually beer. To me, it was undrinkable. So many firsts.

The Au Pair Job

I arrived in Florida as an au pair — a live-in childcare arrangement: the family gets affordable childcare, the girl gets to see the world, tasked with caring for two boys whose names I could barely pronounce and whose rapid-fire English sounded like static.

My English was rudimentary at best. I'd studied it in school in Finland, mostly because I had to.On my first day in the kitchen with the boys, my entire culinary instruction consisted of pointing: "Put that stuff into that thing and heat it until it looks like this." I pointed at a casserole dish, then at the oven, then at a picture in a cookbook. They nodded like they understood. None of us understood. We managed anyway.

The boys were in school most of the day. The house was quiet. The father worked. Mother was a busy housewife, never home. Mostly tennis every day. And happy hours. I was alone with a television, a kitchen I didn't know how to operate, and a growing suspicion that I'd made a terrible mistake coming to America. That's when I discovered soap operas.

This silence had a specific quality I hadn't expected. In Finland, silence is companionable — it sits with you without demanding anything. This was the silence of a house that didn't know me, in a country that hadn't noticed me yet, in a language I couldn't quite catch. I was twenty years old and completely invisible, which sounds romantic and was mostly just lonely.

The show that came on was The Young and the Restless. I had no idea what was happening. A woman was crying. A man was yelling. Someone slammed a door. Then a close-up of another woman's face — shocked, betrayed, furious. I sat down on the couch and watched.

The next day, same time, same channel. Different crisis. I didn't understand all the words, but I understood the story. Betrayal. Lies. Confrontation. Someone wronged. Someone torn between loyalty and truth. The emotions were universal. The English was not.

But slowly, I started catching phrases. I wrote them down. Tested them out loud when no one was home. Soap operas don't talk like textbooks. They talk like people. They taught me rhythm — how Americans actually speak, how emphasis changes meaning, how silence can be louder than words. I learned that "fine" doesn't mean fine. That "we need to talk" means something bad is coming. Within six months, I could argue. Not because I'd studied grammar. Because I'd watched hundreds of hours of people lying, confessing, accusing, forgiving, and falling apart on screen.

The boys noticed. One afternoon, the younger one knocked over a glass of juice. He froze. Looked at me. I said, calmly, with perfect American intonation: "It's okay. Accidents happen." The older one laughed. "You sound like a real person now."

Years later, people would ask how I learned English so fast. The Young and the Restless. They thought I was joking. I wasn't. Soap operas taught me what people mean when they're not saying what they mean. That skill turned out to be useful.

The House

I found myself immersed in a world that was humid, confusing, and nothing like the movies I had watched back home.

I worked six days a week. My routine revolved around the boys: getting them ready for school, feeding them, picking them up afterward. My room was tucked behind the kitchen, and I learned quickly that entering without flipping on the light first was an invitation for disaster. I would turn on the light and wait a full minute, giving the cockroaches time to retreat.

I had never seen a cockroach in Finland. In Florida, they were a design feature—etched into the very essence of domestic life. The house was multi-million-dollar, overlooking the water with a pool glimmering like a promise. But money wasn't an issue for the roaches. Roaches don't care about wealth or façade.

I mailed one home to my parents in a matchbox. Named him Oscar.

***

The family had money. Real money. The kind that buys waterfront views and assumes problems disappear when you throw cash at them. But wealth doesn't mean competence. It doesn't mean accountability. And it definitely doesn't mean the people with power will treat you fairly just because you did the work. I didn't know it then, but I was learning something crucial: systems built on money don't care about truth. They care about convenience. And if you're not convenient, you're disposable.

The Trash Standoff

Two weeks into my stay, the parents announced their plans for a week in Europe, leaving me in charge of the children. Alone. This felt... optimistic.

On the first morning, Courtney—the five-year-old—decided television took precedence over school. I dragged him to the kitchen for breakfast, but he retaliated by kicking the trash can over. Garbage flew everywhere, a chaotic display of childhood rebellion.

In that moment of cultural clash, I stated: "You clean." He shot back: "You are my housekeeper. You clean it." I paused, thinking: Well, this is America. How curious to encounter a mentality so different from my own.

That expectation did not align with my Finnish upbringing, where responsibility was instilled early. So I got the boys on the school bus, leaving the trash scattered across the floor. I followed the Finnish nanny rule: you kick it, you clean it. Courtney, however, disagreed—strongly. Thus, the trash remained. A week is a long time to walk past a pile of garbage every morning. I developed a relationship with it — acknowledged it, stepped around it, refused to touch it. Some mornings it felt like a test of character. Some mornings it just smelled bad. The ants arrived on day four. The flies on day five. I made coffee and went about my day.

A week flew by, and soon enough, ants arrived, followed closely by flies. The smell matured into something distinctly unpleasant, a malodorous challenge to our collective patience.

The night before the parents returned, in a flurry of last-minute panic, Courtney cleaned everything. Thoroughly. I muttered a thank you, suppressing my pride.

That standoff taught me something: waiting works. Not because people suddenly develop integrity, but because consequences catch up. The trick is being willing to let the mess sit long enough that someone else has to deal with it.

Years later, I'd use the same strategy in court. Let the contradictions pile up. Let the forged documents sit side by side with the real ones. Don't clean up their mess for them. Make them explain it.

The next day, as the parents returned, mother inquired about the funny smell lingering in the house. At dinner that evening, father leaned in and asked if anyone had anything to report. We all exchanged glances, the air thick with distrust and unspoken words. I seized the moment, saying: "Everything has gone well. Everyone behaved. No problems."

My honest assessment earned me something resembling respect. It felt like a delicate negotiation, and we avoided further issues thereafter.

***

In the rare moments I had free, I scoured the phone book searching for anything Finnish — a club, a cultural society, anyone who might know what sisu meant without needing it explained. What I found, page after page, was "Finish carpenters." It took me a while.

Longer still to appreciate that English had assigned my entire nationality to the back end of a cabinet. But the phone book had made its point: in America, you finish things. Where you're from is your own business.

My main transportation was a bicycle. I only had one day off a week. Sunday mornings I would get up early and go explore. Disappeared for a day. Loved the coastal bike paths, the endless rows of bars and restaurants. I stayed in good shape putting hundreds of miles on a bike.

Then I graduated and was allowed to use the family's old car, mainly to drive the kids around but then for my days off. My first alone trip was to a mall. I was way too exited to check the license plate, not the make or model of the car either. It was a black car.

When I was done with my shopping spree I come out to the parking lot. Where is my black car. That specific dread — the parking lot panic, the creeping certainty that you have somehow lost an entire automobile — is apparently universal and hits harder in a foreign country where you can't even ask for help without conjugating something wrong. I walked up and down rows of black cars with the focused desperation of someone who has run out of better ideas, peering into back seats like a very obvious criminal.

Hadn't realized that there were four parking lots. Had no clue which one I had parked at. The next four hours was spent from going from car to car, looking for my sweater in the backseat.

Found it. I took off exhausted. Made a left turn somewhere on to a one-way street. Going the wrong way. Naturally. And where did that cop car came from. Immediately. I got stopped.

I showed him my international driver's license that was a mini book, exotic looking. He had never seen one and was very interested. Instead of giving me a ticket he took me out for dinner. I went, because what else do you do. Also I was hungry. Also America was turning out to be significantly stranger than advertised, and dinner seemed like a reasonable response.

When my time was up, I asked about vacation pay. The family laughed and handed me a crumpled twenty-dollar bill — one extra week's pay on top of the twenty a week I'd already been earning, as though six months of work deserved exactly that much ceremony. I didn't argue. But I filed it away: fairness isn't a starting point. It's something you enforce. And if you can't enforce it, you walk away before the insult becomes the injury.

But sometimes, if you're lucky and foreign and carrying the right kind of paperwork, you get dinner instead of a ticket.

Why Quiet Exits Matter

I left Florida without drama. No tearful goodbyes, no promises to stay in touch, no forwarding address beyond "Los Angeles, somewhere." The family didn't ask where I was going and I didn't volunteer. We shook hands, they thanked me for my service, I thanked them for the opportunity. Very polite. Very professional. Very hollow. What doesn't get said when you leave cleanly is everything that matters. I didn't say their son was a tyrant because they'd let him be. I didn't say twenty dollars bonus for six months was an insult and they knew it. I didn't say they'd built a life on the backs of people they could underpay and slept fine because they called it opportunity. None of it. Because saying it wouldn't change anything — it would just make the exit messy, and messy exits follow you.

I didn't really care about the money. I hadn't come to America to get rich off a baby-sitter salary. I came to see what else existed beyond Helsinki winters and predictable summers, and the job gave me that — a foothold, a way in. That doesn't make the twenty dollars any less of an insult. You can be grateful for the opportunity and still recognize when someone's taking advantage of you. Those two things aren't mutually exclusive.

Anger is expensive. You can carry it, let it fuel you, but if it comes out at the wrong moment in front of the wrong people, it becomes evidence that you're the problem. Not the system, not the family that underpaid you — you. The angry one. The ungrateful one. So I packed my two suitcases, said thank you, and got on a bus. I watched Florida disappear through smudged glass. No ceremony. No grief. Just the specific lightness of a chapter ending cleanly. I was twenty. I had two suitcases and a foothold and the bus fare to Los Angeles. That was enough.

The fastest way out is always the path that doesn't require explanations.

CHAPTER 6

Greyhound University

Greyhound University doesn't give degrees. It gives perspective. Harry Chapin called it "a dog of a way to get around," and he wasn't wrong — you sit in a seat that doesn't recline, next to strangers who haven't showered in three days, traveling through states you can't pronounce, learning exactly where you rank in America's invisible hierarchy. Spoiler: if you're on a Greyhound bus, you're not high on the list.

In the summer of 1981, I bought a Greyhound pass for a month. All I had was a map of where the buses went, a red pen to mark the route as I went, and a burning desire to explore—the kind of yearning that gnaws at your spirit until you can't ignore it anymore. I chose my destinations the way you choose words you've heard before. "New Orleans" sounded right.

Leaving St. Petersburg Florida, forty hours later, I arrived—a weary traveler in a world that felt full of possibility yet marred by my naïveté. I uncapped the red pen and drew a thick, crooked line from Florida to Louisiana — the first mark on the map. Forty hours on a Greyhound is its own education in the limits of the human body. You learn which positions are sustainable for four hours versus which ones destroy your lower back by hour twelve. You learn that the smell of the bus at hour thirty-eight is something that stays in your clothes for days. You learn that the fluorescent lights never turn off, that the person three rows back will cough for the entire state of Louisiana, and that arrival — any arrival — feels like a small miracle. You hold onto that feeling longer than you should.

The Hierarchy

Greyhound buses have a social structure more rigid than anything I'd seen in Finland. At the top: people traveling short distances. They're just passing through. They sit near the front, keep to themselves, get off at the next stop. They don't make eye contact. They don't want to be associated with the rest of us. Fair.

In the middle: families. Usually, a mother with kids who are too young to complain effectively but old enough to be exhausting. They take up multiple seats, spread snacks everywhere, and emit a constant low-level hum of chaos. You don't sit near the families unless all other options are gone.

At the bottom: long-haul solo travelers. The people who are on the bus for *days*. No specific destination. No urgency. Just moving because staying still costs more.

I was in the middle-bottom tier. Solo, long-haul, but with a destination. That put me slightly above the people who were just riding in circles, but below anyone who could've afforded a plane ticket and chose not to. The driver didn't care where you ranked. He cared that you didn't cause problems, didn't smell too bad, and got back on the bus within ten minutes of each stop.

Miss the ten-minute window and the bus left without you. No exceptions. No sympathy. Your bag stayed on the bus. You stayed at the truck stop. Efficiency.

New Orleans

Greyhound teaches scale. And humility. It also teaches you when not to ask questions.

For ten hours, I sat next to a Black grandmother who was larger than life in every way that mattered. Her vibrant stories spilled out like gifts from a treasure chest: tales of her ten siblings, her children, her grandchildren—dozens of them. They were poor, loud, and infinitely loved. They were held together with something stronger than money.

At some point she leaned in and said, very calmly, "Honey, when you get to New Orleans, you just stay where the white folk are. No need to wander around and get yourself killed."

That sentence did not come with a disclaimer or footnote. It wasn't political. It was logistical. Survival advice. I trusted it immediately. Something in the way she said it — calm, matter-of-fact, the way you'd tell someone not to touch a hot stove — landed in my chest like a weight I hadn't expected to carry. I was twenty years old and Finnish and had arrived in America believing, in some vague optimistic way, that it was mostly what the movies suggested. That sentence rearranged something.

When I stepped off the bus at 4 a.m., the Greyhound station was deserted — a far cry from the bustling downtown I'd pictured. I stood there with two suitcases and a very European belief that things would somehow work out. My legs ached from the bus. My eyes felt gritty. I had that specific post-overnight-travel disorientation where you're not quite sure what day it is or why you thought this was a good idea. The air was thick and warm in a way that felt almost physical, like walking into a room with too many people in it. Nothing about this resembled a plan.

Around me were people walking, talking, living — none of them white. I had no plan, no address, no idea what my next move should be.

Then, out of the dim chaos, I spotted a glowing Holiday Inn ad at the other end of the station with a phone beneath it. I called. Somehow, we understood each other. They sent a car. For a fleeting moment, I felt safe, then I did the math. One night at a Holiday Inn would consume a heroic percentage of my monthly education budget. I stood in that lobby doing arithmetic in my head, the kind that ends with you choosing between shelter and eating for the next week. The carpet was very clean. The receptionist was very polite. I smiled back and tried to look like someone who had not just arrived on a Greyhound at 4 a.m. with no plan.

In daylight, New Orleans looked less like imminent death and more like a city coming to life. It was messy and vibrant, filled with culture spilling into the streets.

I pulled up my big-girl panties and found a cheaper motel. There, I met a Canadian traveler who was equally lost and therefore qualified as a partner in exploration.

Together, we roamed down Bourbon Street. Jazz clubs. Music spilling out of doorways like an invitation to stay alive. In those moments, life began to make sense again. I stayed two days. Then got back on the bus.

El Paso

Next stop: El Paso, Texas. I arrived in the early afternoon, right in the heart of siesta. It was hot—almost oppressive in its stillness. The streets lay quiet.

I stood staring into the window of a closed art gallery, probably radiating lost foreigner energy. Just then, the gallery owner opened his door, inviting me in as though I were a long-lost friend. We talked art—the kind of conversation that ignites passion and filament.

Then he casually suggested, "Do you want to go to Mexico?" He recommended I leave my luggage and camera behind so I wouldn't be "an easy target." In that moment, a question took root in my mind: *Is this how people disappear?* My heart was doing something irregular.

I was standing in a closed art gallery in Texas with a man I'd met forty minutes ago who was suggesting we cross an international border together and leave my luggage behind. Every sensible instinct I had was filing a formal objection.

I said yes anyway. Because I was twenty and had come this far by saying yes to things that scared me, and it had worked out so far, and also the tacos he'd mentioned.

With no phone, just a few dollars, and my passport tucked safely in my pocket, I somehow found myself saying yes. We crossed the border and immersed ourselves in the atmosphere: street tacos that permanently ruined all future tacos for me, laughter echoing through alleyways, local artists welcoming us into their studios where credentials were unnecessary. I felt human, generous, alive. And more importantly, I came back intact. I stayed friends with Edgar for forty years after that day.

Another lesson emerged in the simplicity of connection. No contracts. No paperwork. Just accountability in real time. People looked at you. People remembered you. If something went wrong, it belonged to someone. There was no escape into plausible deniability. That's how trust is supposed to work. Face to face. Name to name. I stayed in El Paso two days. Then got back on the bus.

The Rest of the Route

Upper Michigan and Sacramento were the only places where I had actual distant relatives. Somehow, the rest of America adopted me anyway.

I stayed a few days with distant family. Nice enough. Polite. The kind of visit where everyone's relieved when it's over. Then I got back on the bus and headed north to Vancouver.

Everyone on the bus connected you forward—not institutions or policies. People. "I have a cousin there." "Call this person." "Stay here. Eat this. Watch your back." I didn't yet know how rare that was.

While I was on a payphone in Winnipeg at the YWCA, I noticed a girl circling. I was using my telephone operator knowledge to make free long-distance calls—payphones had their workarounds if you knew the system. Small rebellion. Zero guilt.

When I hung up, she said hello—in Finnish. I froze. I had been counting on Finnish as my private language. The one place no one could follow me. We became best friends instantly. Spent days partying. Naturally.

***

In upper Michigan, I followed a referral from my godparents to distant relatives who were expecting me. I discovered a massive Finnish community around Lake Superior—second generation, practical, emotionally restrained.

I was paraded around like a prize pony straight from the old country. Everyone had a son. Nice boys. Hardworking boys. Lutheran boys. Sweet, earnest, mildly alarming. One of the first things I learned was to say yes before I fully understood the question. It kept working.

When I bought my next pass, I casually told the agent, "I want to go to Zigago." She stared at me, perplexed. Then, pointing at the map, "Oh honey, you mean *Chicago*." Accents were thick on both sides of the continent.

Chicago

My ultimate goal was the Monet water lilies at the Art Institute. Mission accomplished.

I stared at them for eight hours, letting their beauty wash over me. I cried a little, tears of joy, of reflection. Eight hours in front of a painting sounds excessive until you're doing it, and then it sounds exactly right. The lilies aren't what you expect. They're not calm. They're enormous and restless, color pushing against color, the surface of water rendered in a way that feels more true than a photograph. I sat on a bench until my back ached and then sat some more. This was why I had come. Not to America specifically — to this. To the thing that exists on the other side of forty hours on a bus.

Nobody asked me to leave. Nobody wanted to know why. My soul recalibrated.

Niagara Falls and New York

I made my way to Niagara Falls for my twentieth birthday, raising an imaginary glass to myself. "Good job, girl. Still alive."

Next stop: New York. Then a flight back to Finland. Six weeks. A once-in-a-lifetime adventure that pushed the boundaries of my understanding.

What Buses Teach You

Greyhound University teaches you that America has two versions.

There's the version in the brochures—freedom, opportunity, the open road, manifest destiny, all the promises. And then there's the version you see from a bus window at 3 a.m. in the middle of nowhere. Truck stops. Trailer parks. Towns that died when the highway rerouted. People living in cars because rent costs more than they make in a month. The America that doesn't make it into the commercials.

It also teaches you self-reliance in the most unglamorous way possible. Nobody on a Greyhound bus is waiting to solve your problems — and there's something clarifying about that. You figure out what you need, you figure out how to get it, and when the bus pulls out you'd better be on it. Not because the world is cruel, but because the world is indifferent, and indifference turns out to be a decent teacher.

Greyhound University doesn't issue diplomas. It simply teaches you how systems actually work — and how dangerous it is to confuse paper authority with human truth. I would remember that later. Very clearly.

The Return

I returned to a life that was technically unchanged. Yet internally, I felt like a spirit unwilling to be tamed. Back to work. Back to my boyfriend. Back to the plan I had left behind.

But I was still restless.

My mother had opinions about my travels—why I didn't at least apply for art school, start thinking about a career, or do something real with my life? When the art school application deadline came, I sabotaged it by pulling a drawing. If I got in, I'd have to stay. Easier to fail on purpose. California kept calling.

In 1982, I took another leave—a full year this time, landing in Los Angeles. Kari waited—until he didn't. Eventually, he married someone else.

By 1983, nothing was holding me back anymore. I was free to go, and I moved to Los Angeles permanently.

In 1988, I got married and was happy. Life flowed like a gentle stream, peaceful and rich with promise. Years later, around 1994, I reached out to the sculptor again and accepted his offer to cast a bronze of the piece I had modeled for. Finally, I had the means to make it happen.

When we connected, he told me it was the biggest mistake of his life that he hadn't waited. As fate would have it, shortly after the foundry work was completed, my father built a sturdy crate and shipped the sculpture to me.

The day it left Finland, the artist had a stroke. Three months later, when the piece arrived in Los Angeles, Kari died.

***

I unpacked the crate myself. The bronze was cold from the journey. We set it on the table and sat with it for a while, trying to reconcile the fact that something he had made of me had outlasted him — that his hands had shaped this version of my face and now those hands were gone. That's the strange mathematics of art. The maker disappears. The made thing stays.

The next year, 1995, Kari Ovaska, the sculptor, would have turned fifty. His largest retrospective traveled through Finland. Opening night in Helsinki coincided with my birthday—an uncanny turn of events.

I was living in Los Angeles and wasn't able to attend the show. But as you entered the gallery, my portrait was the first piece you saw when you walked in. I felt a rush of pride and disbelief, like an out-of-body experience.

The next day, *Helsingin Sanomat,* the newspaper, reviewed the show and asked, "Who was that potato-nose woman?"

Fifteen seconds of fame. Perfectly Finnish.

I often wonder about the alternate reality — Mrs. Ovaska, studio helper, sculptor's wife. Whether I'd have faded into the background or fought my way to my own work anyway. Probably fought. That's the honest answer. But I didn't stay to find out, and by the time I understood what I'd walked away from, the question had answered itself.

What I didn't know yet: that chaos would find me anyway. And when it did, I'd need every bit of that independence — and the willingness to fight alone — to survive it.

CHAPTER 7

Los Angeles With No Net

California had already won me over before I arrived — at least with the idea of it. San Francisco was the original fantasy. Fog. Art. Thoughtful people wearing black and having opinions. Then Los Angeles waved. I landed instead in Brea, California. Orange County. Vanilla with a homeowners association. The neighborhood was aggressively suburban. Identical houses. Identical lawns. Identical smiles. No cafés. No sidewalks. No accidental encounters. No life you could stumble into. Without a car, you didn't "live" there—you were **stored.**

I stood at the end of the street that first morning and felt the specific despair of a landscape that offers nothing to walk toward. In Helsinki, you could always walk toward something — a café, a harbor, a person you might accidentally become. Here the street just continued until it became another street exactly like it. I went back inside and made coffee and told myself this was temporary. It was. But temporary has its own weight when you're living inside it.

The bus stop was an hour's walk away. I remember standing on the sidewalk the first morning, looking down a road that went nowhere, thinking: This is what people mean when they say "safe." *Wow. I have made choices.*

I was hired to take care of a five-year-old named Joshua.

Joshua was spirited, that's the polite word. He was a tiny tyrant with unlimited screen time and no boundaries. His mother had surrendered. His father attempted authority in short bursts between business trips. I wasn't a nanny — I was damage control. Joshua was five and had already figured out that screaming worked better than asking. I had the specific exhaustion of someone responsible for a child who does not want to be managed, in a house where no one had ever told him no with any conviction. By week two I understood why the mother played tennis every day. By week three I didn't blame her.

Venice Beach Sundays

Sundays were my only day off. One day to remember who I was before responsibility swallowed me whole. Every Sunday at 7 a.m., I got on a bus and headed to Venice Beach. Four hours each way, worth every minute. Venice was chaos in the best sense. Street art, music everywhere, roller skaters weaving through pedestrians like choreography. Food stalls, noise and laughter. People existing loudly, unapologetically. I didn't need to belong. I just needed to breathe.

By evening, the thought of returning to Brea felt unbearable, so I delayed it. At 11 p.m., I caught the last bus into downtown L.A. The Bonaventure Hotel had a piano bar. Of course it did.

Glass elevators and indoor waterfalls. An international crowd. I became a regular. From 1 a.m. to 4 a.m., I sat at that bar, soaking in a world that felt wide again. Those three hours were the only hours in the week that belonged entirely to me. No Joshua. No obligations. Just the sound of a piano and strangers who didn't know what my week had been and didn't ask. I walked home by 7. Joshua was awake by 8. Reset complete. Rinse. Repeat.

The Night That Changed Everything

One Saturday, I was offered the rare luxury of a local night off. I found a restaurant with live music and dancing. I met a group of people. We talked. We danced. One man attached himself to me immediately. I declined. Repeatedly, calmly and clearly. He ignored it.

When the night ended, the group suggested continuing the party at a nearby house. Against my instincts—and reassured by the size of the group—I went.

The moment we arrived, the group paired off and disappeared into bedrooms like it had been choreographed. It hadn't been choreographed. It had been engineered. I was suddenly alone with the one person I had tried to avoid all night. I said it was late. I said I needed to go. He decided otherwise.

Yes. I was raped.

The word is exact. I use it because the alternatives are all ways of making it smaller than it was, and I spent enough years doing that already.

Afterward, he handed me a phone and said I could report it if I wanted—but no one would believe me. I had come willingly. He was confident, relaxed and certain. I believed him.

I walked ten miles home in a ripped skirt and a fractured wrist. I remember the sound of my own footsteps on the pavement. Counting them. Focusing on the next one and then the next one. The skirt was cold. The air was warm. Nothing made sense in the way that nothing makes sense when your brain is trying to file something it has no category for.

I didn't tell anyone for ten years.

Ten years is a long time to carry something alone. You get good at it the way you get good at anything you practice daily — efficiently, automatically, without thinking about the weight anymore because the weight has just become part of you.

Shame is efficient that way. It keeps the system clean. No paperwork. No disruption. Just silence. Not the family. Not friends. Not anyone who could've done anything about it. I just kept moving.

Sundays to Venice Beach became non-negotiable. Not an escape anymore—survival. If I stayed still too long, the thoughts caught up. The what-ifs. The should-haves. The replaying.

But if I kept moving—bus to Venice, walk the boardwalk, piano bar until 4 a.m., bus back to Brea—the thoughts couldn't land. Momentum became armor. I knew every stop on that route by heart. Which seat caught the morning light. How the bus smelled different at 7 a.m. than at 11 p.m.

I finally told someone. Then the floodgates opened. Not because I'd healed, but because I'd finally accepted that no one was coming to save me. If I wanted out, I had to get myself out.

Orange County taught me survival skills. I learned to read a room in seconds, to trust my instincts, and to leave without explanation when something felt wrong. Better rude than dead.

I learned to document everything — receipts, names, dates, conversations — because memory isn't evidence. If you ever need to prove something happened, you need more than your word against theirs.

That habit saved me decades later in courtrooms, where fraud had to be proven against people who didn't want to see it. Orange County didn't teach me how to win. It taught me how to survive long enough to fight back.

I wasn't a quitter—but Brea was done with me. I didn't last the year. Joshua survived.

I moved to West Hollywood soon after. New house. New family. Same job. I cooked, cleaned, nannied, and learned—thoroughly—that motherhood was not my calling. Consider me cured.

What it really gave me were survival skills. The kind you don't advertise. The kind you use when it counts. Los Angeles was waiting.

West Hollywood

One morning I rushed to drag the trash cans out for pickup. I'd forgotten the night before. One can was suspiciously heavy. I yanked, my lower back yanked back. *Pop.*

That moment quietly redirected my entire future. We renegotiated the terms of my stay. I would take care of the kids for free in exchange for room and board, and they'd hire a housekeeper named Wilma to handle the cleaning. This was my first adult lesson in leverage: injuries could be bargaining chips.

LA City College

With newfound freedom, I wanted to check out Los Angeles City College. While the kids were in kindergarten, I took the bus and explored.

I found the right office. Asked about enrolling. "No. You need a student visa from your country." They told me. I wandered into another office for foreign students. "Finland?" they said. "We've never had anyone from Finland." Then, they huddled together, shrugged it off, and made a small bureaucratic exception. "You can try one semester. Then you have to go home and get the visa." Fair enough. I was in.

I loved it. Attending school while the kids were at kindergarten, just like that—a new life began, patched together with goodwill, bus schedules, and loopholes. Wilma and I became fast friends.

West Hollywood Nights

One night, perhaps a miracle, we both had the same night off. We decided to go bar hopping right in the neighborhood—West Hollywood looked promising. We walked into a bar, eyes wide with anticipation. Wow. So many good-looking men. "Are we in heaven?" we mused. Then it dawned on us—every bar we visited was a gay bar. At some point, we stopped pretending to be confused. "Well," we concluded, "we're not the target audience."

Los Angeles had made one thing very clear: I was useful everywhere. Desired often. Sometimes inconveniently. And somehow still free. For now, that was enough.

In 1983, Third Time Is the Charm

I officially enrolled at LA City College, this time with a student visa — legitimate on paper, at least.

I found a room in a Victorian house run by a ninety-year-old woman from Oklahoma. Turquoise shag carpet and blue floral wallpaper—so bad it circled back to charming. When I said I'd take the room, she leaned in and whispered that she already had a husband picked out for me.

The next night I got a knock on my door. Steve asked if I'd like to have a cup of tea. That was it—we were best friends immediately. It took a couple of years before we started dating. She didn't live to see it, but I ended up marrying him five years later.

Art School

At school, I signed up for every art class I could find—drawing, painting, design. Anything tactile, anything physical, anything that didn't require fluency in English.

And as a delightful twist of fate, I earned straight A's across the board in art. Outside that realm, I also took classes in tennis, philosophy, and business. Somehow, I made the dean's list, which felt absurd given that my English was still held together with duct tape and hope. Nobody asked questions; they just printed my name correctly and moved on.

In one business class, the instructor unexpectedly called me at home and asked if I wanted to wrestle sometime. I said yes. What did I know? I thought America was exceptionally friendly. This sort of thing never happened in Finland. Afterward, I looked up the word in my dictionary.

We never wrestled. He never called again.

I understood later what that moment had been—not confusion but testing. A small reach for leverage disguised as humor. I was young, and he controlled my grades. That imbalance weighed heavily, unnoticed until much later.

Art school wasn't about indulgence; it was practical. You showed up, you worked, you failed in public, and then you tried again. Creativity didn't need protection; it survived structure just fine.

But I overstayed my student visa, something that became part of my survival. I cleaned houses, took a psychological test involving inkblots, and passed. When I showed up for the interview, I didn't get the job because the woman didn't like looking up at me, tall enough to make insecure people uncomfortable.

The Catering Truck

I quit cleaning without a plan. I sold kitchen cabinets, taught art at the Braille Institute, did some interpreting work, and ran a catering truck downtown Los Angeles.

The catering truck became my real education in business, survival, systems, and consequences.

How hard could it be to drive a truck? I was already a captain of my own ship—let's give it a go. I trained for two weeks, sitting in someone else's truck, absorbing everything I could. I took the driving test and nailed it. The company handed me a route and a cook. And I won the lottery.

Yolanda—a beautiful Salvadoran woman—became my cook and my best friend. We were both twenty-four and ready to conquer the world. Construction sites were our main clients, and word spread fast about the "party truck." Breakfast and lunch, music included. We fed the boys and lifted their spirits. The routine was brutal: up at sunrise, buy the food, load the truck, fill it with ice, and stock drinks. At the end of each shift, you'd pay up. We were good. Immediately.

Stopping at each site took exactly thirty minutes. Not thirty-one. Not "close enough." Union breaks are sacred. If the workers came out and you weren't there holding burritos like an offering, you were done.

Miss it twice and you were fired. No appeals. No mercy. Add Los Angeles traffic and you had yourself a daily stress test disguised as a job. A heavy foot developed early. It was never fully cured.

Two years earlier, my parents had visited me and we rented a car in downtown L.A. My dad drove because the traffic terrified me. I remember thinking, I will never drive in this city. This is unhinged.

Fast forward, and I'm threading a catering truck through construction sites on a stopwatch, gambling my income on red lights and faith. Turns out fear is temporary. Deadlines are not.

The Construction Site

There's a brick building at 9th and Figueroa downtown. I can say this with pride: it was built with my burritos. This site had a drive-through layout—enter one side, exit the other. One day, after feeding the crew, my exit was blocked by a fresh delivery of steel bars.

Oh shit.

The only option was to back the truck all the way out. Sweaty hands gripped the steering wheel. One mirror folded in. Six inches of clearance on either side—no scraping, no margin for error. I made it. Then I heard clapping—from about ten floors up. Forty guys watching the whole thing. They'd placed bets. One guy believed in me. He won.

The next day he thanked me for his "retirement fund." For twenty years after that, I got a Christmas card reminding me. Sweet. It couldn't have been much money, but it meant everything.

The Garment District

Not all stops were created equal.

I had one stop at a clothing factory. I had a feeling from day one it was a bad idea. These people made minimum wage—if even that. Sweatshop conditions. Long hours. No official breaks. No official anything. I'd show up and they'd swarm the truck like they hadn't eaten in days. Maybe they hadn't. Yes, I felt sorry for them. But sympathy doesn't pay the bills.

A couple of people asked for credit till the next payday. "Sure, of course." I kept a little notebook. Wrote down names. Amounts. Due dates. The payday came. They never showed up again. Lesson learned: credit is a luxury I couldn't afford.

I wore a money belt for the coins—ease and fast dispensing. Paper money stayed in my hand while I was serving, then got stuffed into the belt when I needed both hands free.

One day I saw a guy eyeing my money. Not glancing. Eyeing. Calculating.

Measuring distance. I knew what was coming. For once, I was prepared. He made his move—lunged forward, reaching for the belt. I slammed him with my knee. Groin. Jackpot. He bent over in pain and crawled away like a wounded animal. That was it.

I called my company that afternoon. "It's not worth going there anymore. I don't have enough eyes to keep them from stealing from me. It's too dangerous." They agreed. Found me another construction site within the week. Problem solved. Mostly.

What stayed with me wasn't the attack—I'd handled that. It was the look on the other workers' faces when it happened. Not shock, not concern. Resignation. Like they'd seen it coming too. Like this was just how things went when you were desperate and someone with money showed up.

I didn't blame them for being desperate. I blamed the system that made them desperate. But I also wasn't going to get stabbed over a breakfast burrito.

Survival math. Cold. Practical. Necessary.

Success attracts attention. Not all of it friendly. The veterans—other catering truck drivers who'd been working the downtown routes for years—didn't love being outperformed by the newcomer with the accent and the party truck. The first time my refrigeration unit died overnight, I thought I'd been careless. Maybe the plug wasn't pushed in all the way. It happens. The food spoiled. Total loss. Several hundred dollars down the drain.

I ate the cost. Restocked. Moved on.

The second time, I knew. Someone was unplugging my truck at night. Deliberately, quietly. After that, I taped the plug to the outlet. Obvious and visible. A quiet accusation to whoever was doing it. It stopped. But the atmosphere changed. In the beginning, the other drivers had been helpful—talkative, giving hints on what to buy and serve, how to change the menu, shortcuts around road construction, which inspectors to avoid.

Then it cooled. Formal. "Good morning." "How are you." The kind of politeness that keeps distance and warns you not to cross it. I learned to park under streetlights and to check the truck every night before I left. Competence didn't always earn goodwill. Sometimes it earned resentment.

The Routes

My route covered about eight stops — construction sites mostly, a few office buildings, one hospital loading dock. Each had its own rhythm, its own cast of characters, its own unspoken rules.

The guys at the high-rise on Figueroa were my favorites. They tipped, they flirted harmlessly, and they placed bets on whether I could parallel park the truck in impossible spaces. I could. I did. They cheered. One of them told me I drove like I was angry at the city. I told him I was angry at traffic. He said that was fair.

The hospital stop was the hardest. Six in the morning, nurses coming off night shifts, doctors who hadn't slept, orderlies working two jobs and still couldn't make rent. They didn't want conversation — they wanted coffee, and they wanted it fast, hot, and cheap. I started having their orders ready before they reached the window, because at six in the morning, after a twelve-hour shift, the kindest thing you can offer someone is not making them wait or talk.

One nurse — older, Filipino, tired in a way that looked permanent — always ordered the same thing. Black coffee, one breakfast burrito, no salsa. One morning she handed me a twenty and told me to keep the change. I tried to give it back. She refused. "You show up," she said. "Every day. Same time. That matters." I didn't know what to say, so I just said thank you. She nodded and walked back inside.

Not every opportunity is worth the risk. You can want to help, feel sorry for people, believe everyone deserves a chance — but if the situation is dangerous, if the math doesn't work, if your gut says get out, you listen. You don't stay out of guilt. You leave, find a better route, survive.

Skid Row Fridays

Fridays became my reset.

After the downtown LA route, I'd load up everything left over and drive to Skid Row.

Before I started working there, that area was the place you locked your doors and rolled up your windows. The first time I drove the truck down there, my hands were tight on the wheel and I was doing the math on exits in my head the way I'd learned to do — where the doors were, how fast I could move. Then a man walked up to the window and said good evening and asked what I had left, and the math stopped. He was cold. I had coffee. That was the whole transaction.

Scary. Dangerous. The kind of neighborhood you drove through quickly and thanked God when you made it out. But once I got to know some of the people, it turned out they were just people. Human beings who'd had things go wrong. Lost a job. Medical bills spiraled. Family fell apart. Mental illness without treatment. Addiction without support.

The kind of third-world-country problems that shouldn't exist in the richest country on earth—but do, because we've decided that healthcare and housing are luxuries instead of rights.

I didn't have much myself. I drove an old Pinto that sometimes needed a pair of scissors under the hood to start. My apartment was a single room with turquoise shag carpet. I was one bad month away from being right there with them. But I could give these people a short moment of kindness. Of being seen. Of being recognized as more than invisible.

I didn't charge them. I just gave away whatever was left. Burritos. Coffee. Fruit. Whatever hadn't sold.vSome people thanked me. Some didn't. Some were too tired or too high or too broken to make eye contact. It didn't matter. It wasn't charity. It was the only part of the day that made sense.

The only part where the math didn't have to work. Where efficiency didn't matter. Where I could just be human without calculating risk. I hope I remember to keep that in my life. Even now. Especially now. When everything's a fight and every system's a trap and trust has to be earned with documentation and witness testimony — I hope I remember that sometimes, the right thing to do is just give someone a burrito and not ask questions.

The Olympics

During the 1984 Olympics, I had trained to be an interpreter for the Finnish team. I just thought I could squeeze that in somehow. And I did. Because apparently sleeping was optional.

During the Olympics, our schedules for the catering trucks moved up an hour to ease the LA traffic. That meant waking up at 3 AM to start the breakfast route. I'd be done feeding my construction workers by noon, then straight to the Olympic Village to work as an interpreter for airports, athletes, dignitaries, and press conferences.

By midnight, I was done. Three hours of sleep, and then rinse, repeat. The month was unforgettable. I'm glad I did it. It was a once-in-a-lifetime experience, the kind you commit to before your brain has time to calculate the math on how little sleep a human body technically needs to function.

I was part of "the flying squad"—which sounds more elite than it was but did come with perks. There were so few Finnish interpreters that we got extra privileges. Passes to go anywhere. Access to everything. The main job was simple: make sure the athletes had everything they needed.

I also got called in to pick up dignitaries from the airport. Thanks to my catering truck experience navigating LA at ungodly hours, I knew the city cold. I could get anywhere, anytime, without a map or a second thought.

Most of the interpreting was straightforward. Until weightlifting. I didn't know much about weightlifting. Actually, I didn't know anything about weightlifting. But I showed up anyway, clipboard in hand, ready to translate whatever needed translating. Then, at one point during the competition, it became clear that Finland was going to win a medal. Silver, specifically. And that's when it hit me: There's going to be a press conference.

A press conference I would have to attend. In front of cameras.

Interpreting. Live. For the media. About a sport I knew nothing about. Using technical terms I didn't know in either language. The fear of public speaking—still deeply rooted from childhood, still very much alive—came roaring back. My hands went cold. My mouth went dry. I looked at the cameras and felt eleven years old again, standing in front of a classroom, every word in every language I knew evaporating simultaneously. The coach was kneeling in front of me feeding me terminology I'd never heard and I was nodding like I understood while internally having what I can only describe as a very polite crisis. Everything after that moment became a blur.

We got silver. Thank God. At least there would be fewer questions than if we'd won gold. The press conference was set up in a room with flashing lights, cameras everywhere, reporters shouting questions I barely understood even in English. The coach knelt in front of the table, feeding me technical terms as fast as he could. I didn't know any of them. Not in Finnish. Not in English. Somehow, we got through it. I have no idea what I actually said. But no one threw anything, so I'm calling it a win.

The main highlight—the thing that made the entire month worth it—was the closing ceremonies.

We accompanied the athletes up to the entrance of the stadium, making sure they were in the right order, checking names, doing the official interpreter thing. And then a few of us looked at each other and thought: What the heck. This is the last day. We're just going to march into the stadium with the athletes. So we did.

We walked right in. The noise hit first — that specific roar of a full stadium that you feel in your chest before you hear it properly. Then the lights. Then the realization that we were actually in it, not watching it, not interpreting it, just in it. I don't remember making a decision to start grinning. It just happened. Three weeks of three hours of sleep and burritos at 6 a.m. and press conferences about sports I didn't understand, and here we were, walking into the closing ceremonies of the 1984 Olympic Games because we decided to. Some decisions make themselves. No permission. No credentials that technically allowed it. Just a handful of interpreters deciding that we'd earned the right to take in the glory of the moment firsthand.

The roar of the crowd. The lights. Athletes from every country flooding the field in a chaotic, joyful mass. The whole world watching.

We were in it. Worth every second.

Somewhere in that month, I proved to myself I could keep going long after I thought I couldn't. The Olympics mattered. The athletes mattered. The dignitaries I drove around, the press conferences I fumbled through, the construction workers who needed breakfast burritos at 6 a.m.—it all mattered. So I showed up. Even when my body wanted to quit. Even when my brain couldn't quite translate "clean and jerk" into coherent Finnish. Even when three hours of sleep felt like a cruel joke. I showed up.

PART II

Becoming an Artist *by Accumulation*

I am not a product of my circumstances.
I am a product of my decisions.
— Stephen Covey

CHAPTER 8

Publishing, Deadlines, and Reality

After a year on the catering truck, I quit. The money was good. That wasn't the point. Money has never been the point for me. I needed more. I wanted more. I didn't come to America to drive a truck full of sandwiches and disappointment. I came for a reason—I just didn't know what it was yet.

So, with that familiar impulse to leap before looking, I moved on. No plan. Again.

A friend connected me with someone at a small publishing company called California Bound. They published relocation magazines specifically for real estate agents—glossy booklets full of smiling agents and aspirational houses that made you believe moving to Thousand Oaks would change your life. They were looking for a housekeeper.

Not exactly the glamorous American dream I'd envisioned, but I needed work and I wasn't above cleaning toilets. Yet. There's a specific quality to cleaning a stranger's bathroom when you have a portfolio from art school sitting in your apartment. You develop a very focused relationship with the task directly in front of you and an agreement with yourself not to think about the larger picture. I was good at that agreement. I'd had practice. I jumped right in. I cleaned their house. I scrubbed their toilets. I washed their laundry like a good immigrant who knew the value of any job that paid.

Here's a funny little detail that stuck with me.

I saw a clothesline in the backyard. The first American one I'd seen—

seems that dryers were everywhere in this country. Everybody in Finland used clotheslines. No dryers. We dried our clothes the way nature intended, with fresh air and sunlight and a vague sense of moral superiority.

So I took the extra step. I thought I was being helpful, maybe even impressive. I hung their laundry on the clothesline instead of being lazy and just throwing everything in the dryer. The fresh smell of laundry that had dried in the open air with a gentle breeze—how can you beat that? The next time, the order came in: use the dryer. The towels were hard as rocks.

Noted. Not everything I think is the best thing in the world is perceived as such by the rest of the world. Put your nose down, girl. Americans like their towels soft and their efficiency mechanical.

A few months into this, I'd had enough. I decided I was not going to clean anybody else's toilet ever again in my life. This was not what my purpose was. I didn't know what it was, but this was not it. I quit.

Again. Nothing lined up. I was sitting at home thinking, how stupid can you be? One should have something planned first. Not me. I thought: I have to get better at this "house keeper" thing if I don't own any houses yet.

In a couple of days, the phone rang. Nikki, the owner's wife, asked if I'd like to come back and work at the office doing shipping. Hell yeah. "When do I start?" "Tomorrow morning?" "I'll be there." I had proved the point: you have to close one door for another to open. Preferably without thinking it through first. Not glamorous. Not art. But it was indoors, and they needed help.

The office was situated in Beverly Hills—a modest setup considering the zip code. A handful of dedicated souls: Ed the owner and sales guy, his wife Nikki as production coordinator, an editor, an art director, a typesetter, and me—the shipping person who showed up with a portfolio from LA City College like I might accidentally need it.

It was a small cog in a larger machine, and for the first time in a while, something sparked inside me. I'm forever thankful for how they "adopted" me. I felt I belonged. I was part of the family.

Till I wasn't.

I watched intently as magazines came together. Articles trickled in, and the typesetter, using a machine that looked like it belonged in a museum, transformed words into formatted columns. The art director worked laboriously, laying out everything by hand—cutting, pasting, aligning with a ruler and wax. Galleys were proofed; corrections were painstakingly made. Everything felt physical, tactile, slow—and I loved it.

I would finish the shipping and find reasons to stay near the production room. Watching the art director lay out pages by hand — cutting galleys, positioning photos, measuring with a ruler — felt like watching someone build something real out of nothing. My hands wanted to be doing it. I didn't say that out loud. I just stayed close and watched and waited.

The Photographer

The magazine needed tons of photos of different neighborhoods—showing the lifestyle, showing the structure of housing, making suburbia look like paradise one lawn at a time.

If I could be bold enough to ask for vacation pay as a nanny, I could ask to be a photographer. I did, offer accepted.

First it was the close-by places. I went crazy. I had an eye for this. I knew it. And apparently, they agreed because I was approved for longer trips with a company car. The first time I drove out of the parking lot with a camera and a company car and a list of neighborhoods, I sat at the first red light and laughed out loud. Nobody heard me. That was fine. Some victories are private.

Okay, now we're talking. You can't stop me now.

Some of the rich areas—Beverly Hills, Bel Air—I found out that it's frowned upon to take photos of people's houses without permission. Apparently the wealthy don't appreciate strangers documenting their fortresses. My excuse became legendary, and this is where the heavy Finnish accent was dialed up a notch for maximum effect.

"My aunt frrrom Finland wants to move here and I want to show her what it looks like. Yourrr house is sooo beautiful and inviting and immaculate—I'm sure she would approve of me finding a good neighborhood for her. But if you don't allow that, I will delete the photos right now." Cue the apologetic Scandinavia smile and the thick accent that made me sound both harmless and charming. Not once did I have to delete a photo. Turns out rich people love being told their houses are beautiful, especially by confused foreigners with cameras.

Production

A few months in, I asked if I could assist in production. They said yes—probably because I was already doing it, staying late, asking questions, volunteering for every task that wasn't just shipping boxes.

Publishing taught me how ideas become objects. Nothing ships itself. Creativity is cute, but deadlines? Deadlines are real. Waxing the galleys of type, cutting them up for columns, leaving room for photos—my photos—inking the boxes the old-fashioned way. Tissue paper on top of the board to spec the color. Rubylith film for color separation.

I had to figure out the enlargement from the slide to fit into the boxes, and we'd order a stat—a black-and-white low-resolution photo to show the position of the image to the printer.

That's where my eye came in handy again. I was able to look at the slide and do a quick sketch of the photo showing the exact enlargement needed. No stats required anymore. Cost savings. Bosses tend to like that.'

The Mac Arrives

Then everything changed when the Macintosh arrived. I had never touched a computer in my life, the company obtained one Mac. Then two. This was around 1984, maybe early '85. The machines were beige, boxy, and notoriously unreliable. The software crashed constantly, and floppy disks failed on a whim like they had personal vendettas. Fonts were limited, and every task took three times longer than doing it by hand.

I didn't care. I fell in hard. Completely and obsessively. The screen was small and the font options were limited and it crashed approximately every forty-five minutes and I didn't care about any of that.

I would sit in front of it after everyone else had gone home and just move things around — a headline here, a photo box there — watching the page respond in real time to decisions I was making. It felt like the most direct translation between thought and object I'd ever experienced. I had been waiting for this without knowing I was waiting for it.

I taught myself MacPaint and PageMaker—design software that felt like magic. For the first time, I could design something, see it on screen, change it instantly, and print it. No wax, no cutting, no waiting for the typesetter. No begging the art director to move something two millimeters to the left.

I stayed late every single night, came in early, and learned through mistakes and repairs and sheer stubborn determination. I devoured every manual, called tech support so often that they eventually recognized my voice and sighed when they heard my accent.

I figured out how to build a dummy book to use as a sales tool—a physical mockup of what the magazine could look like for a new city. I learned to spec type, how to match fonts, how to kern. I created the ads myself, which meant the art director and typesetter were suddenly less necessary.

And that? That went over exponentially well with management and exponentially poorly with the people I was replacing.

However, I became so absorbed that I forgot an important rule: the work wasn't mine. I was family, but not really. I was just a worker bee — not the owner. My possessive nature got in the way. I met every deadline. Every single one. Camping trips were canceled without a thought. Dinner plans, girls night out? Fiction. I ate at my desk. I drove home at midnight and was back by seven.

My eyes had that specific gritty quality of someone who has spent too many hours staring at a screen that wasn't designed to be stared at for that long. I didn't notice the cost because the work itself felt like payment. That's a dangerous equation. I'd learn that later. I didn't notice—my heart was in love with the work itself, not the life around me.

The company began to rely heavily on me for everything: layout, design, production, proofing. I worked faster than the old system ever had, and I was cheaper too—they didn't have to pay the typesetter or art director for all the revisions anymore. Just me. One person, one salary, infinite availability.

The Breaking Point

Eventually, it all came crashing down.

One day, the owner asked me to complete an entire magazine over the weekend. Last minute. Again. I said yes, again. I finished it and delivered my work Monday morning—perfect, on time, exactly as requested. Then we argued about some sections in the book. "You can't do that," I said. "It cuts the flow of the whole book." He yelled back: "I can do anything I want. This is MY book." And there it was. Something dropped in my chest. Not shock exactly — more like the sound a belief makes when it lands wrong. I had been working as though the work was mine because the work felt like mine. That's what happens when you give everything. You forget to keep track of who it actually belongs to.

I had treated it as MY book. I had given everything I had to his business. I'd forgotten, I was just cheap labor with a work ethic and an expired visa. He nodded, thanked me briefly, and handed me my next project. No acknowledgment. No raise. No recognition. Just the next deadline.

That's when it hit me. I was making someone else rich. The efficiency I'd created wasn't mine. The work I had stayed up all night doing wasn't mine. I was useful, I was good, I was, ultimately, replaceable. I drove home that night and sat in my apartment and looked at the Mac I'd bought with money I'd saved from a salary that had never reflected what I actually contributed.

The math was suddenly very clear. I had spent two years making someone else's business work. I could do that for myself instead. The only difference was that failing would be mine too. That seemed fair. It was time for a change.

I began taking clients on the side. Small projects at first, flyers for local businesses, business cards, brochures, ads. Word spread quickly. Designers were scarce in the mid-'80s, but someone who could actually use a Mac and meet deadlines? Even scarcer.

Timing helped. Luck helped. But being early and relentless? That helped even more. One final argument with the boss escalated, and just like that, I quit. Again. But this time I had a plan—sort of.

My student visa had already expired — and it had never given me the right to work in the first place, only the right to open a bank account. My passport was weeks from expiring too. MACnetic Design was born anyway. No safety net, a couple of small clients, no business plan — just me, a Mac, and looming deadlines. It was 1986, I was twenty-six, and I was about to run a business in a country where I had no legal right to do so. Seemed reasonable at the time.

The first week I had one client, a florist who needed a business card. I sat at my kitchen table and designed it in two hours and charged thirty-five dollars and felt like I'd invented something. The second week I had two clients. By the end of the month I had six. The visa situation was a problem I was solving by not thinking about it, which is a strategy with a limited shelf life but an excellent short-term return. I had work to do.

CHAPTER 9

Starting the Studio

Mid-'80s Los Angeles. I started my own graphic design studio the way people start forest fires: accidentally, confidently, and without permits. Just-get-it-done mentality. I had a bank account. I started paying taxes. I followed the rules. Other than one minor detail. No passport.

Why Ownership Mattered

People ask why I didn't just work from home. Or rent a desk at a co-working space. Or stay freelance without the overhead. The answer is simple: **ownership.** Not of the building—I was renting. But ownership of the work. The schedule. The decisions. The success and the failure.

When you work for someone else, you're building their dream. Your effort makes them money. Your late nights pad their profit margins. Your ideas get credited to the company, not to you. I'd done that. For years. I was very good at it. And I was done.

I needed space that was mine. Where I could close the door and think. Where I could spread out a project and leave it overnight without someone touching it. Where I could fail in private and succeed on my own terms.

That's what ownership gives you. Not security—ownership is terrifying. But **agency.** The first morning I opened the studio door with my own key, I stood in the empty room for a moment before turning on the lights. Just stood there. The smell of fresh paint and possibility and absolutely nothing belonging to anyone else. I had cleaned someone else's toilets to get here. That made the moment better, not worse.

The ability to say: this is mine. I made it. It works because I made it work. And if it doesn't work, that's on me too. I'll take that deal every time.

Steve and I had been together for a while by then. He was a quiet, steady presence — a chess player by habit and temperament, the kind of man who thought before he spoke, never raised his voice, and meant what he said. Solid, reliable, trustworthy: qualities that sound ordinary until you spend enough time looking for them and realize how rare they actually are. We were both hard workers who understood the value of showing up, and in that we understood each other completely. Soul mates, in the most practical and genuine sense of the word — not the fairy-tale version, but the real one, where someone simply fits alongside you without friction or performance.

We were already living together, coexisting happily in the way that works until it doesn't: roommates who shared a bed, a life, a routine. We split bills, made dinner together, didn't fight. It was comfortable and easy. But it wasn't moving forward, and I'd already learned that standing still is just a slower way of sinking.

I kept waiting for the romantic proposal — the one I'd imagined as a girl, down on one knee, a question asked, a future offered. It didn't come. Months passed, then a year, then longer. I wasn't unhappy, but I wasn't building toward anything either.

One evening I was at the kitchen table working on a client project — probably a brochure, maybe a catalog — and Steve was on the couch playing chess. I looked up. "Steve." "Mm?" "We need to talk." He looked up from the board, which was the correct response, because that phrase never means anything good. I didn't have a speech prepared and I wasn't angry, just clear. "It's time." He blinked. "Time for what?" "Time to get married. Or time for me to move out."

Silence — not the kind where someone is thinking deeply, but the kind where someone has been handed a binary choice they weren't expecting and is calculating which answer costs less. "I'm serious," I said. "Either we're building something together or we're not. You decide."

Then I went back to my work. I stared at the project in front of me and saw absolutely none of it for the next twenty minutes. My heart was going faster than the situation called for. But I'd said what I meant and I meant what I said and there was nothing left to do except wait and pretend to be working, which is its own kind of discipline.

A week later, he said yes. Not on one knee, not with a ring, not with a speech about love or forever. Just: "Okay. Let's do it." No romance, no grand gesture — just a decision, which suited us both fine.

Steve and I married on Valentine's Day, because irony has excellent timing. When you marry your best friend, the love of your life, you're confident it's forever.

We had a small wedding at a hotel on the beach. I got my green card, which I needed, and which was a practical relief — but it was a byproduct, not the reason. I remember holding it. An unremarkable piece of plastic that meant I could stop doing the mental math every time someone asked for ID. Stop calculating how much time was left. Stop being someone who existed in America on a technicality and a lot of luck. It was the most unglamorous relief I have ever felt and one of the most complete.

I married him because I loved him and believed it would be forever. What I didn't know until much later was that Steve had apparently concluded otherwise — that the card was the point, that the marriage was a transaction dressed up as a commitment. How little you can know about a person you've lived alongside for years. How much can go unspoken between two people sharing a bed, a kitchen, a life — and how different the story can look depending on which one of you is telling it.

***

My thirtieth birthday was big for me. Like by then you have to be somebody, right? I was. I had built my dream—successful career, husband, two cats, real estate, though not the dream house yet. But still. I'd arrived. Celebration was definitely in my mind. I waited for Steve to come home. And waited. By ten o'clock I went to bed. Hurt and mad. Not sure which one dominated, but both were present and accounted for. He forgot.

I heard the door open later. Steve came in, gave me a kiss on the cheek like it was any other Tuesday. I pretended to be sleeping because I'm Finnish and we freeze people out with dignity.

I got up later to get a glass of water. On the kitchen table was a five-foot-tall flower arrangement. I stood there in the kitchen in the dark with a glass of water, looking at this enormous thing that definitely hadn't been there when I went to bed, and felt the specific complicated feeling of being furious and touched at the same time. The flowers were extraordinary. The timing was terrible. Both things were completely true and neither cancelled the other out. The kind that doesn't fit through normal doorways. The kind that required planning.

I had to remember—deadline is a deadline, it happens to me all the time. Birthdays can be celebrated later. Happiness shouldn't be based on a calendar date. Every day should be a celebration. He had his moments.

It wasn't the fairy tale. But it was functional. And at the time, functional was enough.

Looking back, I see the pattern. I told him what I needed. I gave him a deadline. I didn't wait for him to decide on his own timeline.

I captained. Not because I wanted to. Because no one else was steering.

That turned out to be a problem later. I didn't romanticize it then. I don't now. I needed legal status. He needed a nudge. We both got what we needed.

No business plan. No safety net. No inspirational quote taped to the wall. I didn't ask permission. I just worked. It worked back. The business was successful. Long days, deadlines. Invoices that got paid. Not dramatic, just steady.

***

My first real client was Sisterhood Bookstore. Wood floors. The smell of paper and coffee. A community hub disguised as a retail space. Women, ideas. Books that changed lives. Naturally, it was eventually eaten by a big-box store with better lighting and worse intentions.

Decades later, while outlining this book, I wrote the owner's name down — Simone Wallace. The next day she texted me. My name had come up in a history project where a women's organization is building a website about Sisterhood Bookstore history.

Some people call that fate. Others call it coincidence. I call it irritating — the way intention tugs on the world in quiet ways. Hard to prove, harder to ignore. That question — coincidence or cause — comes back later, when judges decide which truths count and which are just inconvenient patterns.

Meanwhile, ceramics happened. The ceramics started as a distraction. A way to use my hands for something that wasn't client-driven, deadline-dependent, or tied to someone else's vision. My mother-in-law introduced me to it. She made adorable rabbits, chickens, trinkets. Very sweet. Very not me.

Then one day she had a plain mug. No animals. No personality. I asked if I could paint that. That was it. Hooked.

I don't dabble. I acquire infrastructure. Within six months I had: molds, pouring table, a kiln, every glaze known to man. I used plates as canvases and painted with resist wax like it was normal. Painted abstract designs, geometric patterns, occasionally something that looked like intention but was really just me seeing what happened when cadmium red met cobalt blue at 2,200 degrees. I did ceramics at night, because apparently I don't believe in hobbies. Only secondary careers.

But here's the thing: ceramics wasn't a career. Not at first. It was peace.

When I was painting a plate, I wasn't thinking about deadlines. I wasn't worrying about invoices or difficult clients or whether my English was good enough to negotiate a contract.

I was just painting. My hands knew what to do before my brain caught up. That's rare. In design work your brain is always slightly ahead, planning the next decision, anticipating the client's reaction, calculating whether the choice you're making will hold up under scrutiny. With ceramics, the hands led. The glaze went where the brush went. The piece became what it became. There was something almost physiological about the relief of that.

The glaze went where I put it. The kiln didn't judge. The piece either survived the firing or it didn't, and if it didn't, I made another one.

No one was grading me. No one was paying me. No one had expectations. It was the first creative work I'd done in years that didn't have to justify its existence. And that freedom—that lack of external pressure—unlocked something.

I started experimenting. Trying techniques I didn't know were "wrong" because I'd never been trained in the "right" way to do them.

I mixed glazes that weren't supposed to work together. I layered wax resist in ways that made the ceramics instructor at the community college wince when she saw my work.

"You can't do that," she said once. "I just did." "But it's not—" "It's not what?" She paused. "It's not traditional." "Good."

***

The best pieces came from mistakes. From accidents. From trying something that seemed impossible and discovering it worked anyway.

That lesson—that the best work comes from ignoring the rules you're told can't be broken—would save my life decades later.

When people told me I couldn't challenge a foreclosure without an attorney, I did it anyway. When experts said pro se litigants don't win against banks, I kept fighting.

When the system said the rules were the rules and I should accept them, I said: show me where it says that. Prove it. Make me believe you.

Ceramics taught me that authority is often just tradition wearing a fancy hat. And tradition doesn't mean truth. It just means no one's questioned it yet.

The Studio as Sanctuary

The studio became more than a workspace. It became a sanctuary. A place where I could close the door and the world stayed outside. No one asked me where I was from or how long I'd been here or whether my visa was still valid.

No one cared that my English had an accent or that I did things differently than they'd been taught. The work spoke for itself. The ceramics either sold or they didn't. The design projects either landed or they didn't.

And when they did, it was because I'd earned it. Not because someone gave me a chance. Not because I was lucky. Because I showed up. I delivered. I kept my promises.

That's what ownership gives you that employment never can: the certainty that your success is yours. Not your boss's. Not the company's. Yours.

And when you fail—because you will, often—that's yours too. But at least you get to learn from it. At least you get to try again. At least you're not waiting for someone else's permission to fix what you broke.

I shared an office with my husband, Steve. He ran a phone company installing business systems. The office had a huge patio. I put my kiln out there. Steve built a smokehouse and started smoking salmon. Soon we were known for our monthly business parties. Design people, tech people, smoked fish. "Totally Smoked" salmon developed a following. Orders happened. Of course they did.

Around this time, my friend and co-worker asked me to accompany her to a meeting with a medium. She had just lost her parents and was desperate to find somebody who could talk to them. I wasn't really a believer in talking to the dead, but I was curious.

To my surprise, I was the first one to receive a "message." The medium asked me what I do.

"Graphic designer," I replied.

She paused. "Is your office at La Cienega and Robertson Boulevard?" "No."

"What's at that corner?" "I don't know. Some design store, I'm sure."

She leaned forward. "This is a very important address for you." And that was it. She moved on to the next client. I was surprised how specific she was. We were sitting some fifty miles away. I filed it under weird but irrelevant and forgot about it.

***

A couple weeks later, my production guy delivered salmon to a design store in Beverly Hills and casually mentioned that his boss made ceramics.

The owners came to visit my studio. They pointed at pieces. "I like that one." "And that one." "And that one." I smiled politely and assumed this was just one of those friendly visits people make before disappearing forever. I waited for them to leave so I could get back to work.

"So… aren't you going to write this down?"

Oh. Oh. This was a buying meeting.

I found a scrap of paper and a pen with the careful movements of someone trying very hard to look like this kind of thing happened all the time. It did not. My studio was dead quiet, and I briefly wished I had hooked up the speakers first, just to give the room a little dignity. Instead I stood there, embarrassingly underprepared, pretending I had invoices and inventory sheets somewhere in my life.

My brain was still catching up while my hand tried to keep pace. Apparently, this was how real business happened now: one minute you're making pottery, the next minute you're a person with an impromptu wholesale order and a serious need to look less surprised.

They bought everything. I had barely finished building my display shelves and was still in the process of deciding how to display everything. The whole collection — earth tones, black and white, plates and vases, all painted in my newly discovered wax-resist style — was gone. What a difference five pounds of salmon can make.

Forty-something pieces. Cleaned me out. The store was at *La Cienega and Robertson Boulevard,* and just like that, I had a new account, a new audience, and a new business I had not planned for. That's how it went: design studio by day, ceramics by night, smoked salmon on the side. No roadmap. No branding strategy. Just momentum, curiosity, and the occasional misunderstanding that worked out spectacularly in my favor.

And apparently, psychic real estate tips.

I still don't know what to do with the psychic real estate tips. I've decided to leave that part where it belongs: in the same category as all the other things that happened exactly when they needed to and absolutely refused to be planned.

CHAPTER 10

Success, Concurrently

My first big client came as a referral from my husband, who had a company installing phone jacks and phone systems. *Lexicon School of Languages* found him through the *Penny Saver.*

That should have been my first clue.

They wanted someone to turn their idea—teaching English to Hispanics through books, manuals, and videos—into something real. Quickly. Cheaply. I fit the bill.

I was one of the first designers in Los Angeles with a Mac and working knowledge of what was then called "desktop publishing." I hated that term. I was a designer. But labels aside, I had the tools. A $4,000 black-and-white scanner. A $3,500 black-and-white laser printer. Today, you can buy both—better quality—for about $400. Progress is insulting.

***

Inglés Sin Barreras — English Without Barriers, a comprehensive video-based language program marketed heavily to Spanish-speaking audiences across the United States and Mexico — was born. The ads were everywhere, running on Spanish-language television for years, promising English fluency to a generation of immigrants and their families who needed it to navigate work, school, and daily life on the other side of the border. The program wasn't cheap, and the contract that came with it read like a mortgage — multi-year payment plans, fine print, the full architecture of a commitment you didn't fully understand until you were already in it.

The irony wouldn't fully land until years later, when I found myself living in Baja, surrounded by people who had grown up watching those ads on TV.

Whenever the title comes up, I become an instant minor celebrity — my name is on the books, listed as the designer. It's an odd kind of recognition, arriving decades late, in a language I once helped package but never learned fluently myself.

Dell and the HiBobs

I had a number of tech clients. Apple. Toshiba. My biggest break was Dell catalogs.

With Merisel—a software and hardware distributor—we approached Michael Dell. I flew to Austin, Texas to meet him.

I remember sitting in their lobby waiting, flipping through their corporate brochure to kill time. There was a little blurb about how they were a global company with reach everywhere.

And then I saw it: "Even in Finland they have Dell computers at Lindström's laundromat."

I stared at the page. This million-dollar, worldwide company would mention my little country as proof of their global dominance. And not just Finland—a laundromat in Finland. Their absurdity trumped mine. Serendipity at its best. This was meant to be.

The meeting went well. They asked if I could handle the production for a mail-order catalog.

"If you can do the production in one week, we'll do it." Sure.

I made the commitment with no idea how to pull it off. I worked forty hours straight. Didn't sleep. Didn't stop. Mission accomplished. I remember standing up when it was done and my legs not quite working right for a moment. The kind of exhaustion where your eyes feel like they've been sandpapered. I ate something — I don't remember what — drank three cups of coffee that landed wrong, and sent the files. Then I sat in the quiet of the studio and felt the specific satisfaction of having done something that shouldn't have been possible and done it anyway. That feeling. That's the one I kept chasing.

One of my big selling points was my background as a production artist who'd done everything by hand. I had the knowledge of color separation—how to break an image into cyan, magenta, yellow, and black plates. That translated directly into creating printable files when you did color jobs on the Mac. I knew everything about PMS colors, four-color process, trapping, bleeds—all the technical details that separated designers who could make pretty pictures from designers who could actually get things printed correctly.

Most Mac designers at the time were learning design and production simultaneously. I'd already spent years doing it the hard way with wax and X-Acto knives. The computer just made me faster and more dangerous.

***

One of the things I added to the catalog was a little filler box where Dell employees could introduce themselves and say something about the company.

The sample read: "Hi, my name is Bob. I'm the shipping manager at Dell Computer." So "HiBobs" became a thing. People loved them. They humanized a tech catalog in a way that felt personal and approachable. The HiBobs outlived the catalog by years.

I was ridiculously proud of that. Not the design itself— it was a simple text box. But the idea that something I added as a small human touch outlasted the project, that people remembered it, that it changed how a corporation communicated with its customers — that felt like the best kind of success. The kind that doesn't announce itself.

The Hollywood Foreign Press

I connected with the Hollywood Foreign Press and started doing their invitations, membership books, tickets to Golden Globes, hot commodity, and advertising material.

Deadlines were brutal. Last-minute changes. Always.

The office was on Robertson Boulevard—the same street where years earlier a psychic had told me would be very important to me. She'd been right about new client that launched my ceramics business. And now here I was, working out of that exact location, though not quite the way I'd imagined. The universe has a sense of humor about predictions.

The office was impressive, very fitting for the glamour clients they served. The hardwood floors were to die for—inlays, handmade, precious woods. No Home Depot products here. This was craftsmanship that made you embarrassed to walk on it with regular shoes.

As a perk, I got to go to the Golden Globes. Met every celebrity there was. It was exciting, yes, but just not my cup of tea. I couldn't understand why people lined up for hours just to get a glimpse of their favorites. The room was very loud and very bright and smelled like money and anxiety in roughly equal proportions. Everyone was performing something. The celebrities were performing accessibility. The executives were performing importance. The journalists were performing neutrality. I was performing someone who belonged there, which I mostly pulled off except for the moments I caught myself looking at the room and thinking: I'd rather be home.

I'm Finnish. We don't do fanfare.

Besides, I'd already met celebrities before. They're just people with better lighting and worse problems. I offered to buy Harrison Ford a drink as a joke — everything was open bar. He actually took me up on it. We stood at the bar for maybe ten minutes. Had a quick drink with me and said he was nervous about presenting somebody an award. Go figure. He ended up being just a really nice guy with a really big name.

The excitement wore off fast when you realized you were working harder to meet their deadlines than they were working on their actual jobs.

What I did appreciate was the craftsmanship. The invitations, the programs, the attention to detail — that mattered. The celebrities were just delivery mechanisms for good design work.

I still kept them as a client for a little while after I moved to Julian. I let the Golden Globes invitations go — the woods, the country style, the slower pace fit me better. But one thing kept me going back a bit longer.

I would haul a stack of Julian apple pies to their office every time I visited. Turns out bribery works better when it's baked. I did still want to make one more splash for my portfolio: their 75th Anniversary Golden Globes program.

I had envisioned an elaborate cover with an embossed golden globe statuette locking the foldout. I made a mockup. Presented it. I was impressed with myself. A few days later, I got a message: they'd hired another company to make the program. Just like that, I was fired. I sat with the email for a while. Not grief exactly — more like the flat, specific feeling of effort that didn't land. I had made something I was proud of. I had envisioned their

75th anniversary and built it into something worthy of the occasion. One email erased all of that without a word of explanation. I filed it. Moved on. But it left a mark I didn't fully acknowledge for years. Note to self: loyalty means nothing to these people.

To my amusement, their program came out looking like a corporate annual report. Beige. Boring. Nothing like what they deserved for a 75th anniversary celebration. Oh well.

The First Warning I Ignored

Getting fired by the Hollywood Foreign Press should have registered as a warning. Not because I cared about the job, I didn't — but because of how it happened. No conversation, no feedback, no courtesy. One email. Decision made elsewhere. Door closed.

I noticed it. Filed it away. Then promptly minimized it. "They're corporate, that's Hollywood." "Not my people anyway." All true. Also irrelevant. What mattered wasn't who they were. It was the pattern: years of delivery erased instantly, without consequence or reflection.

I told myself it didn't count because I had other work. Because I was busy. Because I didn't *need* them. That's how warnings survive. You contextualize them until they stop feeling like signals. I was very good at rationalizing away discomfort. It's a useful skill when you're building something. It becomes dangerous when you're ignoring structural truths. The lesson wasn't about ego. It was about disposability. I just wasn't ready to learn it yet.

The Six Degrees

A few months later, I was trying to get new clients in Julian. I showed my portfolio to a potential client and had the Hollywood Foreign Press office invitation in there—the one on Robertson Boulevard with the fancy floors.

Pat looked at it and said, "Hmmm. I designed the custom-made hardwood floors for that building." The six-degree separation thing at work again.

Twenty years of steady work. Real contracts. Real deadlines. I showed up. I delivered. Clients came back because the work held up. My success wasn't luck. It was delivery.

The invoices were clean. The costs were not. I paid for success in small, unglamorous ways. Sleep was the first casualty. Then rest. By year five, I had a permanent low-grade tension headache that I'd stopped noticing because it had simply become the baseline. My shoulders lived somewhere around my ears. I stretched them down deliberately every morning and they climbed back up by nine a.m. I thought this was normal. I thought this was just what working felt like. Then the ability to be bored—which is underrated and essential for creative people.

I was always "on." Always reachable. Always solving something. Even my downtime was preloaded with contingency plans. My body absorbed this quietly. No dramatic breakdowns. Just tight shoulders. Shallow breathing. A permanent sense of urgency even when nothing was technically wrong.

I didn't think of this as sacrifice. I thought of it as professionalism. That's how it sneaks up on you. When you normalize strain, you stop recognizing damage. Success has a sheen to it that makes people stop asking questions. From the outside, my life looked organized and predictable. Ascending. I had real clients, real invoices. A calendar booked months out. That's the version people saw—the one that reads well in bios and introductions.

What success hid was how narrow the margin actually was.

I didn't have a safety net. I had momentum. Which looks very similar until it suddenly doesn't. Momentum depends on one thing: that nothing interrupts it. No illness. No delays. No bad actors. No system failures. No personal emergencies. No violence. No banks behaving badly. No courts shrugging. Success doesn't warn you how fragile it is when it's built on uninterrupted performance.

I was producing a newsletter for Merisel. It didn't matter if I was on a honeymoon—the phone had to be answered. Romantic dinners were interrupted by layout emergencies. Sunsets waited while I found a fax machine. I faxed a newsletter from a hotel business center while wearing clothes I'd packed for a honeymoon. The man running the machine looked at me with an expression that translated clearly: this is not what marriage is supposed to look like. He wasn't wrong. But the newsletter went out on time. This did not impress my parents.

Finns take holidays. Finns believe in proper vacations, scheduled rest, and the radical idea that no one should die because a newsletter is late. I did not share this belief. My American husband understood. He married into it.

On my trips to Finland I got one of the first MacBooks—a laptop, two inches thick, that required a transformer the size of a hefty brick. The whole setup felt like fifty pounds of extra weight in my luggage, but it got the job done. My mother watched me set up the transformer and the laptop and the phone connection on her kitchen table and said nothing for a long time. Then: "You came all this way to do this?" I explained about the client. She made coffee and went to watch television. She had reached the stage of accepting that her daughter was a particular kind of person and that arguing with it accomplished nothing. I appreciated that about her.

And that distinct melody on the dial tone, waiting to hear "You've got mail"—pure dopamine hit. Worth every pound.

I'd sit in my childhood home in Helsinki, connected to clients in Los Angeles via a phone line that cost more per minute than the work was worth, uploading files at speeds that would make modern internet users weep. But I could work from anywhere, which meant I was expected to work from everywhere. We are so spoiled these days.

I sacrificed sleep first. Then weekends. Then, slowly, my health. No drama—just the math of responsibility. Their goals came first. Mine waited.

That's what built my career. Not talent alone. Reliability, endurance. Showing up when it hurt. Talent might open a door, but delivery decides whether it stays open. The first ten years were total bliss. I was thriving. I ran around LA in meetings, picked up new clients with ease. Got to a point where I could decline a client because I didn't like them—a luxury you can't afford in the beginning.

I trusted professionals because professionalism had worked for me so far. Designers, printers, clients, vendors — all playing their roles. I assumed that extended to banks. To courts. To institutions. Why wouldn't it? I had no reason not to trust yet. That trust wasn't foolish. It was earned — just not protected. I followed the rules I could see. I signed where I was told. I trusted professionals whose job it was to know better. That trust would turn out to be the most expensive thing I owned. I didn't know that yet. I was sitting in a studio I'd built, with clients who called back, in a country that had finally made room for me. Everything was working. That's the moment you don't see the bill coming — when the lights are on and the invoices are paid and there's no reason to look up from the work.

PART III

The House
Where The Story Turns

A man's house is his castle.
— Edward Coke,
Institutes of the Laws of England, 1628

CHAPTER 11

The Promise of Stillness

By 1988, I had a husband, graphic design studio, a ceramics business, a salmon side hustle, and something I hadn't planned on: a reason to stay.

My first car was a used Pinto. Predictably terrible. Second was a new Colt. Fine, functional, paid in cash. Then I got my dream car: a white convertible Mustang, license plate MYPONY1. Because I could. Paid in cash. I drove it off the lot with the top down in January because why wouldn't you. The air was cold and I didn't care. There's a specific kind of happiness that comes from a thing you earned entirely yourself — no financing, no cosigner, no one's name on it but yours. I drove home the long way. I was high on life and gasoline.

Paying cash felt smart. Responsible. No debt, no interest. No one owns you.

Turned out the system doesn't reward that. Years later, when we tried to buy a house, I learned the hard way that paying cash for everything means you don't exist. No credit history. No proof you can manage debt. The bank looked at me like I'd been living off the grid in a bunker. I sat across from the loan officer while he explained credit scores and debt-to-income ratios and the importance of having borrowed money before in order to borrow money now, and felt the specific frustration of a system that rewards the behavior it claims to discourage. I had been careful. I had been responsible. Apparently those were the wrong moves.

The system doesn't want you debt-free. It wants you leveraged. Tracked, predictable. You get a loan, you build credit, you become real. Pay cash? You're a ghost. I didn't know the rules. I thought avoiding debt was winning.

What Stillness Felt Like (Before I Knew It Was Temporary)

Stillness wasn't dramatic. That's what made it convincing.

It looked like coffee in real mugs, not travel cups. Keys that lived in the same bowl every night. A body that didn't brace when the phone rang. Silence that wasn't charged.

We didn't talk about safety. We lived inside it.

There were routines. Steve liked to revisit the unfortunate chapters of his life, as if repetition might improve the ending. I pretended this didn't bother me. He practiced guitar at night, played chess with his computer. I worked late, but not frantically.

We argued about normal things. Money sometimes. Whose turn it was to cook. Whether smoked salmon counted as dinner again. Nothing existential. Nothing that made you scan the room for exits.

This is what I thought adulthood was supposed to reward.

Not happiness—just relief. Relief from contingency, from improvisation. From always calculating the next move. I didn't feel triumphant. I felt finished. That should have scared me more.

We built something. Not just a marriage—a life. The studio expanded. The ceramics business grew. The smoked salmon became a legitimate side revenue stream. We weren't wealthy, but we were solvent. Clients. Contracts. A rhythm that worked. Steve wasn't flashy. He was steady.

One Ordinary Day That Later Mattered

There was a Tuesday—no reason to remember it at the time.

I woke up early, not because I had to, but because my body did. Sunlight through the window. The sound of Steve in the kitchen, already up, already functioning. The smell of coffee I hadn't made. I stood in the doorway for a moment before going in. Just stood there. The light was doing something ordinary with the kitchen tiles. Steve was reading something. The coffee was ready. Nothing was on fire. After years of calculating exits and next moves and backup plans, the absence of urgency felt almost physical — like pressure you'd been living under so long you'd stopped feeling it, and then suddenly it lifted.

I remember thinking: *This is it. This is the landing.*

I worked in the studio that day. Finished a client job early. Took a walk without purpose. Bought groceries without checking my bank balance first. That was new. Nothing happened. That's why it mattered.

Years later, I'd understand that the most dangerous assumption isn't optimism—it's continuity. The belief that tomorrow will resemble today because today feels earned.

That Tuesday taught me what I stood to lose, even though I didn't know it yet.

After years of movement — buses, borders, temporary rooms, student visas — steady felt like an achievement. Two businesses sharing an office. Referring clients back and forth. Two people who understood deadlines. We worked side by side, ate smoked salmon on the patio in private, and didn't need constant reassurance that this was real. For the first time since leaving Finland, I wasn't planning the next exit.

We ventured into selling smoked salmon at the Scandinavian festival in Ventura. Huge success. Sold out in two hours. Naturally, we did it again the following year in Santa Monica—our neighborhood. This time we brought enough salmon to feed a small Nordic army.

I'd made a sign, a banner, a menu, business cards with the coolest logo. We looked legit. Professional. Successful. Apparently, that was the problem.

Before the festival opened, the health department showed up to check our permits. We didn't have any. The prior year? No one cared. No one asked. Half the vendors were working out of home kitchens and garages. But now? Shut down. No commercial kitchen. A hearing in two weeks. Five-thousand-dollar fine.

We packed up every piece of salmon and went home. We drove home in silence with the back of the car full of salmon we'd smoked for three days and a banner I'd stayed up late designing and a logo I was genuinely proud of. The salmon smelled exactly right. Everything else felt wrong. I stared out the window and ran through the inventory of what we'd done and couldn't find the mistake, which was its own kind of frustrating.

The First Hairline Crack

The salmon incident should have registered as more than annoyance.

It was my first encounter with a system that didn't care how hard you worked—only whether someone complained loudly enough. No investigation. No consistency. Just enforcement triggered by visibility. We didn't break new rules. We broke the unwritten one: *don't stand out.*

What stayed with me wasn't the fine—it was the speed. How fast legitimacy evaporated. How quickly success flipped into suspicion. I told myself it was small. A fluke. Bureaucratic noise. That's how you survive early warnings: you shrink them until they fit into the life you want to keep believing in.

I showed up to the hearing alone. We decided I was better at talking our way out of disasters. Fair assessment.

I sat in front of the panel, feeling like a criminal. The first words out of their mouths: "We received a call saying you do not have a commercial kitchen." Everything after that blurred.

Someone had ratted us out.

Déjà vu. Again. We were too successful. Too visible. Jealousy had picked up the phone.

I explained: it's just the two of us. We set up at the festival like everyone else working out of their garage. The reason we looked good? Because that was my job. I was a graphic designer. Making people look like a million bucks was the entire point.

My story stuck. The fine was forgiven. Slap on the wrist. Don't do it again. I walked out into the parking lot and sat in the car for a minute before starting it. My hands were slightly unsteady — the aftermath of performing calm for an hour while internally calculating how bad this could get. It hadn't gotten bad. But I'd felt, for the first time, what it was like to sit in front of a panel that had the authority to make my life difficult and wait for their decision. That feeling would become familiar.

We spent months wondering who'd been evil enough to call the health department. Never found out for certain. Lesson learned: you can't look too good. Success makes you a target.

I'd been in America for seven years. I'd gone from cleaning houses to running a successful design studio. I'd proven that Finnish teacher wrong in every measurable way.

The next step was obvious: buy a house.

I thought responsibility was about provision. Pay your bills. Show up.

Don't be reckless. Build something solid and it will hold. I didn't yet understand that responsibility also means anticipating betrayal—not paranoia, just literacy. Knowing where the weak joints are. Understanding that systems don't fail evenly. They fail downward.

I assumed adulthood came with insulation. It doesn't. It just gives you more to lose.

The Seduction of Ownership

Buying a house felt like a punctuation mark. A period. A settling of accounts. Proof that we had crossed into the adult class of people who stop moving. I didn't crave luxury. I craved stability. Walls that wouldn't disappear. Neighbors who stayed put. A future that didn't require backup plans. I didn't see ownership as leverage. I saw it as sanctuary.

Since the beginning, every time we had a day off—which didn't happen often—we'd escape. Mountains. Desert. Mexico. LA wasn't a vacation. It required get-aways.

One trip took us to Palmdale. A new, upcoming desert town. Beautiful. Quaint. Small-town charm. We looked at a development on 38th Street, butting into open desert.

Wouldn't this be perfect? Quiet desert living. Drive to work over the mountains. Idyllic.

We bought a house. Moved in a month later over a long weekend. Our own house. Life was perfect. Then came Monday.

We headed out to go to work. The freeway was a parking lot. Twenty thousand other people had the same idea: commute to LA. How did we not know this? We had stood on that development on 38th Street and looked at the open desert and somehow failed to ask the question that should have been obvious: where do the twenty thousand other people who live here go on Monday morning? The answer, it turned out, was directly in front of us, at five miles an hour, for ninety minutes each way. We are very smart people who made a very preventable mistake. After a week, the mountains sucked.

We bought a condo in West LA. Palmdale became the weekend house. My parents visited from Finland and spent a couple of months there during winter. So it all worked out. For a while.

Palmdale was the fastest-growing city for a few years. Then, suddenly, our 38th Street get-away was in the middle of the city. We'd bought a second house to rent out since things were booming. How fast things change. Palm-dale started turning into a slum. We sold just to get out of there.

Palmdale taught me that geography lies. Quiet is not stability. Space is not protection. Growth curves don't care about your intentions. We adapted quickly—because we could. That reinforced the illusion that adaptation was strength, not warning. Every pivot worked just well enough to keep me trusting the process.

That's the danger zone. When survival masquerades as success.

The Weight Before the Turn

By the time my mother was dying in Finland, the stillness was already thinning.

Grief does that. It pulls focus inward. Makes you sloppy about the future because the present is heavy enough. I was doing the math constantly — how many flights, how much time, whether I'd get there before or after. Grief in advance is its own specific exhaustion. You're mourning something that hasn't happened yet while still trying to function as if everything is normal. The work kept coming. I kept doing it. But I was somewhere else. I was tired in a new way. Not burned out—*weighted.* Carrying loss in advance.

But I could feel something shifting. A low-frequency hum. The sense that the pause was ending. Stillness doesn't announce its departure. It just stops holding.

By 1999, LA started to feel claustrophobic. Burned out was real. We started thinking about moving. My mother-in-law had just passed away in San Diego. Life was heavy.

I was waiting for the call from Finland. The one that said it was time.

It came in February. I already knew. You always know, before the phone rings, when it's that call. The house was very quiet.

CHAPTER 12

Julian, Borrowed Stillness

I thought stillness was something you earned. It felt permanent at the time. That was the mistake. I didn't yet know it was something you borrowed.

After coming back from my mother's funeral in Finland, we started looking for a place to move. Santa Barbara? Out of reach. The coastline? Also out of reach. Turns out beautiful California real estate costs actual money.

Then I discovered Julian—a little mountain town in San Diego County that most people only knew for apple pie. Steve had grown up in San Diego and was familiar with Julian. I looked up houses for sale and found a blue house with a white picket fence in the middle of majestic pines. Such a cliché I had to see it just to confirm it was real. Off we went.

We ended up looking at houses every weekend for weeks. Couldn't find the one. Each place had something wrong—too small, too dark, too close to the road, too much like settling. So we decided this wasn't for us. We picked up sandwiches and a six-pack and found a quiet road in the middle of nowhere to have our last meal before heading back to LA and admitting defeat.

There was a fresh For Sale sign. How had no one shown us this? We drove up the driveway. I got goosebumps. I felt it in my bones, in my chest, in the way the light hit the trees. This was it.

We ran back to town and put in an offer without seeing the inside. The house had gone on the market that morning. We didn't care what the kitchen looked like or if the plumbing worked. Sometimes you just know. Or you think you do. That's usually how it starts. I remember standing at the top of the driveway looking down at it and feeling something I can only describe as recognition. Not déjà vu — more specific than that. The feeling of a place you haven't been before that already knows you. I didn't need to see the kitchen. The kitchen was irrelevant. We made the offer in the car on the way back to town. It was ours. We got the key on my thirty-ninth birthday.

Best present I ever gave myself. I didn't question it. That part matters.

The land didn't just sit there looking pretty. It participated.

Mornings arrived quietly. No sirens. No car alarms. No neighbor rehearsing their life crisis through drywall. Just wind in the pines and the occasional bird making a very serious point about something. The kind of silence that isn't empty—it's occupied, but politely.

I didn't realize how much noise I'd been carrying until it stopped. My shoulders dropped without being asked. My jaw unclenched. My thoughts stopped racing each other to the front of the line. I remember the first morning I woke up and didn't immediately start calculating what needed to happen. Just lay there. The light was coming through the curtains at an angle I hadn't seen before — slower, different quality, trees instead of buildings. I stayed in bed for twenty minutes doing nothing. That had not happened in years. Maybe a decade. It felt suspicious, then wonderful, then like something I wanted to protect. This wasn't relaxation. It was recalibration. I didn't realize how much I needed it until it stopped.

In Los Angeles, everything required momentum. You had to keep moving or risk falling behind. Here, the land didn't reward urgency. It rewarded attention. That's a different skill. I had to learn it. If you rushed, you missed things. Light shifted differently through the trees depending on the hour. Weather announced itself early. Seasons didn't sneak up on you—they arrived with paperwork.

Steve had a gift for finding things the land had swallowed. Spearheads, metates, artifacts — he could read the ground the way some people read faces, and he was rarely wrong. One afternoon we came across a circle of rocks, unmistakably a firepit, with two larger stones positioned like a chair and a table. I sat down in it and felt something shift. This was a kitchen. Someone had sat in exactly this spot, doing exactly what kitchens are for. I sat very still for a moment. The rock was warm from the sun. The trees were the same trees — different trees, but the same trees. Someone had sat here, maybe a thousand years ago, with the same view and the same light and the same need to eat something before the day continued. That continuity felt enormous and also very quiet. The important things usually are.

I looked around and said it was bad design — if you turned to your left, your elbow would knock a pot right off that table. Then I pointed at the ground and said if we dug there, we'd probably find something. We dug. Broken pottery pieces, exactly where they should have been.

The people who left them behind were the Kumeyaay, who wintered in the desert lowlands and moved up into the mountains each summer to hunt and grind acorns. We had a large flat rock on the property with multiple metate grinding holes worn into its surface — I called it the first fast food restaurant.

Elsewhere on the land, Steve kept turning up spearheads and fragments that had been waiting in the dirt for centuries. History in our own backyard, completely undisturbed, because nobody had thought to look.

I started walking the property every day after that. Not for exercise — for inventory. Learning where the ground softened after rain, where the oaks dropped their leaves first, where the deer crossed without asking permission. Show up enough times and the land starts to reveal things. Not quickly. That's part of the deal.

***

We moved to Julian in 1999. Fresh start. New chapter. This was my American dream, finally real and mine.

The house played a trick on you. From the driveway it looked like a simple one-story farmhouse tucked into the trees. Then you walked around it and realized it wasn't. The land dropped away, revealing a full downstairs built into the slope.

Upstairs felt domestic and intentional—fireplaces, warmth, rooms that suggested permanence. Downstairs was possibility. High ceilings. A big open room begging to be a studio. A former woodworking shop that immediately became mine.

There was space. Actual space. Physical proof that my life had expanded. I thought this was the end of the rainbow. I had finally found my pot of gold. It's easy to confuse arrival with permanence. That should have been suspicious.

Rootedness didn't feel accidental. It felt earned.

I hadn't drifted here on a whim or followed a fantasy brochure version of mountain life. I'd worked my way into this stillness. Years of deadlines. Years of saying yes when it would've been smarter to say no. Years of responsibility stacked so high it became structural.

This wasn't hiding out. This was collecting payment. Or so I told myself.

I didn't worry about being bored. Boredom is a luxury for people who haven't had to survive on momentum. I was curious what would happen if I stopped bracing for impact. If I let my nervous system retire from its second job as a fire alarm. Stillness didn't make me smaller. It made me clearer. Clear enough to notice what I'd been ignoring.

I could think without interruption. Decide without urgency. Work without the constant hum of background panic that passes for productivity in cities. The land didn't ask me to perform. It didn't care what I'd accomplished or what I planned to do next. It just required that I pay attention. And I did.

Every tree felt like it had tenure. Every rock had clearly won an argument at some point and stayed. The property was covered with majestic oaks — living on it felt like living in a park, which was exactly what I'd wanted without knowing how to ask for it. We had a seasonal pond, and in years following a heavy winter the snowmelt would fill it into something that deserved to be called a lake. My own lake. I put fish in to keep the mosquito population down, which was practical, but watching them move through the water was something else entirely. I'd also insisted on lilacs — whites and pinks — and we got plenty of those, which reminded me of my grandmother's house in a way that caught me off guard every spring when they bloomed. Permanence was everywhere. It rubbed off on me. I thought this was what adulthood rewarded when you did everything right.

After my mom passed away, my dad sold the Helsinki condo we'd moved into when I was born in 1960. He'd wanted out of the city for a while, but Mom was a city girl. Once she was gone, he didn't waste time.

We'd had the same phone number for forty years. Still imprinted in my memory: 765-171. Disconnected. When I ordered a new landline in Julian—yes, a landline, because it was 1999 and cell service in the mountains was a joke—the number was (760) 765-1774. What are the chances of the first five digits being the same? The universe was nodding. I stood in the kitchen with the phone in my hand staring at the number they'd just read me and felt the specific unreasonable certainty of someone who has just received a sign they didn't ask for. I wrote it down twice to make sure I hadn't misheard. I hadn't.

I wanted it to mean something. That's how people read patterns.

Narrator: The universe was not nodding.

***

I got lucky and found someone who would buy all our office furniture in one deal. I moved into the new house within weeks. Steve had to stay in LA, waiting for the sale of his business to go through. He moved his business operations into the condo and we became weekend spouses.

I got very domesticated, very fast. I baked my first cheesecake in my dream home like I was auditioning for a lifestyle magazine. My days went like this: work on computer, walk in the woods, paint walls, repeat. I made the cheesecake from scratch because I had time for that now, and it came out perfect—I ate it standing at the kitchen counter looking out at the oaks and felt genuinely, uncomplicated happy in a way I hadn't felt since I was eleven years old on open water.

There was no one to perform for. The cheesecake was mine. The view was mine. I couldn't believe how happy one person could be. This was it. I had arrived. I didn't consider what would happen if it didn't last.

The house felt permanent in a way people sometimes don't. I didn't notice it right away. I was too busy being grateful. Too busy settling in, unpacking not just boxes but identities. But the land welcomed me immediately, without conditions. It didn't need reassurance. It didn't second-guess itself. I fit here easily. That should've been another clue. People don't always work that way.

Steve liked visiting. I liked staying. There's a difference, and it matters. I mistook shared weekends for shared vision. Mistook quiet acceptance for contentment. The land never asked me to explain myself. It didn't negotiate. It didn't stall. I thought peace was contagious. It isn't.

I didn't yet understand that some people experience stillness as suffocation. That what feels like arrival to one person can feel like an ending to another. You adjust to it.

The first winter brought just a dusting of snow—perfect, just enough to get a sense of winter without the Finland-level commitment to misery I'd grown up with. I did not want those winters anymore. I wanted the postcard version, and Julian delivered.

Business was good. I started a studio tour in Julian because I wanted the little town to be known for more than just apple pies. I got more into fine art. The tour grew from three artists to fifteen in no time. Everything was clicking into place. That's usually when you stop checking.

We spent a year as weekend couples. Then Steve's company sale fell through. And soon after that, my husband decided peace and quiet wasn't for him.

He wanted a divorce. By email. No warning. No buildup. Just a decision already made.

***

That came from left field like a meteor nobody saw coming. What just happened?

My life crumbled in real time while I stood in the house I'd thought was the happy ending, holding a printed email that said our marriage was over in fewer words than it takes to order a sandwich. I read it twice. Then I set it down on the kitchen table and looked out at the property — the oaks, the pond, the lilacs that were just starting to come back — and felt the strange dissociation of a life that looks exactly the same as it did five minutes ago but isn't. The house was still there. The trees were still there. Everything outside the window was exactly where I'd left it. Only the story had changed. That's all it takes.

How does one get over something like this?

Slowly. It took a while and I'm not going to pretend otherwise. There were mornings I walked the property because standing still was worse. The land didn't care that I was heartbroken. That indifference was useful. The deer still crossed at the same spot. The oaks were entirely unmoved. That indifference was useful — it insisted that the world was continuing whether I kept pace with it or not. Eventually I did.

A couple of years went by in separation before the final decision. In 2003, we were divorced.

Slowly I started getting back in the swing of things. Painted more. Worked more. Walked in the woods more. The house stayed. Steve left. The dream adjusted. It didn't disappear. It changed shape.

Funny how what attracted him in the beginning—the woman who knew what she wanted and went after it—became the reason he couldn't stay. The world revolved around me too much, I was told. Apparently making decisions and moving forward is "selfish" when the other person has decided that standing still is a personality. I hadn't seen that as a problem. Still don't, actually. But he did.

The house was mine now. That should have felt like control. Fully, legally, emotionally mine. I kept the phone number. Kept the studio. Kept the life I'd built. What I didn't know yet was that keeping it would become the hardest fight of my life. The house stood exactly where it had always stood. The oaks didn't know what was coming. Neither did I. We were all just continuing — the land, the trees, the woman who had mistaken arrival for safety — waiting for the next thing, whatever it was. It always comes. You just don't know the form yet.

CHAPTER 13

Loss Compounds

Homeownership after divorce is sold as empowerment, but in practice it's just you, a roof, and a stack of papers daring you to blink. I kept busy with existing design clients, though finding new ones was harder after the move to the mountains. The property was beautiful—pines, silence, space—but very hard to explain to corporate clients why the internet cut out when a deer walked past the modem. So I adapted the way I always do.

I was buzzing around in my convertible with the top down, wind in my hair, living the dream. I got a dog—an Alaskan Malamute named Wahnee. I went from Queen Bee in LA to Mountain Queen in Julian, and honestly the upgrade was worth it.

Wahnee loved the back seat with the top down. She'd stick her nose up in the air and howl like a wolf, and tourists would stop and stare like we were some kind of traveling wilderness show. We were majestic.

Grief hadn't entered yet, but its scaffolding had. This was the stage where people assume you're fine because you look fine. Because you're smiling. Because you made a bold move and pulled it off. What they don't see is how much energy it takes to keep the narrative clean. Reinvention doesn't erase what came before it; it just asks you to carry it quietly. I didn't feel lonely yet, but I was already learning how to manage solitude so it wouldn't notice me first.

This is the part people later romanticize. They point to it as proof of resilience, as if resilience is something you choose once and keep forever. In reality, it's a series of small refusals to collapse, most of them invisible. I wasn't healed. I was functioning. Those are not the same thing.

Then my first winter alone in the mountains, we got two feet of snow. WHAT? I didn't sign up for this. The real estate agent had conveniently left out the part where Julian occasionally remembers it's in the mountains and behaves accordingly.

I was stranded at the house for a week. My little convertible pony couldn't negotiate that much snow—turns out sports cars and alpine conditions don't mix. Who knew. Everyone. Everyone knew. As soon as I could get out again, I ran down the hill and came back with a brand spanking new Ford Expedition. License plate: BIGFOOT. Problem solved.

Control became a theme. Not obsession — strategy. When enough things happen without your consent, you start collecting leverage wherever you can find it. A vehicle that could handle snow. A schedule that bent around my needs. Work that answered to me. Control wasn't about dominance; it was about preventing surprise. Loss teaches you that what hurts most is not the impact but the blindside.

People expect recovery to be visible. They want a before-and-after. What they don't expect is the in-between state where you're hyper-competent because you're afraid of what happens if you're not. I didn't call it fear. I called it preparation.

***

I got serious about photography and switched the camera from automatic to manual — a small revolution for someone who liked control but had been letting machines make the decisions. I learned light, depth, and patience. I used the property for boudoir shoots and published a few photography books. Kept up ceramics, started mosaics, and sculpture followed naturally. Then I opened a gallery. Apparently, I had no understanding of the concept of resting.

What looked like ambition was really accumulation. Each new skill was another layer between me and the ground. If one thing failed, something else could hold. That's how it started — not as success, but as redundancy.

And yes, people started saying things like, "You're so strong," as if endurance were a compliment instead of a weather report. Strength, when required too often, becomes a job description.

Wahnee turned out to be the perfect ambassador for the gallery. I'd say in the morning, "Wanna go to work?" and she'd get excited and run to the car like she had appointments to keep and people to impress. She was better at customer relations than most humans.

One day I had to go down to San Diego for the day. Wahnee got left behind. She had a doggie door out to the fenced-in backyard, so I wasn't worried. Few hours later somebody called me and said Wahnee was running on the highway towards the gallery.

It just broke my heart. She must have thought: Mommy forgot to take me to work. I better go find her. I drove back as fast as legally possible—and maybe a little faster than that—picked her up, and brought her home. She was fine. I was a wreck. I sat in the car with her for a few minutes before driving anywhere, one hand on her back, just breathing. After that, she came with me everywhere or I didn't go.

This is how grief negotiates. It doesn't demand ceremony; it demands proximity. It narrows your tolerance for risk. It makes you choose certainty over convenience. People mistake that for attachment or overprotection. What it really is—is memory management. I had already learned how fast something can vanish when you assume it will be there when you get back.

***

In 2003, the Cedar Fire broke out. It was a massive wildfire in San Diego County, started by a lost hunter trying to signal for help, which grew to become the largest fire in California history at the time. My first fire. I didn't quite know what to expect.

We watched it for two days from a distance. Little panic, saw some flames on the horizon, but it looked like we'd dodged the bullet. Friends in town started packing and I thought they were overreacting. I'm going home.

I was sitting on my patio having a beer, thinking that could have been bad.

Then the wind changed direction. Within minutes the smoke had covered everything. The sun disappeared behind an orange haze that turned noon into dusk. Oh my god. Pure panic.

Luckily I'd gotten all the important paperwork ready in boxes—organized and Finnish and prepared like a responsible adult. Now I had to throw everything into my car like a lunatic. I heard the chopper flying around with speakers blasting: "IMMEDIATE MANDATORY EVACUATION!"

Holy shit, this is for real. Mind starts to race. What if the house burns down? I have to be able to work. So I rush back inside to grab my computer—easier said than done. CPU manageable, but the monitor was one of those massive CRT screens from before the flat-screen era. It's amazing how strong you get with adrenaline coursing through your system.

Dang, I'm gonna need some clothes. Back inside. By now the electricity is out and the phones are dead.

Oh, I love that—my first framed photograph. I have to take it. Oh, I love my big Iittala glass bowl I brought from Finland. I have to take it. And this, and this, and this. Now my car is so full I couldn't fit another toothpick in there, and Wahnee is looking at me like I've lost my mind.

I get to town and see my friends. They thought I'd already left. There are only two ways out of Julian, and the other one was already closed—it was burning. So we had to head down to the desert with the remaining thousand people in a convoy that wasn't moving. Needless to say, blood pressure sky high. But we got out the back way.

For four horrendous days the mountain was closed. We stayed glued to the TV watching any news we could get. I saw so many of my friends' houses burn to the ground on the screen. I got one glimpse of my road — nothing but smoke, couldn't see my house through it.

My heart sank. I thought it was all gone. On the fifth day we were allowed to return. Steve drove down from LA to drive up with me as emotional support. What a good ex-husband I had. I also had company of a different kind — a Finnish news reporter who had heard about the fires and wanted to document what it looked like when a Finn came back to the disaster area. It turned out to be my fifteen minutes of fame in the old country, my burned mountain road broadcast back to Finland as though Julian, California were briefly worth knowing about.

We drove up and my little road was still smoldering. I was shaking, tears in my eyes, the camera probably catching all of it. I turned the corner and saw the house — the back looked okay. Where was the fire? I continued around the property to the driveway and saw a manzanita bush by the entrance burned black. We pulled up to the garage. Everything was there. The house was fine. I got out of the car and kissed the ground.

Survival doesn't reset the clock. It adds a layer. From that point on, every sense was calibrated differently — I noticed wind direction, tracked weather, listened for sirens even when none were coming. People say trauma lives in the body; what they don't say is that it also lives in your planning. I didn't feel lucky. I felt warned.

This was the first time I understood that disaster doesn't have to take something from you to change you. Sometimes it just proves that it could have. I must still have a purpose.

***

Then my brother Seppo died. Forty-nine years old, alcoholism generously padded with denial. I went back to Finland. Again.

I traveled alone. Seppo's death was unexpected even though I'd known for years he wouldn't last long. The drinking had been killing him slowly and publicly, and no one wanted to name it. Why the rest of the family couldn't acknowledge what was right in front of them was beyond me.

When I arrived at his house, my sister-in-law had set up a twin bed in a tiny spare room. The room felt claustrophobic — too small, too close, with everything pressing in — and with the state I was already in, I couldn't stay in it. I ended up on the couch. I couldn't sleep, tossed and turned all night with this anguish that was physical, something dark and restless pressing into my chest. The next morning someone mentioned in passing that the couch where I'd spent the night was the couch where Seppo died. I could feel his distress in the fabric. I never touched that couch again.

The day of the funeral was freezing with ice everywhere. The funeral home arrived with the casket and the men struggled to get it out of the hearse on the slick driveway. One of them grunted that it was heavy as hell and I snapped at them—how dare you, that's my brother you're talking about, mind your manners. They went silent and carried him inside like properly scolded children.

At the reception, Seppo's friends spoke about him like he was someone I'd never met. What a good friend, always ready to help, the kind of guy who'd drop everything if you needed him. Kenny Rogers' "The Gambler" played in the background, the Finnish version with something about dying in your sleep, the way he went. He was six months short of retirement from the railroads after twenty-five years as a conductor, and I sat there in conflict because for the past twenty years every time I visited Finland, Seppo took vacation time and stayed home drunk. I hadn't seen him sober in years, so who was this person they were mourning, and if he was that person to them, who was I to him?

I sat with a plate of food I didn't eat and smiled at people who wanted me to confirm their version of him, and felt the specific exhaustion of being the only person in the room who seemed to notice the gap between the story being told and the one I'd lived.

This is where grief multiplies instead of deepens. You don't just lose the person; you lose the version of the story you thought you shared. Competing narratives don't cancel each other out—they coexist, and you're left holding all of them. People expect closure from funerals. What I got was disorientation. There's a special kind of loneliness that comes from realizing the person you loved was many people, and you only knew one of them. That realization doesn't resolve. It lodges.

One summer years earlier I confronted him directly and asked why he drank. He said it was because Mom always said why don't you do anything with your life, look at Leena, Leena this, Leena that. So what was I supposed to do with that information? I was the reason. Or the excuse. Pick your poison. Either way it didn't matter now.

While I was in Finland burying my brother, I lost something else: the coastal property where I was made captain at eleven, where I learned to fish and water-ski and navigate open water, where my childhood made sense. The house and land had been built by my father and uncle — every brick carried by boat, every piece of lumber hauled across the bay — but paperwork now outranked all of it. Sibling rivalry, jealousy, greed, alcohol doing what it does best—turning memory into entitlement.

When Seppo died, he left the property to his wife and her family. Strangers would own the place my father and uncle built with their hands, every brick carried by boat, every piece of lumber sailed across the bay. I arrived too late to fight for it, or maybe just in time to understand that some things can't be fought for and can only be lost. I thought about the dock. The sound the boat made against it. The way the water looked at six in the morning when no one else was up yet. Those things don't transfer with the paperwork. They just disappeared.

At the time, I only knew that something important had been taken without anyone asking whether it should be.

***

My father had gone to the property that winter alone. It was mainly a summer place, locked up during the cold months, but he'd driven out to check on things and make sure the pipes hadn't frozen and the roof hadn't collapsed under snow. He heated the sauna by himself — his last act a completely Finnish one. My sister-in-law had been wondering for days because he wasn't answering his phone, and she finally sent someone to check. He had died there, sitting peacefully in the corner of the sauna bench. Eighty-three years old. There are worse ways to go, and he would have known that. That's the way I want to go.

I can't imagine how hard it was for him to visit that place after Seppo's death, to sit in the sauna he'd built knowing it no longer belonged to us, knowing the place we'd made together brick by brick and summer by summer now belonged to strangers. Maybe that's why he didn't leave. Maybe the sauna was the only place left that still felt like his. The month to die in Finland seems to be February—Mom, Seppo, Dad. He went the way a Finn should, quietly with no drama and no warnings. Just finished.

I had tried more than once to talk to him about what he wanted when the time came, but he refused the conversation the way only a stoic can. Finally he said no funeral, no cemetery, no burial, no reason to take up real estate after you're gone. He'd donated his body to science and everything was supposed to be handled.

Except it wasn't. Science, it turns out, has standards. After five days in a sauna, they politely declined. So now what, Dad.

I arranged the cremation before flying back to Finland and closed my gallery because not knowing how long I'd be gone made it impossible to pretend stability was sustainable. My first task was to pick up my father's ashes, and I'd made the urn myself because of course I had. Simple and clean, built from birch, a leftover box that once held a Finnish vase—a return to roots whether I intended it or not. I painted a design on the box, attached branches of rosemary, and covered it with a sheer black veil for his final fishing trip.

The rosemary was fine. The handmade urn was not. Regulations prefer grief to be factory-issued, standardized and pre-approved and accompanied by receipts and respectable markups for the funeral industry.

No you can't use a handmade urn, no you can't pick up the ashes yourself, no you can't ship it. Red tape has excellent lung capacity and zero sense of irony.

I didn't take no for an answer. My sisu outlasted their policies and eventually everything worked out.

I drove through Helsinki with my father strapped into the back seat and surreal doesn't quite cover it. I was speeding, not on purpose but just not paying attention, and a cop pulled me over. I apologized and explained I had my dad's ashes in the backseat, and the officer told me to step out of the vehicle. I thought he was being rude until I saw his face—confusion, then alarm. He thought I said I had my dad's radar in the backseat.

Tutka versus tuhka. One letter. Finnish matters.

We both started laughing, and I said that's my dad — still a joker, even dead, even from inside a birch box, he was teaching me something—language matters, one letter changes everything. The Finnish language is unforgiving that way, and so is everything else that matters.

***

We had a funeral my way. We drove across Finland to places we'd been together and I talked while he listened, or at least didn't argue which was already an improvement over most of our relationship. He rode shotgun, seat-belted and dignified and silent, and for once he agreed with all my decisions. But he wasn't done.

I packed him in my luggage for the flight back to Julian, and I've never lost a suitcase in my life but this time my father went somewhere else. I waited two days in Los Angeles with nothing, and a month later the airline called to say they'd found my bag.

A young Mexican delivery driver brought it to my driveway and asked what was inside because it was heavy.

"My dad," I said. He crossed himself three times while backing away from the house like I'd just told him it was haunted. Typical Dad. One last unscheduled trip. Hope he enjoyed it.

Dad had always wanted to visit Machu Picchu but then he saw a documentary about how tourism was destroying it—buses grinding up the mountain daily, wearing away what had survived centuries—so he never went. I decided I'd go for him and packed part of him in a salt shaker for easier customs. Practical. Discreet. The TSA doesn't ask questions about seasoning.

I arranged to be at the top before sunrise and stood on the edge of the ruins as the sun crested the mountain, the light spilling gold across ancient stone. I whispered happy trails Dad and opened the salt shaker and tilted it toward the valley.

And of course a gust of wind caught the ashes and blew them all over me. Thanks Dad. Grief doesn't resolve. It trains you.

My father was my last living relative in Finland. After him there was no one to go back to — the strangest feeling of being a person without a country. I didn't fit the old one anymore, but in America I was still unmistakably a Finn. Freedom and loneliness arrived together and never separated. Some days the space was exhilarating. Other days it crushed me flat. Is this what midlife crisis is? I latched on to my friends, some more than I probably should have. I'm grateful for the few good ones.

What I was becoming was someone with a high tolerance for instability and a low tolerance for bullshit. My hands had gotten steadier. The things that used to make me flinch had stopped being surprising. Grief doesn't soften you. It clarifies. At the time, I thought I was just surviving. In retrospect, I was being trained for something much larger.

CHAPTER 14

Trust the Professionals, They Said

All of this — the funerals, the flights back and forth to Finland, the lost property, the ashes scattered across two continents — took a serious bite out of my savings. So I did what responsible adults are told to do and refinanced, consolidated everything into one loan, my first mortgage entirely in my own name.

My ex-husband had always handled contracts, read the details, paid attention to fine print. I signed with bold strokes and optimism, trusted the professionals and trusted the documents and trusted that the system worked the way it said it did. At the time that still seemed reasonable.

I met the mortgage broker from Pickwood Mortgage at a restaurant in Orange County, which should've been the first red flag — a mortgage closing in a booth at lunch. He slid a stack of papers across the table with tabs everywhere marking where to sign and initial and date. I signed and initialed and dated everything he pointed to while he made small talk about interest rates and market conditions and how this was a great time to refinance. He smiled and said we'd be in contact. I drove home with the top down and felt vaguely that something had been too easy. I filed that feeling under: you're being paranoid. Refinancing is supposed to be simple. This is what professionals are for.

Two weeks later a FedEx box arrived and it was done. Everything finalized, recorded, official. I put the package in a drawer and got back to work.

The drawer was in my studio, under the window that looked out at the oaks. I didn't open it again for five years.

A subprime loan is what banks sell to borrowers they've decided are too risky for standard financing — higher interest rates, adjustable payments, terms designed to look manageable until they aren't. The broker told me that in five years I could easily modify it, piece of cake, no problem at all. Five years later the payment doubled. That detail hadn't come up over lunch.

I tried to do the responsible thing and apply for a modification. That's when I finally opened the package and started reading. I remember sitting on the floor of the studio with the documents spread around me, the light coming through the window at the wrong angle — late afternoon, too bright. I kept thinking I was misreading the numbers. I checked again. I hadn't misread them. My income on the application was a number I had never earned in my life. I sat there for a long time.

There was "my" loan application, doctored to show my income as ten times higher than it actually was. Not a rounding error. Not a clerical mistake. Ten times. There was also the loan cost estimate we'd agreed on — two thousand dollars — and then, buried in the paperwork, an additional $26,000 broker fee quietly added to the balance of the house. Not mentioned. Not discussed. Just there, already spent.

Then there was the notary stamp. "Personally known to me — Shane Thomas Case, Notary Public." I had never met Shane Thomas Case. When I tracked down his bond and oath and compared the signatures, they didn't match. No notary journal on file for that date. Because of course not.

I think I'm royally screwed.

I filed a claim against his bond to collect fifteen thousand dollars for the fraud. Two weeks later a letter from Merchant Bond's attorneys denied it — two weeks past the five-year statute of limitations. It would've taken another lawsuit to recover that money, and I was already neck-deep in litigation on two fronts. I didn't have the bandwidth for a third fight, so the notary fraud went unpunished, just like everything else that was about to follow.

I called Specialized Loan Servicing and explained that my payment had doubled, that I was struggling to keep up, that I wanted to apply for a modification. The woman on the phone was cheerful and efficient. She said I'd need to be three months past due before they could consider my application. "But I'm current. That'll destroy my credit." "It's fine," she assured me. "It's part of the process."

Following their instructions I stopped paying.

Ninety days later they sent the modification packet. I filled it out meticulously, attached every required document, faxed it back. For six months every submission vanished — confirmation numbers and all. Then with great formality they denied the modification, citing incomplete application and failure to provide required documentation.

Let me be clear about the sequence: they qualified my fictitiously inflated income for the loan. They then used my actual income to deny the modification. The same institution. The same property. Two different versions of my financial reality, deployed selectively for maximum extraction.

I didn't understand yet why this was happening. That answer took seven more years to fully assemble. It's in Chapter 39. But the short version is this: my default was worth more to them than my payments ever were.

Day ninety-one wasn't about qualifying for help. It was about triggering the insurance. Banks had bundled mortgages into securities, then taken out insurance — credit default swaps — that paid out when those loans failed. In 2009, President Obama told struggling homeowners to ask their banks for loan modifications. Millions did. What no one mentioned was that servicers were being rewarded for pushing borrowers into default, not keeping them housed. A performing loan was worth less to them than a defaulted one. Foreclosure wasn't a failure of the system. It was the system working exactly as designed.

"Go three months late," they told us. "Then you qualify." We listened. They foreclosed. Funny how that worked.

The Big Short — Michael Lewis's book, later a film — pulled back the curtain on all of it. The mortgage industry had built a global financial machine on top of loans it knew would fail, sold to borrowers it knew couldn't sustain them, insured by instruments designed to profit from the wreckage. Homeowners weren't the customers. We were the raw material. And the house always wins.

In 2012, five major mortgage servicers reached a $26 billion settlement with the federal government over illegal foreclosures, forged documents, fabricated signatures, and robo-signing. Twenty-six billion dollars sounds like accountability. What it actually was is a rounding error against the profits generated, and not one executive went to prison. The settlement didn't give people their homes back. Mine was not among them.

Washington Mutual was its own separate disaster. A Senate subcommittee investigation found that WaMu had flooded the market with shoddy loans using high-risk lending, lax controls, and compensation structures that rewarded volume over quality. On September 25, 2008, it became the largest bank failure in U.S. history — seized by federal regulators and sold to JPMorgan Chase for $1.9 billion. JPMorgan later paid $13 billion to settle claims over the mortgage securities WaMu and Bear Stearns had sold to investors. No criminal charges were ever filed. The Justice Department concluded the evidence didn't meet the standard. It never does. *(Sources: CNBC Investigations, HistoryLink.org, The Seattle Times)*

I kept thinking someone would step in — a regulator, a judge, some higher authority who still believed the rules applied to everyone. Instead I watched judges acknowledge fraud on the record and rule for the bank anyway. I watched attorneys argue that forged notary signatures didn't really matter because the debt was still valid. I watched procedure used to smother substance until the truth ran out of oxygen.

You don't call it broken. You call it designed.

There's a version of this story where I'm the villain. She didn't pay her mortgage, she deserved to lose the house. And technically, that's true — I stopped making payments. On the instructions of my loan servicer, who told me I had to be ninety days delinquent before they would even consider a modification. I did what they told me to do. That trust was the weapon they used against me.

What that version of the story leaves out is what happened next — all that time I spent in courtrooms proving that the documents used to take my home were forgeries. But sure. She didn't pay.

I thought about the drawer. The package I'd put away without reading. The trust that had seemed so reasonable at the time. I wasn't going to put an thing in a drawer again. And I'm Finnish. We don't do permission.

CHAPTER 15

Nobody Would Take the Case

I didn't want to be my own attorney. I wanted my house not stolen. These are different ambitions. When I realized foreclosure was coming, I assumed I'd hire a law firm. I had evidence. Documents. A clear timeline showing forgery. This felt solvable. Unpleasant, expensive, but solvable. It wasn't.

I made more than twenty calls to law firms in San Diego and up to Los Angeles. No one would touch the case. "It can't be won." "Banks always win." "Unless you have a $20,000 retainer."

One attorney was more direct: "You're probably right about the fraud. You'll still lose. The system protects the banks, not you. Walk away."

Walk away. As if that were advice. As if abandoning my home to documented forgery was the reasonable choice. I kept calling. The rejections developed a rhythm. By the tenth call I had stopped expecting anything different. I'd sit at my desk in Julian with the phone and the list and work through them methodically, the way you work through a difficult problem — not because you believe the next one will be different, but because stopping feels worse than continuing. The oaks outside the window were indifferent. The deadlines were not.

Polite at first. Then rushed. Then silence—attorneys who stopped returning messages the moment they heard the basics. Foreclosure. MERS. Forgery. Click. Some didn't even let me finish the sentence. "We don't handle foreclosure defense." "We don't take cases against major banks." "We don't represent homeowners in—" [line goes dead] Finally, one lawyer said the quiet part out loud. "If MERS is on your title, representing homeowners against banks can get us disbarred."

MERS. Mortgage Electronic Registration Systems. I had never heard of it. Apparently, everyone else had—and they were terrified of it.

The gap wasn't just fear. It was ignorance. Most attorneys had never studied foreclosure defense or quiet title in law school — it wasn't part of the curriculum. They didn't refuse my case because they thought I was wrong. They refused it because they didn't have the vocabulary to evaluate whether I was right. The knowledge simply didn't exist in the profession yet. I was asking specialists who didn't exist to solve a problem nobody had named.

I wrote the name down and looked it up. Then I read it again. Then I sat back in my chair and looked at the ceiling for a while. A private database, created by the banks, tracking ownership of something as fundamental as your home — outside the public record, inaccessible, answerable to no one. I had signed documents referencing this entity without knowing what it was. Most people had. That was the design.

***

The Company That Isn't a Company

MERS is not a lender. It's not a bank. It's a database.

Created in the 1990s by the mortgage industry to avoid county recording fees and speed up foreclosures. Instead of recording each transfer of a mortgage in public records—where ownership is traceable, transparent, and costs money—banks created a private registry.

MERS appears on deeds as "nominee" for whoever owns the loan. The problem is: nobody knows who that is.

The promissory note gets sold on Wall Street. Bundled. Sliced. Securitized. Traded like baseball cards. The debt moves. The money moves. The mortgage stays behind, frozen in the name of a company that never loaned anything, never collected a payment, never had any actual relationship to the borrower.

Legally, that matters. A lot. The law is clear: before a notice of default can be filed, the party enforcing the loan must have perfected title. That requires a real, documented chain of ownership. Paper that proves you own what you're trying to take.

Securitization breaks that chain by design. The note and the deed are separated—sometimes intentionally, sometimes through sheer incompetence—and suddenly no one can prove who actually holds the debt. Courts know this. They proceed anyway.

MERS solves the inconvenience by pretending continuity exists.

The Vice Presidents Who Aren't Vice Presidents

MERS claims to have thousands of "vice presidents." You don't get promoted. You get stamped. For about twenty-five dollars, employees of loan servicers, foreclosure mills, and title companies are "authorized" to sign documents as MERS officers. They don't work for MERS. They don't work for the lender. Many of them work in document processing centers, signing their names hundreds of times a day without reading what they're signing.

They sign documents transferring property they don't own, on behalf of entities that may no longer exist, for loans no one can produce the original note for. This isn't a glitch. It's the business model. And once the model exists, anyone can use it.

NBC10 Philadelphia reported the same mechanics in 2019 — a North Philly landlord whose rental property was stolen outright when someone forged her signature on a deed, stamped it with a counterfeit notary seal, and sold it. Investigators bought a functioning notary stamp online in five minutes for $26. The county recorder's office filed it without question, because verifying signatures isn't something they do — or, as Philadelphia's Records Commissioner put it, something they're capable of doing. A retired FBI agent called it a game anybody can play. Two hundred and forty-seven deed fraud allegations in Philadelphia alone, in just two years. And the Pennsylvania Department of State — the agency responsible for regulating notaries — wouldn't show up to the task force meetings set up to address it.

So I Did What Desperate People Do

I couldn't find an attorney to fight the foreclosure — twenty-plus rejections, nobody would touch it. So I filed Chapter 7 bankruptcy, not because I understood bankruptcy law, but to buy time. To stop the trustee sale. To create space to figure out what came next.

I found a bankruptcy attorney willing to take the case. Not a foreclosure defense specialist, just someone who could file the paperwork correctly and get me through the hearing. That distinction would turn out to matter enormously. She filed my mortgage as secured debt. It should have been filed as unsecured.

I didn't know the difference. I trusted her to know what she was doing.

Here's why it mattered. Secured debt means the court assumes the creditor has a valid lien on the property — the debt is legitimate, the foreclosure is enforceable, and once the automatic stay lifts, the bank can proceed without having to prove anything. Unsecured debt is a different world entirely.

The creditor has to prove they have a valid claim. They have to produce the original note. They have to demonstrate standing and show the chain of title is intact. If the debt is unsecured, the bank has to fight for what it's trying to take.

My attorney filed it as secured, which meant the court never questioned whether U.S. Bank actually had the right to foreclose. Never asked for the original note. Never required proof of standing. The automatic stay lifted, the bankruptcy was dismissed, and the foreclosure resumed.

I was $2,000 poorer, the chain of title had never been examined, and I had just learned that trusting professionals to do their jobs correctly was a luxury I couldn't afford.

I remember the specific quality of that realization. Not rage—something quieter and more permanent. The understanding that I had been careful, I had hired someone, I had done exactly what you're supposed to do when you don't know how to do something yourself—and it had made things worse.

That's the part that stays with you. Not the mistake. The fact that you did it the right way and it still didn't protect you. It doesn't feel dramatic in the moment. It feels small. Practical. Like adjusting to a new rule you didn't know existed until it cost you something.

There was no one to complain to. The bankruptcy was closed. The deadline had passed. The only direction was forward.

Learning the Hard Way

I learned the difference between secured and unsecured debt the way you learn anything in litigation when you're representing yourself: by failing first, then reading the statute that explains why you failed. By the time I understood what should have been filed, it was too late to fix it.

The bankruptcy case was closed. The foreclosure moved forward.

That's when I realized: if I was going to lose my house, it wouldn't be because I didn't fight hard enough. It would be because I trusted someone else to fight for me.

I fired her. Went pro se. I cleared the studio table and covered it with paper. Case law printed from legal databases. Statutes highlighted in three colors. A timeline on a roll of drafting paper tacked to the wall — the kind I used to use for design projects — now tracking motions and deadlines instead of page layouts. I had designed catalogs on impossible deadlines for twenty years. The skills transferred. The stakes were different.

Started learning bankruptcy law, foreclosure procedure, and civil litigation simultaneously while the sale date kept approaching. I filed an appeal—that disaster gets its own chapter later.

What mattered then was stopping the foreclosure. Everything else was noise.

The System's Design

The bankruptcy court didn't care about fraud in the underlying foreclosure. That's "not their jurisdiction." You have to fight that battle somewhere else.

Where? Good question.

The system is designed so that no court actually has to address the fraud. Bankruptcy court says it's a foreclosure issue. Foreclosure court says it's a contract issue. Civil court says you should have raised it in bankruptcy.

Round and round. And I was learning—fast—that procedure kills you long before facts ever get a chance to matter.

The David v Goliath Group

Somewhere in the chaos, I found a David-versus-Goliath group in Los Angeles. Smart people. Strategic thinkers. They were mapping foreclosure fraud long before it was fashionable, before the 2008 crash made it a headline. They taught me how to show up in court, how to assert my rights, how to file a motion that wouldn't get laughed out of the room — and most importantly, how to use the system's own rules against itself.

That education was priceless. Years later, I turned it into something. Together with Richard Mendez, I co-created David v. Goliath: The Homeowner's Guide to Fighting the Mortgage Machine — a nine-module online course built for pro se homeowners navigating exactly the kind of fraud I'd lived through. Everything I'd learned the hard way, organized into something someone else could actually use before losing their home instead of after.

Also terrifying. Because once I understood the rules, I also understood how badly the deck was stacked. Litigation is a special kind of violence — polite, slow, expensive, designed to outlast you. Nobody raises their voice. Everyone drains your time, money, and nervous system with immaculate manners. The goal isn't justice. It's attrition.

Learning to Speak the Language

I wasn't a lawyer, I was a person who refused to disappear quietly. It turns out those require the same skill set.

While I was learning—writing briefs around the clock, teaching myself legal formatting by trial and error—the unlawful detainer courts moved fast. Five days to respond. Conveyor-belt justice. No time to think. No margin for error. If you miss a deadline, you lose. Even if you're right. Especially if you're right.

I started reading California Civil Procedure like it was a novel I'd be tested on. California Evidence Code. Federal Rules of Civil Procedure. I kept a legal dictionary open at all times, cross-referencing terms I thought I understood but didn't.

"Demurrer." "Estoppel." "Res judicata." Words that sounded like spells because, in court, they basically are. I read case law with obsessive focus. Line by line. Over and over. Trying to answer the only question that actually mattered: Who won.

Not who was right. Not who had better facts. Who won. Because in appellate case law, the facts don't always matter. What matters is procedure. Whether the trial court abused its discretion. Whether the standard of review was correctly applied. Whether someone filed the right motion at the right time using the right language.

You can have all the evidence in the world and still lose because you cited the wrong subsection.

Seven years in, it got easier—but never easy. There were nights I'd read the same paragraph ten times and still not be certain which way it cut. My eyes would stop tracking. I'd make coffee I didn't drink, step outside, stand under the oaks for a few minutes, and come back to it.That was most nights for years. Even now, reading a case, it's not immediately clear whether it helps you or destroys you. That ambiguity isn't accidental.

The other side counted on that. They'd quote a sentence that sounded airtight, devastating, case-ending. Then you'd read the full opinion and realize the meaning flipped entirely. The sentence they quoted was describing the losing argument. Or it was dicta—commentary, not binding law. Or it applied to a completely different fact pattern. Context was everything. Omit it, and you could make case law say almost anything.

I learned that trick. And I learned to catch it when they used it on me.

The education came the hard way. I memorized statutes I couldn't pronounce but had to cite perfectly or lose on a technicality. I learned margins, font sizes, line spacing, the difference between a motion and a petition, how to serve opposing counsel, how to request a hearing, how to lodge an objection, how to appeal.

I learned to read the language they used on purpose. "Meet and confer" means pretending to negotiate before the court makes you negotiate.

Court clerks had no patience for pro se litigants who didn't know which form unlocked which door. "You can't file that here." "You need Form CM-010, not CM-040." "This needs to be lodged, not filed." I learned to take notes on the spot, standing at the counter, because my hands were usually shaking and writing something down steadied them.

***

I made mistakes. A lot of them. Procedural mistakes that cost me hearings. Evidence mistakes that cost me motions. Strategic mistakes that I didn't even recognize as mistakes until months later when I understood the rules better.

But I kept showing up, because what else was I going to do? Walk away?

Let them take my house with forged documents and call it legal? No.

The documents I'd found so far — the doctored loan application inflating my income tenfold, the notary stamp from a man who had never met me and whose signature didn't match his own bond — were only the beginning.

I didn't know that yet. What I knew was that the paper trail used to take my home had been manufactured, and that manufactured paper, filed in a county recorder's office, carries the same legal weight as the real thing until someone fights back hard enough to prove otherwise. The system doesn't distinguish between a legitimate document and a convincing forgery. That's not a flaw. That's the opportunity.

If I was going to lose, I was going to lose fighting. And if I was going to fight, I was going to learn how to do it right. I was fifty-nine years old, living alone in the mountains, learning civil procedure at two in the morning. The house was quiet. The deadline was real. I made another cup of coffee and kept reading.

And then the universe threw in another curveball.

Let's see what she's made of.

CHAPTER 16

Violence Arrives

While I was learning courtroom procedure in San Diego, I was also learning how to fight with a PVC pipe in Mexico.

Only one of those systems cared about truth.

I had been coming down to Baja for years before any of this. The first trips were my own idea, on my own terms — Julian was still mine, the house was earning income on VRBO, the appeals hadn't started, and Baja was the place I went when I needed the kind of quiet you cannot buy in California. I had a place near the Sea of Cortez. The desert there is honest about what it is. It does not pretend to be hospitable. The wind comes off the water in the afternoon, the light goes flat and pink, and then the dark arrives all at once. I painted when I could. I drove back to Julian when I needed to. For a while I had two lives and they fit together.

Then in 2018 the tenant from hell moved into the upper floor and stopped paying. In 2019 the locks on Julian were changed by people who knew the courts would not put them back. That is a particular kind of dispossession. Not the clean kind where a sheriff arrives with paperwork and you are given a date. The kind where one morning the keys no longer turn and the law you believed in declines to notice. The house was still legally mine. The foreclosure was contested. The appeals were live. None of it mattered to the locks.

After that, Baja stopped being the place I chose and started being the place I had left. Same desert. Same wind. Same light. Different posture. You stop unpacking boxes because you are not sure how long you will be where you are. You stop hanging things on walls. The body adjusts to the possibility of sudden departure and it does not unadjust just because the address has stayed the same for a few months. I thought distance might buy safety. It didn't.

***

Violence doesn't arrive with music. It doesn't build suspense. Real violence is quieter than that. Sometimes it arrives thirsty. Sometimes it walks out of the desert asking for water.

May 14, 2019. 9:00 a.m.

My twenty-pound, four-legged doorbell went off — not the lazy bark for rabbits, not the curious one for distant trucks. This was sharp. Urgent. Someone was here.

I stepped outside. The desert morning was already warming, sunlight spreading across pale sand. Behind the house runs an arroyo — a dry wash carved by storms that rarely come, most days silent, a ribbon of sand winding between mesquite. Not that morning. Three people were walking up it. Two men, one woman. Moving slowly, not like travelers trying to reach a road. Moving like people deciding something.

When you live alone in a remote place, instinct becomes your early warning system. There are moments when your body knows before your mind catches up. This was one of those moments. I knew something wasn't right. No neighbors for miles. No passing traffic. No witnesses. Just desert, wind, and three strangers walking closer. I locked the garage. Sat down. Waited. Sometimes waiting is the only move you have.

They saw me. For a moment we stared at each other across the arroyo. One of the men raised his hand. Not quite a wave. More like acknowledgment. They spoke briefly among themselves. And then they changed direction and walked straight toward the house. My dog pressed close, low growls rumbling in his chest. Animals know.

The footsteps came slow. Unhurried. A soft knock. A voice through the door.

"Agua."

Maria Guadalupe Gonzalez Toledo, you came to my door asking for water. I gave you a bottle. You wanted more. I gave you another. Instead of thank you, you threw it in my face, ripped my phone from my hand, and ran. I took a few steps after you. You were already gone.

I turned around. Moises Medina Duran, you were standing a foot away from me. Close enough that surprise didn't register — no warning, no escalation, no moment where I could have changed what happened next.

You stabbed me in the stomach. I folded over and thought, very calmly: Did you just kill me?

That calm is strange to describe. No screaming. No life flashing. No dramatic inventory of regrets. Just a body taking stock — pain sharp, then dull, then spreading, warmth moving through fabric that was probably blood — and a mind that had somehow gone very quiet and very practical at the same time. Did you just kill me? Is this how it ends? Here, in my driveway, in the dirt?

I have never been happier to have extra body fat. It kept the blade from reaching anything that would have ended the question permanently.

You could have run, but didn't. You came back for my face. My throat. You came again and again like finishing the job was the only thing left on your agenda that morning. I am sixty years old. I am big and strong, and I grabbed the only thing within reach — a five-foot PVC pipe — and I defended myself. If I had been smaller, slower, or weaker, I would have died right there in the dirt. No question. No drama. Just gone.

You climbed onto the retaining wall and started throwing rocks. Your aim was terrible at first — rocks scattering wide, any of them heavy enough to kill. Then one almost did. It came straight for my head. I stopped it with my hand. That's what broke the finger and put a big hole in it. Blood running down my wrist, pain stacking on top of pain, and still that strange quiet in my head that refused to let me fall apart.

You paused — just long enough to check if I was dead. I wasn't. So you kept going. I tightened my grip on the pipe and knocked you off the wall.

And then I heard myself.

"You motherfucker. Get the fuck out of here. Go fuck yourself. Do you know what that even means? Well, you've got my phone. Google it."

I didn't used to swear. My mother didn't raise a woman who swears. All that time of litigation turned me into a truck driver — the stress cracked the language open and something older climbed out. By the time I stood on that wall with a broken finger and my own blood on my hand, the words arrived fluently. I meant every syllable. You ran. Limping.

You lost. I survived. Again.

***

This memory came back to me years later. First it was gone — the kind of gone that isn't forgetting, the kind where your brain puts something in a drawer and doesn't tell you which drawer. Then one afternoon it came back whole. The wall. The rocks. The pipe. The sentence I didn't know I had in me until it was already out of my mouth.

Sisu isn't polite. That was the lesson. I had always thought it was — some quiet Nordic endurance, some dignified refusal to quit. It isn't. Sisu is a broken finger and a stolen phone and a woman on a retaining wall telling a man who just tried to kill her to go look up the word she used, because she was too tired to explain it herself.

Survival doesn't feel victorious in the moment. It feels administrative. The body switches into inventory mode — count what still works, count what's leaking, count what can wait.

I noticed small things first. The dust on my knees. The way my dog's bark had shifted from warning to panic. The smell of iron in the air. Blood has a smell. You never forget it.

Time didn't move correctly. It stretched, then snapped back, then stalled again. I remember thinking I should sit down before my legs decided for me. I remember being annoyed that I was bleeding on my own ground. That detail mattered more than it should have.

I did not cry. That came later. Much later.

Shock is quiet. It doesn't scream. It whispers instructions. Sit. Breathe. Don't faint. Stay upright. The most unsettling part wasn't the pain — it was the clarity. A strange calm settles in, the kind that only shows up when the body has already decided it's not done yet. I remember thinking: *this is inconvenient.* Not unfair. Not tragic. Just deeply, offensively inconvenient.

Violence expects gratitude afterward — for being spared, for surviving, for not getting it worse. You're supposed to feel lucky. The bar gets set by whoever hurt you, and then you're expected to thank them for not clearing it. I wasn't grateful. I was alert.

Survival isn't about winning. It's about refusing to hand yourself over.

I stood there taking inventory. Stabbed. Bleeding. Broken finger. Rocks everywhere. My dog barking like she'd been trying to tell me this would happen.

Cesar Alejandro Lopez, El Ranchero — you were there too. Holding a golf club. Watching. You didn't intervene. You didn't stop it. You didn't leave. That choice lives with you.

What changed wasn't just my sense of safety. It was my understanding of proximity. Violence doesn't require consensus. It only requires permission through silence. One person acts, another watches, a third decides not to interrupt. That is how harm becomes social. I didn't just lose trust in strangers — that would have been simple. I lost trust in the assumption that presence equals protection. The woman who asked for water wasn't desperate. She was testing access. The man with the golf club wasn't neutral. He was choosing outcome without fingerprints.

I stopped believing in bystanders after that. Not because they don't exist — but because the system trains them. Don't get involved. Don't escalate. Don't make it your problem. That logic shows up everywhere. In neighborhoods. In courtrooms. In institutions that pretend neutrality while outcomes repeat.

I didn't become paranoid. I became precise.

When they ran, I didn't chase. I sat there. Bleeding. Shocked. Doing inventory.

Phone: gone. Blood: present. Guts: still inside. Good sign.

How do you get help when the attackers steal your phone?

Survival rarely follows protocol. There is no checklist for what to do when your phone is gone, your hand is broken, and you're bleeding on your own property. There is only improvisation. I didn't post on Facebook because it was clever, I did it because it was available.

Systems don't fail all at once. They fail in layers. When one collapses, you reach for the next.

This instinct would become familiar later—when motions were denied, when evidence was acknowledged but ignored, when official channels closed ranks. You learn to reroute and to ask the question that still has oxygen in it.

You learn that survival favors the person who keeps moving laterally when forward is blocked. That morning taught me something that court would later confirm: procedure is optional when momentum is on your side. The trick is making momentum yours.

You grab your iPad and post on Facebook.

If you read this, please send police. I've been attacked.

Social media. Not just for cat photos.

Within fifteen minutes my friend Jan Hastings showed up with the police. Jan took care of my dog Friska and got her out of there while I gave my first police report. The rest of the day is fog. Trauma does that. It blurs the edges. The police offered to call an ambulance. I declined. I decided I could drive myself. My guts hadn't spilled out. Seemed manageable.

By noon the police were done. I told them not to waste time babysitting me and to go find the assholes. I'd drive myself to town, file another report, and get my hand stitched. Because obviously that's what you do after being stabbed.

Somewhere in this genius plan, I got a message that a doctor from town was willing to drive out to my house. I told him I'd come to him instead, since I had to go to the station anyway. This was not my best decision.

The body keeps score long before the mind catches up. I was still negotiating with reality—telling myself I was fine, that I'd handled worse, that I could manage a short drive. That's the lie competence tells you. Lightheadedness isn't dramatic, it's polite, it gives you a warning. I remember the edges of the road softening, like a bad photograph slipping out of focus.

The realization arrived without panic: *You don't get to decide this part.* Survival sometimes means stopping mid-sentence, it means pulling over. It means accepting that strength has a shelf life measured in minutes, not pride. I didn't feel weak—I felt human. A few miles in, I started getting lightheaded.

Oh shit. I'm not going to make it. I pulled off at a friend's house by the highway.

CHAPTER 17

What Surviving Actually Looks Like

Chello, I said, "the banditos got me, can you help." Grandma gave me a glass of water with sugar. My hand shook so badly I spilled it everywhere. Very dignified. She watched me with the particular stillness of someone who has seen trouble before and knows that what a person needs in that moment isn't words — it's water, and sugar, and someone who doesn't panic.

Eventually, we made it to town. Twelve stitches on the finger, the kind of careful needlework that requires you to hold very still while someone threads a needle through the part of your hand you use for everything. We stopped for food afterward, because apparently shock needs tacos. That's when it hit me — the delayed reckoning that trauma saves for the moment you finally sit down and something ordinary happens, like a plate of food arriving. I could have died. There's something almost insulting about the body choosing tacos as the moment to tell the truth. Not during the attack. Not while driving. Not at the police station. Tacos.

I broke down right there at the table, crying into my tacos, which is not how I imagined this day going.

Next stop: police station. Wrong jurisdiction. San Felipe sits on the Sea of Cortez side of the Baja peninsula, and jurisdiction followed geography — I'd have to cross the mountains to Ensenada, on the Pacific coast. A four-hour drive. Not happening. I had to leave at 8 a.m. the next morning to drive to San Diego for a court hearing over my house in Julian. The legal machine doesn't pause for stabbings. I don't say that for effect. I mean it literally. Blood loss, stitches, police reports, no sleep — and the calendar still expected me to show up polished and coherent.

On the way home, I saw a man walking along the highway. We made eye contact. The recognition was instant and physical — a full-body certainty that landed before the thought had finished forming. Shit. That's him. "Chello," I said, "run him over." He declined. Apparently vehicular homicide is frowned upon even under the circumstances.

We stopped. Moises ran into the desert. Chello flagged down a four-wheel-drive truck and explained the situation to two strangers who, without hesitation, took off after a man who had just stabbed someone. Absolute heroes. I drove home and called the local police. "He's here," I said. "Go find him." Silence all night. I lay in the dark, hand throbbing, mind cycling, wondering if he was still out there in the desert or if he'd circled back. Wondering if the door was locked. Checking twice. That's what fear becomes after violence. Not drama. Repetition. Door. Window. Gate. Again.

At 7 a.m., police showed up. "You can't leave yet." They had Moises handcuffed in the back of a truck.

I needed the doctor's report before I could go anywhere. I followed them to the little local station — no jail, just an office with a ceiling fan and fluorescent light and a folding chair that someone had decided was sufficient furniture for a crime scene. They handcuffed him to an ATV wheel. Mexican-style. He sat there looking at the floor while I sat three feet away looking at him, both of us waiting for bureaucracy to finish its paperwork.

I picked up the report. We met at a 7-Eleven in town. Then things escalated. Sirens on.

A hundred miles an hour through sleepy San Felipe, where nothing moves faster than forty. The police car ahead of me took corners on faith, passed cars on the left, on the right, occasionally what I'm fairly certain was a sidewalk. I followed in my Honda Element, high on painkillers, full of adrenaline, shock doing the actual driving. I remember thinking that if I died in a car accident on the way to file a police report about being stabbed, that would be an extremely annoying way to go.

There's a ten-mile stretch where local police lose jurisdiction. Backup from Ensenada had followed in case state police pulled me over for speeding — one cop to stay with me and explain, one to keep the handcuffed man moving. They had four hours from the time of arrest to get him to jail. The four-hour drive took two.

At the station I waited three, maybe four hours. Made another report. Waited some more. The police doctor arrived. Another report. He pulled off my bloody bandage to count the stitches. Twelve. Measured the wound with the focused efficiency of someone who has done this many times and stopped being affected by it. I needed a fresh dressing. They didn't have one. The bloody bandage went back on. Excellent. Infection roulette, with a court appearance in twelve hours.

***

By six o'clock it was dark. No phone. I borrowed one and called my friend Bonnie. "Can I come over?" A pause. "I'm broken." She didn't ask questions. She just said yes. Sometimes that's the whole miracle. Not advice. Not analysis. Just someone opening the door.

I drove to the border — a drive I'd done a thousand times, muscle memory, automatic. That night I couldn't find my way. Something in my navigation had gone offline along with everything else. Midnight. Finally San Diego. Safe. Someone taking care of what was left of me.

Two days later they released him. The next day I stayed in the fetal position. That's not a metaphor. I pulled my knees to my chest and stayed there, which is the body's honest answer to what had happened and the only response that made any sense.

The day after that my finger doubled in size and turned bright red. ER. Impressive — within fifteen minutes I had a bed with an IV of antibiotics flowing in. Turns out it wasn't infected. The finger was dislocated, blood flow cut off. They reset it, but the damage was already done — another hour or two and they would have had to amputate. Six-week splint. Ligaments stretched, scar tissue took over. The finger stopped bending. Three months of physical therapy, painful, no effect. Another three months. Still a sausage. Surgery, more therapy, more pain. "It's just a finger," people say. It's never just a finger when you work with your hands.

All of this happened while I was fighting for my house and attending hearings in San Diego. I drove to Ensenada over and over trying to get the police to arrest them again. Within a month I went back to my house in Baja. I had to kill the witch. Fear only gets stronger if you let it live.

A year passed. They were still free. Everyone in the neighborhood knew who they were. I reported it. Nothing happened. The particular helplessness of being believed and ignored is its own kind of violence.

Then Governor Jaime Bonilla came to the neighborhood with promises and an entourage. I pulled him aside and told him my story. I told him I could kill Baja tourism in five minutes with a press conference in San Diego about how dangerous it was and how ineffective the police were. He summoned his DA on the spot. "Take care of this woman," he said.

Within a week I received a call from the Ensenada DA's office. They wanted me to identify the attackers from photos. I couldn't go — I had a court hearing in San Diego. "No problem," they said. "We'll come to you." We met outside IKEA in Mission Valley. Garden section. Patio furniture. The DA crossed the parking lot toward me and I said, "Pull up a chair. This is my office." I identified all three and signed the statement. They left. Within a week, all three were in jail. So that's how things work — not through procedure, but through leverage applied to the right person at the right moment.

Another year passed. I entered the victims' unit. Counseling. On Zoom. With a translator app. Sentence by sentence.

September 28, 2021. The Criminal Trial — Mexico

When I first saw them on the Zoom screen months earlier, my body shut down completely — no voice, no movement, just full panic. Trauma doesn't care that you're safe now. It drags the past into the room and locks the door. I sat in front of a screen in Baja, looking at the faces of the people who had tried to kill me, and my nervous system treated it as if they were standing in the room.

After that, I made a decision. They had too much power over me and I needed it back. Another witch to kill. The shaking, the panic, the way my body hijacked itself at the sight of their faces — that was weakness I couldn't afford and wouldn't tolerate. I decided I would testify, but only on one condition: I wanted to speak to them directly. To look at them and say what happened, out loud, to their faces.

That day, I was completely calm. I went through the entire attack from beginning to end — step by step, blow by blow — looking them in the eye the whole time. Asking why. I knew they weren't allowed to answer. That wasn't the point. The point was that I was the one speaking, and they were the ones who had to sit there and hear it. Every thought went through a translator, one sentence at a time, and those pauses — waiting for the words to cross from one language to another — turned out to be exactly what I needed. Long enough for each moment to land. Long enough for me to feel it and release it and move to the next one.

By the end, the shaking had stopped. I was free. I was in control again. That's all it took — not a verdict, not a sentence, not an apology they were never going to give. Just my own voice, in a room where they had to listen.

They had two years to come forward, two years to apologize when it might have actually mattered. I might have chosen peace over prosecution — I've thought about that. They showed no remorse and confessed only when it benefited them, which is not the same thing as accountability. My Sharp Hospital invoices weren't admissible — they should have been obtained by the court through Mexico City, which would have meant another year of waiting. I gave up on that front. I wasn't asking for money. I needed it to end. They were convicted, sentenced to five years each. That saga was finally over.

Justice wasn't satisfying. It was procedural. I think people imagine justice feels clean when it arrives. It doesn't. Mostly it feels late, partial, and administrative. I never agreed with five-year sentences, but I agreed to close this chapter. There's a difference between the outcome you wanted and the outcome you can live with. I took the one I could live with.

I later learned they were released in March 2025 — no notice, no warning, despite the court's legal obligation to inform me. Mexico-style accountability: mañana doesn't mean tomorrow, it just means not today. I also learned two of them had been in a car accident. Karma has a timing issue. She eventually shows up, usually without paperwork.

The three of them permanently changed my life. I lost a year of work — not from fear or weakness, but because trauma rewires the brain and surgeries take time. The first time I went back to the property after the attack, my body remembered before my brain did.

That's the part no one explains about survival. The event ends. The body keeps voting.

Heart racing. Hands shaking. Scanning every shadow for movement before I'd consciously decided to. I forced myself to stay, to walk the same path, to prove I could. It took months before I stopped checking over my shoulder every thirty seconds. Some part of me is probably still checking.

I work with my hands. I sculpt, build mosaics, paint, type. Every finger matters. They left me with permanent damage.

What followed was another education. As a foreigner, I pressed criminal charges inside the Mexican legal system with no affordable attorney and a constant language barrier — navigating police reports, investigators, prosecutors, forensic doctors, psychiatrists, victims' units, and eventually the governor, who held final authority. Two years of showing up, testifying, waiting, and refusing to disappear.

Afterward, I started a neighborhood watch group on Facebook for San Felipe South Campos. At first it was practical — who heard what, which road, which gate. It now has over nine hundred members.

We don't trade paranoia. We trade data. What happened to me scared people because it wasn't random. It was ordinary — it could have happened to anyone. That may be the most frightening category of all: not rare, not targeted, just available.

Tourism fuels Baja's economy, and safety fuels trust. When trust cracks, word travels faster than sirens.

When you accept that you might be dead in ten minutes, the nonsense evaporates. Fear of public speaking? Gone. Tolerance for bullshit? Zero. Only real things survive — truth, work, art.

That chapter is closed. There is a new one.

October 29, 2024. Another Break-in.

My house again. While I was tied up in court in San Diego — fighting banks and judges who prefer clean records to clean hands — another couple broke in. The security cameras caught everything — time-stamped, clear, uncontroverted. I pressed charges. Again.

I don't hesitate anymore. I don't freeze. I don't wait for permission. That sounds like strength. Mostly it's adaptation. I document. I file. I follow through. I've learned the systems on both sides of the border, and I use them until they work.

The footage caught both of them. The woman pled guilty and received a shortened sentence — four years, plus one year of probation with mandatory monthly drug testing. I also pushed, through multiple attempts and back-and-forth I didn't fully understand between the prosecutor and the judge, for something I'd never heard requested before: she is required to visit every school in San Felipe once a month to speak to students about the dangers of drugs. Twelve opportunities a year to get the message through to kids. I don't know if that's ever been asked before. I think it succeeded.

The man is pleading not guilty. There's irony in there somewhere, given that he's on the same footage. He's counting on a technicality, on the government failing to prove what the camera already showed. I'll be subpoenaing the woman to testify at trial. That should complicate his math. I think he's screwed.

A Mexican friend taught me the perfect courtroom confession: "No lo hice y no lo volveré a hacer." I didn't do it, and I will not do it again. It's the attorney joke that somehow captures an entire legal strategy. I've been watching defendants run that play for seven years. Apparently it travels well across borders.

What matters here is the contrast. While one system explained away forged documents as clerical errors, another treated violence exactly as what it was. Make of that what you will.

Scars don't end art. They edit it. Some things leave the body and stay in the work. It speaks back. The captain never left. She just learned quieter commands.

I didn't ask for this education. But I graduated anyway. You will not get away with it. That's sisu. I didn't know how much I had until I desperately needed it. It didn't feel noble at the time. It felt like there was no alternative.

That is the long arc of it. The trial, the convictions, the second break-in, the woman in the schools — all of it took years. I am telling it to you here in one piece because violence does not belong in fragments. But the calendar of this book has to go backward now, because the next thing that happened, happened first.

Nine days after Moises stabbed me, I had a hearing in Pasadena.

CHAPTER 18

The Appeal Where Reality Blinks

Back on the U.S. side, I headed straight into bankruptcy appeals court.My hearing was set for May 23, 2019. I was ready. The bank hadn't stated a claim. No standing. No evidence. On paper, this was unlosable.

I was discharged from the hospital the day before.

My hand was in a splint, throbbing. My abdomen had swollen into a grapefruit-sized bubble—internal bleeding that, according to the doctors, could have ruptured and ended both my legal career and most of my organs. I was grateful for the bubble. It was doing its job. Life, I was learning, has a fondness for surreal timing. The emergency room doctors had been clear: "You need to stay for observation. If that ruptures—"

I signed the release against medical advice. Again. There's a checkbox for people like me on those forms. Patient aware of risks. Patient leaving anyway.

The drive from San Diego to Pasadena typically takes two hours. In a storm, with one functional hand and organs that might decide to quit mid-freeway, it felt like navigating a ship through a hurricane while the hull was already taking water. I drove through Los Angeles in a storm. Biblical rain. Traffic from hell. I repeated, *You can do this. You can do this.*

The bank had filed a proof of claim in my bankruptcy with no evidence, no standing, no chain of title. Under bankruptcy law, that's not just improper—it's a violation that should result in sanctions.

I'd raised multiple grounds for reversal: the bank's failure to file proper proof of claim forms under the revised 2017 Bankruptcy Rules (Forms 410,

410A, and 410S), standing issues because the claim wasn't presented by the actual creditor or its authorized agent, Common Law contract principles under UCC 1-103.6, and the fundamental problem that you cannot assign a mortgage without the underlying debt. This was supposed to be simple. That's what I thought the law was for. You follow the rules, you get a predictable outcome. That assumption doesn't survive long.

The Night Before: When Curiosity Becomes Evidence

I was at my friend Suzanne's house in Santa Monica. I had driven up from San Diego that day, discharged from the hospital with instructions I had ignored and a prescription for painkillers I was actually taking, because the alternative was not driving at all. Suzanne told me later she had never seen me so frazzled. Suzanne has known me for decades. She has seen me through divorces and deadlines and the year my mother died. Frazzled was not in her standard vocabulary for me. That night it was.

The hearing was the next morning in Pasadena. I should have been sleeping. I should have been doing a lot of things. What I was doing instead was sitting in her guest room with my laptop, the splinted hand resting awkwardly on the keyboard, the abdomen reminding me at intervals that internal bleeding was still on the table. There was something I wanted to check before I walked into court.

There's a public website called the MERS Servicer ID system. MERS — Mortgage Electronic Registration Systems — is the private database that tracks mortgages in America. It was created by banks in the 1990s to speed up securitization by eliminating the need to record assignments at county recorders' offices. In theory, MERS is supposed to track who owns what. In practice, it's a black box where mortgages multiply like digital rabbits. You enter an address. It tells you how many active mortgages are tied to it. Simple, efficient, and terrifying.

I entered my Julian property address. Six active mortgages. On one house. That I'd owned before the 2007 refinance.

I stared at the screen. The painkillers were doing their job in some places and not others. The room was very quiet. Suzanne had gone to bed hours earlier. I could hear the refrigerator cycling in her kitchen, two rooms away. That's the level of quiet I am describing. And on my screen, six active mortgages on a house I had owned for thirty years, on a night when I was supposed to be lying down.

Curiosity is a disease, so I kept going.

I tried other addresses. Friends' homes. Properties I knew were paid off. The numbers were random, chaotic—sometimes zero, sometimes three, sometimes more. Then I thought: What about public property?

I ran the Julian cemetery. County-owned, free and clear. Tax-exempt. No mortgages possible. It had more than twenty mortgages. Too many to display. The system just said: "20+ records found." Apparently even the dead are leveraged. I sat back in my guest room chair, hand throbbing, abdomen pulsing with each heartbeat, staring at this impossible data.

Then, just to see, I ran the address of the federal courthouse in Pasadena, the United States Court of Appeals for the Ninth Circuit. 125 S Grand Ave, Pasadena, CA 91105. Four mortgages. On a federal building. Owned by the United States government. I printed it out. All of it. Screenshots, timestamps, property records showing government ownership, MERS listings showing four active loans secured by a courthouse.

The absurdity was so complete it became evidence. This wasn't about my house anymore. It stopped being personal. That should have made it easier. It didn't. This was about a system that had broken so thoroughly that it was now claiming ownership of everything—homes, cemeteries, courthouses, reality itself.

May 23, 2019: The Hearing

The bankruptcy appeals court sits in what was once the Vista del Arroyo Hotel and Bungalows—a Spanish Colonial Revival resort built in the 1920s for people who had money and time to spare. Now it houses the Richard H. Chambers U.S. Court of Appeals in Pasadena.

Walking in, I understood immediately why it felt so different from state court in San Diego. This wasn't designed to process people. It was designed to pamper them. Calm. Polite. Civilized. Wood paneling that whispered money and permanence. I hadn't gotten the memo on dress code. I felt overdressed for vacation and underdressed for power. The black robes were the same, but everything else had changed.

Security was airport-level. Metal detectors. X-ray machines. Federal marshals who looked like they'd been trained to remain expressionless in all circumstances. I passed through with my splinted hand, my boxes of documents, my printouts of impossible mortgages. No one asked why I looked like I'd just escaped a car accident. That's part of the culture. If you show up, you're fine. Whatever it took to get there is irrelevant. Professionalism is a kind of silence.

The courtroom itself was beautiful in that specific federal way—high ceilings, expensive wood, acoustic tiles designed to make voices sound authoritative even when saying nothing of substance.

Three judges sat at the bench. Not one, like state court. Three. A panel.

The Honorable judges names I've since memorized: Judge Kurtz presiding, with Judges Faris and Brand flanking. I took my seat at counsel table. The bank's attorney—a different one this time, because they rotate through firms like relief pitchers—sat across from me. Pressed suit. Leather briefcase. The casual confidence of someone who'd never had to argue in a splint.

I asked the panel if I could be seated during my argument because I would faint if I stood, and they said yes.

Something else was different. My heart wasn't racing. Fear was gone. Near-death has a way of simplifying things. For the first time, I spoke to judges without apologizing for existing. They listened. When you've been told your organs might rupture, judicial disapproval stops registering as a threat.

The Argument

None of it mattered. I'd prepared for months. The law was clear.

"Your Honors, the bank has failed to comply with the revised Bankruptcy Rules that took effect in 2017. The new rules require secured creditors to file a proof of claim on the proper forms for the claim to be allowed. The bank filed none of these. Without an allowed claim, they lack standing to participate in this bankruptcy proceeding."

Judge Kurtz interrupted. "Ms. Hannonen, proof of claim is not required in Chapter 7 bankruptcy for a secured creditor to preserve its lien."

I felt the ground tilt. That wasn't what I'd argued. I'd said "allowed claim," not "preserve lien." But the distinction evaporated in that courtroom the moment the judge spoke.

"With respect, Your Honor, I understand the lien isn't voided by failure to file. But the 2017 rules require filing for the claim to be allowed — to participate in distribution, to have standing — "

"The creditor can seek relief from stay without filing a proof of claim."

The door had closed. My main argument — months of research into the revised rules — dismissed in seconds. The judge had conflated "preserving a lien" with "having an allowed claim," and once that conflation happened, there was no walking it back.

I pivoted. There was nothing else to do.

"Then we move to standing on other grounds. The claim wasn't presented by the creditor or its authorized agent. MERS purports to assign this mortgage in March 2017, but MERS is just a database — a nominee. It never held the note. It never received consideration. It can't assign what it doesn't own.

"And the entity MERS claims to represent — Chevy Chase Bank — ceased to exist in 2009 when it was acquired by Capital One. In 2017, MERS is claiming to act as nominee for a bank that hasn't existed for eight years."

The judges listened. I could see them processing, but the energy had shifted. The proof of claim argument had been my strongest weapon.

"You cannot assign a mortgage without the underlying debt. The mortgage is worthless without the note. But the note the bank claims to hold is undated, and there's evidence of duplicate notes — one allegedly in Minnesota, one allegedly in Colorado."

Then I pulled out my last card—the one I'd discovered the night before in the guest room.

"Your Honors, there's something else. The MERS database shows multiple mortgages on properties that cannot possibly have mortgages. The Julian cemetery—county-owned, tax-exempt—shows more than twenty active MERS mortgages. My property shows six."

I held up the printouts, my splinted hand making the gesture awkward. "And this courthouse. This building where we're standing. 125 South Grand Avenue, Pasadena, California. Owned by the United States government. The MERS database shows four active mortgages secured by this federal building."

Judge Kurtz leaned forward slightly. "Four mortgages. On this building."

"Yes, Your Honor. On this very building. Government-owned. And according to MERS, it currently secures four different mortgages. I've also documented more than twenty mortgages on the Julian cemetery, which is county-owned public land. The system isn't just unreliable. It's meaningless."

Another pause. Longer this time. Judge Brand glanced at the printout I'd submitted. He didn't pick it up. "We'll take that under advisement."

That phrase does a lot of work. Under advisement sounds like consideration—like the system is processing information, applying judgment.

What it actually means is simpler: the information has been received and will not be acted upon.

A federal courthouse. Four mortgages. A cemetery with twenty. I had handed three federal judges proof that the system tracking mortgage ownership in America had become a fiction—and the response was the legal equivalent of setting down a coffee cup and changing the subject.

If you assume that proving something changes the outcome, this is where that assumption breaks.

The papers were set aside. Literally. Like a napkin someone didn't want on the table. No follow-up questions. No request for the bank to respond. No curiosity about how a federal courthouse could be collateral for four loans. Just: We'll take that under advisement.

Which is judicial code for: We see the problem. We're not touching it.

The bank's attorney stood. She argued procedure, standing presumptions, the prima facie validity of recorded documents. She acknowledged the MERS courthouse issue was "certainly interesting" but irrelevant to whether her client had standing to foreclose. "The assignment is properly recorded. The note is in our client's possession. That's all the law requires," she said.

I had been told a year earlier that U.S. Bank held the original note in an office in Minnesota. At the same time, the servicer, SLS, claimed it was in their vault in Colorado. Two locations. One original note. No one in the courtroom seemed troubled by that.

She didn't explain the four mortgages on the courthouse. No one asked her to. When it was over, the panel thanked us both. Professional. Polite. No indication which way they were leaning.

I gathered my boxes and walked out into the California sun.

My main argument had been dismissed in the first two minutes—not because it was wrong, but because the judge had reframed it in a way that made it irrelevant. And my evidence of systematic fraud—mortgages on a federal courthouse—had been noted, acknowledged, and carefully set aside.

I'd shown them something they couldn't unsee. But seeing and acting are different things. To this day, I'm not sure Judge Kurtz was technically right. The new rules said one thing about allowed claims and another about preserving liens, and I'd argued the first while he ruled on the second. In that courtroom, the distinction didn't matter. Once the judge said it, it became true.

The Aftermath

The court took the matter under submission — meaning a written decision later, no ruling from the bench, no immediate resolution. They needed seven days. Not to research the law, but to figure out how to avoid addressing the evidence. I went home unsettled. Not because they disagreed. Because they didn't engage at all. No questions, no curiosity, no disbelief — just a collective decision not to touch it.

The MERS evidence was the kind of thing that should have provoked outrage, or at least inquiry. This was direct proof that the entire system of mortgage tracking in America had degraded into fantasy. My property showed six mortgages where there should have been one. A cemetery in Julian — a cemetery — showed more than twenty. Cemeteries don't take out mortgages. Dead people don't refinance. What phantom debt was being laundered through the dead? I can't prove money laundering. I'm not a forensic accountant and I have no subpoena power. But I am someone who spent thirty years reading documents for a living, and I know what legitimate paperwork looks like. This didn't look like that. It looked like volume. It looked like velocity. It looked like someone needed the numbers to exist on paper regardless of whether anything real existed behind them.

Instead of inquiry — nothing. Radio silence.

That night, back by the computer, I couldn't let it go. So I did what any reasonable person would do next: I screen-recorded the MERS website, so I'd have solid evidence. Not screenshots this time — video, with timestamps, with my cursor moving through the interface in real-time so no one could claim it was fabricated. I ran the same searches, same addresses, same courthouse. 125 S Grand Ave, Pasadena, CA 91105.

The listings were gone. Not hidden, not altered — gone. Scrubbed clean within twelve hours of the hearing. The federal courthouse now showed zero mortgages. My property still showed six, because mine was in active litigation. They couldn't delete that without raising questions. But everything I'd demonstrated as evidence of systemic dysfunction? Erased. I ran the recording again. Then again. I sat in the dark. I did not move for a long time. It was the feeling of the earth opening up and the sky falling, something that does not happen to people who run database queries on Thursday nights.

This wasn't a glitch. This was a response. Someone — MERS, the banks, some algorithm designed to detect exposure — had seen my filing, seen the screenshots, and sanitized the database. Within twelve hours. On a Thursday night. That was the moment I knew I had touched something real. Systems don't move that fast for mistakes. Only for exposure. They needed seven days to write three pages. They only needed twelve hours to scrub a national database. Priorities.

The Denial: Mootness as Exit Strategy

Seven days later, on May 30, 2019, the Bankruptcy Appellate Panel issued its decision. Three pages. Not "Affirmed." — "DISMISSED as MOOT."

They weren't ruling on the merits. They weren't addressing standing, the missing proof of claim forms, the backdated assignment, or the MERS evidence showing mortgages on federal courthouses. They were dismissing the entire appeal on a technicality.

The reasoning was simple and evasive: I had received my discharge after filing the appeal. Under Section 362(c)(2)(C), the automatic stay terminates when a discharge is granted. Since there was no longer a stay in effect, the court couldn't grant me effective relief even if they ruled in my favor. Therefore: moot. Therefore: dismissed.

The procedural exit ramp had appeared, and they took it. It looks technical. It isn't. It's how you avoid answering the question.

I had raised multiple substantive grounds for reversal — standing, improper proof of claim forms, failure to comply with new Bankruptcy Rules, the backdated assignment creating a retroactive standing problem. Any one of those issues could have established reversible error. But mootness rendered all of them irrelevant. The court didn't have to rule on whether the bank proved its case. They didn't have to address whether the lower court erred. They just had to note that the automatic stay had terminated by operation of law. Done. Appeal dismissed.

What Mootness Conceals.

This sequence happens in every Chapter 7 bankruptcy where relief from stay is appealed: discharge is granted, stay terminates, appeal becomes moot.

Which means appellate courts almost never have to rule on whether banks proved their cases in bankruptcy court. The procedural structure guarantees non-review. It's not a bug. It's a feature.

The three-page memorandum made no mention of the four mortgages on the federal courthouse, the twenty-plus mortgages on the Julian cemetery, the systematic unreliability of MERS data, the bank's failure to file required forms, or the backdated 2012 assignment for a 2008 foreclosure. None of it mattered.

The memo simply noted: "We cannot exercise jurisdiction over a moot appeal." Translation: *We're not looking. We don't have to.*

What Changed

After that, the machine stopped pretending to idle. Notices came faster. Deadlines tightened. The process no longer wandered. It marched.

Before the MERS evidence, the foreclosure process had been chaotic—starts and stops, deferrals, delays. Banks seemed content to let cases drag for years. They had time. They had resources. They could wait.

After I showed them I could see the system itself? Everything accelerated. New motions from the bank. New counsel appearing. New foreclosure notices. The unlawful detainer that would eventually force me out was filed within months.

It wasn't retaliation in the legal sense. You can't prove that a bank speeds up foreclosure because you exposed something. But the timing was clear. The system had been alerted. Not to me. To the fact that someone was paying attention.

Not to my case—my case was irrelevant. To the method. To the idea that someone pro se, with a laptop and a MERS login, could pull back the curtain and show that the emperor wasn't just naked—he was a hologram. Mootness isn't a doctrine. It's a trap door.

CHAPTER 19

The IT Guy Who Was a Vice President

I started investigating the documents myself. If no attorney would help me understand what was happening, I'd figure it out alone. That sounds empowering when you say it out loud. It isn't. It just means there's no one left to ask. I pulled every recorded document tied to my property: Assignment of Deed of Trust, Substitution of Trustee, Notice of Default, Notice of Trustee Sale, Trustees Deed Upon Sale. I read them line by line, then started calling the names printed at the bottom, assuming, naively, that people who sign legal documents might be reachable.

The Assignment of Deed of Trust

The Assignment transferred my mortgage from MERS to U.S. Bank National Association as Trustee relating to Chevy Chase Funding LLC Mortgage Backed Certificates Series 2007-2— whatever "relating to" is supposed to mean. Read the name out loud. It takes breath. It takes two lines, a series number with a hyphen — forty syllables of institutional presence, stacked like a title on a vault door somewhere in Minnesota.

It is the only part of this bank that ever touched my case.

U.S. Bank doesn't originate loans like mine. It doesn't send statements, collect payments, answer phones, or walk into court. What it does — for a fee — is lend its name to securitized trusts assembled on Wall Street. Trust 2007-2 needed something credible on paper. U.S. Bank rents one out. Everything else — the servicing, the filings, the phone calls, the signatures on the forged documents, the motions, the courtroom appearances — belongs to Specialized Loan Servicing and The Ryan Firm.

The pattern wasn't unique to my case. The National Consumer Law Center describes as standard industry practice how Fannie Mae and Freddie Mac routinely foreclose through their servicers' names rather than their own. The right to enforce the note is transferred to the servicer, the servicer conducts the sale, and the foreclosure deed reverts to the GSE at the end. The owner of the loan never appears in the courthouse. The borrower never sees who is actually taking the house. What happened in my case is the same architecture. The rented name is not an accident of my file. It is the operating system.

No employee of U.S. Bank ever signed a pleading in my case. No representative from U.S. Bank ever walked into the courtroom. When the plaintiff was called for, an attorney stepped outside and came back with a realtor. That was the closest anyone came.

The bank wasn't foreclosing on me. A costume was.

Years later, I watched the costume work in real time. The unlawful detainer case — the case U.S. Bank filed to evict the tenants living in my house — rested on a verified complaint. California law requires that an unlawful detainer complaint be verified by the plaintiff, under penalty of perjury. Not the attorney. The plaintiff. The complaint in my case had been verified by the attorney.

I raised it. The judge brushed it off and told me the plaintiff didn't have to show up until trial. That wasn't the point. An unverified unlawful detainer complaint is subject to dismissal — not because the plaintiff is absent, but because nobody has sworn to the facts. The complaint is hearsay on its face. The court proceeded anyway. I was dismissed out of the case before the verification issue could be tested.

The plaintiff didn't show up at trial either. No one from U.S. Bank ever walked into that courtroom. Not once, across all those years.

After I was dismissed, I ran into Richard Coombs, the U.S. Bank attorney, in the hallway outside the courtroom before the trial for the tenant. I asked him, pleasantly: "How do you feel about the case now that you've gotten me out of the way?" He said, "I feel very good. But if the opposing attorney brings up the verification, I'll lose." I stood there in the hallway and felt the ground tilt.

Verification was the argument I had been preparing to make. It was the strongest thing I had, and the court had dismissed me out of the case on a procedural technicality before I could ever say the word — which I now understood, standing in that hallway, was not an accident. They had taken my civil rights, my due process rights, and my one clean shot at winning, and they had taken them all with the same move.

The opposing attorney was the tenant's. He never raised it. Nobody brought it up. A stipulation was reached. Everybody got paid. The tenant got paid to leave. The attorneys got paid. The servicer got paid. The only person in that hallway who didn't get paid was the person whose name was on the title.

Coombs knew the case was broken. He said so out loud to the homeowner he had just finished dismissing. He knew because he had been watching it work for years. Unverified complaint. Absent plaintiff. Costume bank. None of it mattered as long as nobody with standing said the words out loud.

That is what I mean when I say the bank was never there. The bank didn't need to be. The bank had attorneys who could win cases the bank could never have won on its own.

***

The Assignment itself was signed by Norman Edward Gottschalk, listed as Vice President of Mortgage Electronic Registration Systems, Inc. on a document created by Visionet Systems, Inc.

I commissioned a forensic securitization audit through Certified Forensic Loan Auditors — the CFLA mortgage audit[1] — to understand what MERS actually was and what it could legally do. The answer, stated plainly: nothing it could enforce on its own.

MERS has no legal interest in the note, no beneficial interest, no financial interest in whether the loan is repaid, and was never entitled to foreclose. The MIN status on my loan showed "Inactive" at the time of the audit — the loan was no longer active in MERS — yet foreclosure proceeded using a MERS assignment anyway. So who was this man signing on its behalf?

The document was prepared by Visionet Systems in Pittsburgh and recorded electronically. Visionet lists a main number on the Assignment. I

1 *Appendix A, available at www.leenadesign.com/mybook-pdf*

called it. Voicemail. I called the Pittsburgh corporate line. Voicemail. I called every publicly listed number I could find for Visionet Systems and for MERS. Voicemail. I left twenty messages over several months. I asked friends to call with different pretexts. Not one call came back.

I started keeping a log. Date, time, number dialed, duration before voicemail. It became its own kind of document — proof that the people who sign documents transferring American homes operate behind a wall of hold music and dead extensions. Somewhere in Pittsburgh, a phone rang twenty times in an empty office, and a house changed hands.

A document processing company that signs assignments transferring real property cannot be reached by any member of the public through any publicly listed number, by any excuse, at any hour. That isn't a gap in customer service. That's a design choice.

Something about Norman's signature felt off. Titles like that don't usually belong to people who hide. So I looked him up. I found him in about four minutes. That should have been harder. Four minutes. That's how long it takes to find the man who signed away your house. I've spent longer choosing paint colors. LinkedIn showed Norman Edward Gottschalk worked at Visionet Systems. Not MERS. Visionet is a mortgage document processing company. A mill. His role? CTO — chief technical officer. IT department. Fourteen years.

This is what I want you to understand: how ordinary it is. A name. A title. A signature. Filed, recorded, enforced. Nobody asked. Nobody checked. That's not a conspiracy. It's a system that assumes no one will read closely enough to notice. I noticed because I read everything carefully. It's a design habit. It saved me nothing—but it told me the truth. (Appendix B)

I kept digging. A Pittsburgh obituary surfaced—Norman Edward Gottschalk, Sr., steel industry, wealth, prominence. For a moment I wondered if they were using a dead man's name. By then, strange was the baseline. More records clarified it. Senior was gone. Junior was alive, employed, quietly signing documents that moved houses from homeowners to banks. Which raised its own question: why does the son of a steel magnate work IT at a mortgage document mill? Every family has its secrets, I guess.

I don't judge him for working there. I judge the system that made his signature worth more than mine on my own property.

Bloomberg report confirmed it: Norman Edward Gottschalk had worked at Visionet for fourteen years. He signed the assignment "without disclosure of true employment." So why was he signing as a Vice President of MERS?

I contacted MERS directly and asked them to verify his status as Vice President. No response. Not a denial. Not a clarification. Just silence. Which told me everything I needed to know. A legitimate company, asked to verify an officer's credentials, answers. The silence was its own kind of signature.

The Notary Problem

But there was another problem. The Assignment had been notarized in Pennsylvania by Autumn R. Carnegie. The Substitution of Trustee had been notarized in Colorado by Agnes Bradshaw. (Appendix C) I requested their official notary records from both states.

What came back told me everything I needed to know: neither signature matched their official exemplars on file. Neither notarization appeared in their required journals. Neither notary had any record of signing documents for my property.

Pennsylvania law requires notaries to keep a journal of every notarial act. Autumn Carnegie's notary journal doesn't exist, her digital log showed zero entries during the three-week window when my Assignment was supposedly notarized. Zero.

I reported it. The Pennsylvania Secretary of State received a formal complaint in October 2022. Case number assigned. Nine to twelve months to process. Fourteen months later, the Senior Prosecutor declined to prosecute, noting the information would be retained in case a pattern emerged. I wrote back and pointed out that 93 violations in Carnegie's own log, plus zero journal entries during the exact window my document was notarized, was already a pattern. The case was assigned for second review. I never heard from Ashley Murphy.

I wrote to Governor Shapiro. His office replied that the Governor cannot provide legal advice and suggested I contact the Pennsylvania Bar Association's Lawyer Referral Service.

I wasn't asking for legal advice. I was asking him to investigate a crime committed in his state, documented in his state's own records. He sent me a phone number for finding a lawyer. (Appendix T)

I hired a handwriting expert. Court-qualified. Decades of experience. The kind of expert banks themselves rely on when they need proof to stick. Her conclusion was unequivocal: forgery. Not "irregular." Not "inconsistent." Forgery, Carnegie was not the author of the signature.

Agnes Bradshaw confirmed directly: she never signed the Substitution. It wasn't in her journal. That wasn't her signature.

The Pattern

I went to the San Diego County Recorder's office. You can't search by notary name—you have to sift through thousands of documents manually by servicer name.

So that's what I did. San Diego, Orange and Los Angeles Counties. It took me days. What I found wasn't isolated. It was systematic. Seventy-five additional documents. Same forged signatures. Same notary names. Same jurisdictional problems—out-of-state notaries on California documents without the required penalty of perjury language. Some weren't even hand-signed forgeries. They were digital copies. The same exact notary signature, duplicated pixel-by-pixel across multiple documents. Photoshopped. This wasn't a mistake. This was infrastructure.

I need you to understand what I was at that point. Not a lawyer, not a crusader, not someone with a team or a budget or a plan. Just a woman standing at a county recorder's counter, in a county where I didn't live, pulling documents while fighting for a house I had already been locked out of.

The same signatures kept appearing. Different documents, different dates, but the same names, the same notaries, the same errors repeating with a consistency that made them impossible to dismiss as coincidence. It didn't look dramatic. It looked routine. That was the problem.

I wasn't uncovering a conspiracy. I was reading. That's all it took. I read, and the system revealed itself.

The Substitution

A Substitution of Trustee is a document that replaces the original trustee on a deed of trust — the neutral third party responsible for conducting a foreclosure sale — with a new one, usually chosen by the servicer. It's how banks install their own foreclosure machinery on your property. Whoever controls the trustee controls the sale.

I called Simplifile next—the company listed as requesting the Substitution of Trustee. They explained their role carefully, like someone used to this question: "We're like UPS. We receive the package, we deliver the package. We don't create it. We don't request it. We don't know who requested it." I appreciated the honesty. It was the most honest thing anyone in the chain had said to me. UPS doesn't ask what's in the box. Neither does the county recorder. Neither, apparently, does the court. The documents were clean enough to record. Official enough to foreclose. Vague enough that no one was expected to question who actually signed them—or whether they had any authority to do so.

What I Understood

That's when I understood something critical: The problem wasn't that the documents were sloppy. The problem was that they were confident. They didn't fear scrutiny because scrutiny wasn't part of the process. These papers weren't meant to withstand challenge. They were meant to pass unnoticed, like background noise in a system designed to keep moving.

The foreclosure didn't rest on ownership. It rested on compliance. On everyone agreeing not to look too closely. I wasn't asking *who signed this* anymore. I was asking a harder question: What happens when signatures don't belong to the people whose names are on them—and everyone involved knows it? That's when the word nobody wanted to say started to matter.

Forgery.

***

I brought it into court—actual documents, expert reports, notary records. Not theory, not speculation. Evidence that should have required an answer. No one from the "bank" appeared to defend any of it. When I asked where the actual plaintiff was, the judge told me they didn't have to be there, and the case moved forward anyway. The case didn't turn on what was true. It turned on what was allowed to be said out loud.

I remember standing there holding documents that proved exactly what had happened, realizing none of it required a different outcome. That was the part no one explains to you.

That was the strangest part. Not the documents. Not the signatures. The fact that it all continued as if it made perfect sense.

PART IV

The Siege
Seven Years and Counting

The most common way people give up their power
is by thinking they don't have any.
— Alice Walker

CHAPTER 20

How Far Can a Bank Push Before an Artist Becomes a Litigator?

By 2012 I had done everything right and lost anyway. It doesn't feel dramatic. It feels like something isn't adding up. I had followed their instructions, trusted the professionals, filed the paperwork, shown up to the hearings.

What I got in return was an education in a language I hadn't known existed — one where words are split, stretched, and repurposed to serve whoever holds the microphone, where bank witnesses lie with professional calm, attorneys lie without blinking, and judges do something more refined: they simply ignore the law and behave as if gravity were optional. I would later recognize the genre as administrative gaslighting. At the time, I just thought something was wrong with the documents.

I was right about that part. Not proof yet. Just a problem I couldn't ignore.

I started this case as a pro per, which is Latin for how hard could it be?

I spoke English well enough. I wasn't hiding anything. I had documents—proof, receipts, actual paper. I honestly believed that if you showed up with evidence, someone in charge would look at it and say, "Well, that's a problem."

Adorable.

I got my ass handed to me. That was faster than expected.

What I didn't understand yet was that I wasn't stepping into a neutral courtroom. I was stepping into a system already in motion—roles assigned, outcomes anticipated. I wasn't there to be heard. I was there to be processed. Think DMV, but with Latin phrases and consequences that ruin your life.

I sat in that courtroom so many times it blurred into a single endless morning. While I waited for my case to be called, I watched others lose theirs. Five minutes, sometimes less. Families. A woman clutching a folder she clearly thought would save her. "Your Honor, I have kids. I have nowhere to go." "Your Honor, they threw everything out of my house onto the street — where am I supposed to take my children?" Denied. Next case.

The judge didn't even look up. The machine didn't pause between people. It just kept processing. I sat there watching American families get fed into a wood chipper.

Every time I went in, I had my talking points typed up, neatly double-spaced so I could read them straight into the record. Prepared. Organized. Professional. As if that mattered. The funny thing about unlawful detainer court is the bank's attorneys rarely show up. They send "rent-a-mouths", hungry lawyers who hang around the courthouse waiting to pick up a few hundred dollars and step in cold, knowing nothing about the case. They haven't read the file. They don't need to. They bank on the fact that the pro se litigant doesn't know how to object, doesn't know the rules, doesn't know that the game has rules. They're usually right. The system isn't built on knowing. It's built on procedure.

My first hearing was devastating. I was making my argument and after every sentence this attorney interrupted — "Objection." Not because anything I said was objectionable. Because interruption is the strategy. The goal is simple: disrupt, destabilize, shut you down. It works.

You stand there with your neatly typed pages and your evidence and your belief that truth has some kind of weight in this room, and a man who learned your name five minutes ago dismantles you with a single word, repeated on cue.

Had I known then what I know now, I would have told him to hold his objections until I finished. I would have objected under California Evidence Code §702—lack of personal knowledge—and stopped him cold.

But I didn't know that yet. Motion denied. I left with tears in my eyes, which I hated more than losing. Outside the courtroom, the attorney hesitated. Just for a second. "Sorry you got the short end of the stick," he said. He knew I was right. His job was to bulldoze me, and he'd done it well.

That was the first time I understood the outcome didn't depend on what I could prove.

***

In 2018, I stopped Airbnb and rented the upper floor of my house to a tenant. Seemed like a good idea at the time. I needed the income. He needed a place. Simple transaction between reasonable adults.

He moved in. Paid for one month. Then stopped. But he knew exactly what he was doing. This wasn't amateur hour. This was preplanned predation.

He became a "friend." I met his kids. He cooked dinners. We made small talk about the weather and life in the mountains. All while he was planning to backstab me the entire time.

The rental income was my income, and when he stopped paying it had a huge impact. So I did what landlords do—I filed an unlawful detainer against him.

I had another "hmmm" attorney at this point who said I could file, I had a right to evict him. He showed up for the hearing. I told him he needed to be prepared to argue title because I knew the bank was circling. He waved me off and said title wasn't an issue, but we should refile the UD to fix some procedural defects and make sure we won. So I did. Refiled. Served him again. Followed instructions like a good client.

At the hearing, the tenant's attorney Christian Curry strode in like he owned the place and announced immediately: "I want to cut through the chase. This woman is not on title. She has no right to file a UD against my client." My attorney didn't know what to say. Case dismissed. Five minutes. Four hundred dollars. Thank you, you win some you lose some. Professionalism at its finest.

Curry asked me on the way out how I was going to pay for his attorney's fees. "How much?"

"Fifteen hundred dollars." "I don't have the money right now." He leaned in. "I'm going to fuck you up good." And he did.

He filed a motion for attorney's fees. Not fifteen hundred dollars. Sixty-eight hundred dollars. Judge Bowers looked at the motion and said, "Sounds reasonable to me."

Two months later, Curry froze my bank account for the little money I did have. I was left with twenty-five dollars to my name. It took three months to get it reversed. And the police can't just reverse it—oh no, that would be too easy. They have to get a check from the county. Another month. Four months. Twenty-five dollars. An artist trying to survive while a red-faced attorney played financial terrorism for sport.

The Voicemail

On April 25, 2019, I received a voicemail from Christian Curry that I will never forget. I'm including it verbatim because his words matter:

> *"Hi Miss Hannonen, my name is Christian Curry. I'm your tenant's attorney. We met at trial where you lost because you're not the owner of the property. You don't own the property at 3252 Pine Hills Road in Julian. You have no right to enter that property. You have no right to demand rent. You have no right to show up on that property. You don't own it. You have no privity of contract with my client and privity of estate with my client. He has a right to be there. The bank has a right to be there. You have no more right to go to that property than you have to come to my property. You need to get this through and understand—you lost that property in foreclosure. Not yours. You are not the landlord. Bank owns everything in that property that doesn't belong to my client.*
>
> *Please, please, please, please, please do not make good on your threat to come back and try and enter the property. My client will call the sheriffs because you are trespassing. If necessary, we will file a restraining order. I know you had a lawyer and you fired your lawyer. I don't know if you necessarily remember this—you're acting like you don't—the judge told you not to go to the property because you have no reason to go there. My number is 858-505-xxxx. My client specifically does not give you permission to go to the property, does not want you to come there, and does not want to see you on the property. You're not welcomed. You have no business there. Do not go there."*

Mind you, this was three months **before the unlawful detainer case was even filed against me.** And as a good citizen—which I still was at the time—I complied. I tried to go through the courts to clear this up like a reasonable person. Today's Leena would not have stood for this bullshit. Live and learn.

Instead of holding the lease while I fought the foreclosure—which was the entire point of having a tenant—he started working with the bank. Against me. He became a professional squatter, paying no one for three years. A bold business model — not entirely unlike the one the bank had been running on me. I was still learning that trust has to be earned. Preferably before you hand someone your house.

The Lockout

In April 2019, I returned from a short trip to find myself locked out of my own house. The tenant called the sheriff and claimed I was trespassing—that I no longer lived there. An impressive level of confidence, given the facts.

There was no unlawful detainer case filed yet. I hadn't been served a summons. But Sheriff Anderson from the Julian substation decided to act as judge, jury, and locksmith—way beyond his authority. Had I known then what I know now, I would have gotten him fired.

But I was still operating under the delusion that being reasonable mattered. I tried working through the system to get back in. I filed a motion to quash. Judge Matthew Brower kindly informed me I was "too early"—nothing had been filed yet. "I suppose I'll see you back here in the near future," he said. It sounded friendly. It wasn't.

The near future arrived in June. I still hadn't been served the unlawful detainer complaint, but I kept checking the court records online. I didn't dare wait—I'd already seen how the bank played. So I filed another motion, asking to be dismissed for lack of service. I showed up. Judge Brower looked at me and said, "Well, you're here." Then he handed the bailiff the complaint and summons right there in the courtroom and said, "Now you've been served."

A judge practicing law from the bench. A procedural violation that should have ended the case right there. I didn't know that yet. The court, of course, did. Everything I filed after that was denied.

Then I filed a motion to consolidate the unlawful detainer case with my civil case against the bank. I was transferred to Judge Katherine Bacal, who was already presiding over the civil matter.

She didn't consolidate the cases—she deemed them "related." Which was her first mistake. She shouldn't have been able to rule on the unlawful detainer case at all. This meant we were juggling two cases simultaneously:

the unlawful detainer case where I was the defendant, and the civil case where I was the plaintiff. Confusion. Extreme deadlines. Constant pressure to the point of almost giving up. Then *sisu* kicked in.

It also didn't seem to matter that the complaint was verified by the attorney, not the plaintiff. The bank's name was on the paperwork, but no one from the bank had signed under penalty of perjury. The judge forgot to follow the law again. This would become a theme.

January 24, 2020 — Dismissed from My Own Case

The jury trial date finally arrived for the unlawful detainer case — the eviction proceeding U.S. Bank had filed to remove occupants from the property after the foreclosure. I would finally be heard.

The U.S. Bank attorney stood and announced that it had come to their attention I was no longer in possession of the property. Therefore, I was no longer a necessary party. I was dismissed from my own case.

Efficient. Tidy. Wrong.

I tried to protest. "I need my day in court. I need to defend my title. There's forgery — I can prove it." Judge Bacal cut me off. "The plaintiff has the right to dismiss a defendant at any time." Technically correct. Procedurally devastating. My due process rights weren't bent or delayed. They were eliminated with a single sentence.

A bench trial was then set for the tenant: January 29, 2020. A bench trial means no jury — just a judge deciding the outcome alone, without twelve citizens who might ask uncomfortable questions. The tenant who had been living in my house rent-free for three years, working with the bank against me, would get his day in court.

I would not. I had owned that property for twenty years, my name was on the title, and I had proof of forgery sitting in a folder. None of that mattered. I decided to go and observe anyway. I still believed watching mattered.

The Stipulation

The tenant's attorney, Christian Curry, appeared alongside Richard Coombs from U.S. Bank's foreclosure mill. Together, they presented Judge Bacal with a settlement stipulation. She didn't accept it. It was signed by an attorney, not the plaintiff.

Here's where it gets interesting. The ruling was based on California Code of Civil Procedure § 664.6—which at that time required the plaintiff, not the attorney, to sign the stipulation. Judge Bacal asked, "Is the plaintiff still in the building?" Attorney Coombs stepped outside.

I sat there, stunned. Who exactly was out there? There was no bank representative involved in this case. Just servicers and attorneys orchestrating fraud in real time. Apparently, that counted.

A few minutes later, Coombs came back in with a signed stipulation. Judge Bacal accepted it.

Why didn't the "plaintiff" come into the courtroom? Why wasn't he identified? Why was there no power of attorney presented? Why the secrecy? Now I know.

I tried to get a copy of the stipulation. I was denied—it was sealed, and I was no longer a party to the case. A neat trick.

It took me months to obtain a copy. When I finally did, I saw that it had been signed by Jason Lipovsky—a realtor. Not the plaintiff. Not anyone with legal authority to bind U.S. Bank. Just the listing agent. Bold. Consistent. That fraudulent stipulation—signed between U.S. Bank's realtor and my disgruntled tenant—was what removed me from my own house.

A year later, when I tried to contest this stipulation, Judge Bacal pointed out that the statute had been changed. Attorneys can now sign stipulations on behalf of the bank. I smiled. I wondered how much my case had to do with that change. I'd made such a big stink about § 664.6—filed motions, cited case law, pointed out the violation in every brief I could.

And then, quietly, the law changed. Convenient. Almost like someone realized I was right—and decided to make sure future homeowners couldn't use the same argument.

Years later, Judge Bacal would admit it was fraud upon the court. Comforting. Slightly late.

I cited California Constitution Article XX, § 3—the oath judges take to uphold constitutional rights and judicial integrity. I wasn't asking for a favor. I was asking Judge Bacal to do her job.

The motion was denied. The reason? I had no "standing." I had no standing. As the title holder. Of my own house. Let that sink in.

I was dismissed from my case because I'd been locked out by a trespassing tenant. And because I was no longer "in possession" due to an illegal lockout orchestrated by the bank and enforced by an overreaching sheriff, I had no standing to challenge the fraudulent judgment that removed me from the property I still legally owned.

Total due process violation. I was never allowed to have a say in my own case. Denied trial. Denied the ability to present evidence. Denied the constitutional right to defend my property.

The court protected the fraud and called it procedure.

Everything Gone

When the tenant finally moved out, I went back inside. Everything was gone. My art. My tools. Personal items. My life, minus the walls. Not packed. Not stored. Gone. Heartbreaking doesn't begin to cover it. Vocabulary fails here.

This time, the realtor called the sheriff. I was handcuffed for "illegal entry" into my own house. I laughed out loud. Fine, I'll go to jail. We'll add it to the damages. Then they said my friend—who had come to support me—was also going to jail. And my dog was going to the pound. That's where the line appeared. You can take my house. You can lie about documents. You can handcuff me in my own home. But nobody touches my dog. I said I would leave. After that, the gloves came off.

Becoming a Litigator

I had filed a civil case against U.S. Bank back in 2018. The first complaint was drafted by one of my "expert" attorneys—a joke I didn't recognize yet. I didn't even know if I was a plaintiff or a defendant. I didn't speak legalese. I was still polite. So I started learning the law. Really learning it.

Two years later, in 2022, I understood courtroom procedure, evidence rules, and how to stand upright in front of a judge without apologizing for breathing. I filed an amended complaint that was full of piss and vinegar. I showed up. Again. And again.

CHAPTER 21

The Cost of Hiring an Attorney

After the amended complaint was filed on June 7, 2022, we entered the phase politely known as normal motions. Defendants filed motions to dismiss, demurrers, objections—everything except answers. I responded promptly. And thoroughly. And then some.

November 7, 2022: I served discovery on US Bank and MERS.

December 14, 2022: No response.

When attorney Rusty Gore, The Ryan Firm, finally responded in late December, his answers amounted to thirteen variations of copy-paste objections. "Vague and ambiguous." "Attorney-client privilege." "Unduly burdensome and oppressive." Zero substantive answers. Just legal Mad Libs designed to run out the clock.

I contacted Gore. Email first, then postal mail. I suggested we meet and confer to resolve this before dragging the court into it. Professional courtesy. Reasonable attempt at resolution.

Gore was confident. Arrogant, even. He'd filed a demurrer on behalf of all three defendants—US Bank, MERS, and Specialized Loan Servicing—and he was certain Judge Bacal would sustain it and dismiss the case entirely. Why waste time responding to discovery when the whole complaint would be gone in a few weeks?

He slept on his clients' rights. Gambled. And lost.

February 3, 2023: The demurrer hearing.

Judge Katherine Bacal sustained five of the six causes of action. The case wasn't dismissed. Gore's confident little strategy collapsed in real time.

The court asked Gore if twenty days was enough to answer the complaint.

"Yes, Your Honor." Twenty days. On the record. He agreed.

February 18, 2023: Gore contacted me requesting an additional forty-five days to answer the complaint.

I reminded him that two weeks earlier, he'd told the court twenty days was sufficient. I granted him five additional days. Not forty-five. Five.

During this exchange, Gore also requested sixty additional days to respond to discovery.

I reminded him he'd had the discovery since November 2022. Four months. Plenty of time.

Gore's response? "The Ryan Firm has three corporate clients and it's way too much work to answer in this timeframe." Interesting problem. Not mine.

If Gore couldn't meet statutory deadlines, he should have outsourced the work or hired additional attorneys. Instead, he took on three corporate clients simultaneously, banked on a demurrer that failed, and then acted shocked that deadlines still applied.

January 3, 2023: The meet and confer.

We spoke by phone. I'd sent Gore a detailed letter ahead of time outlining the underlying issues — questions about standing, beneficial interest, the validity of the Assignment, Norman Gottschalk's role at Visionet Systems versus his claimed role as MERS Vice President, the handwriting analysis proving Autumn Carnegie didn't sign the document.

I asked Gore to discuss these issues so we could clarify why the discovery requests were relevant.

Gore refused. He stated these issues would be "handled at trial."

Then he said something remarkable: answering my discovery would require him to "launch a federal investigation."

He meant it as a complaint about scope. I heard it as a confession. Standard discovery in a foreclosure case — questions about who signed what, who held what interest, whether the documents were real — and the attorney defending those documents was telling me, out loud, that answering honestly would trigger a federal investigation. He wasn't describing my overreach. He was describing his problem.

I said, "We have some serious issues to resolve." He agreed. Then he filed objections anyway.

January 30, 2023: I sent out revised discovery — the version Gore and I had agreed to during the meet and confer. I served it on US Bank, MERS, and SLS simultaneously.

Pursuant to California Code of Civil Procedure § 2030.260, all defendants were required to respond within thirty days. There is no provision in the statute allowing extra time for firms representing multiple corporate clients.

March 6, 2023: Responses were due.

Instead of answering, the Ryan Firm—a $300-million-a-year operation—filed a 556-page emergency motion for protective order. Against me. A pro se plaintiff.

The motion wasn't about protection. It was about time. They bought themselves another week while the court reviewed their complaint that I was being "unreasonable and oppressive" by enforcing statutory deadlines.

Gore's declaration, filed March 6, 2023:

"In this case, to respond to twelve simultaneously served sets of discovery against all three entities is a massive project that simply could not be completed within thirty days—especially while Defendants were occupied drafting three separate, approximately 75-page verified answers to Plaintiff's massive SAC. Here, each entity is being asked to respond to anywhere from 85–110 separate discovery requests, for a total of about 400+ requests. Many requests require investigation, tracking down people, information, or documents, and analysis. This is something that requires at least two months to accomplish, if not more."

Two months. He'd had it since November. But sure. Two months.

My opposition, filed March 30, 2023:

I pointed out that Gore had received the original discovery on **October 27, 2022** (MERS) and **November 9, 2022** (US Bank). Over **120 days** before the protective order was filed.

I reminded the court that Gore chose to file a demurrer instead of answering. He bet the complaint would be dismissed. When it wasn't, he panicked.

I noted that the Ryan Firm—representing three defendants simultaneously—was nobody's problem but their own. If they couldn't handle the workload, they should have planned better. Hired help. Managed resources.

Besides, I was doing the same work. Pro se. Alone. With a laptop and a PO box. Researching case law, drafting motions, responding to their endless objections, tracking down notaries across state lines, cross-referencing seventy-five forged documents. If a $300-million-a-year firm with paralegals, legal databases, and support staff couldn't manage three corporate clients in four months, maybe they should have outsourced to me. I was clearly more efficient.

Instead, they spent their time drafting a 556-page motion filled with procedural theatrics and boilerplate objections, clouding the real issue: **they didn't want to answer because the answers would be damaging.**

The court denied the motion.

The defendants were ordered to respond. And they did. Three sets of answers. Over a hundred paragraphs each. Dense, evasive, technically responsive while saying absolutely nothing of substance.

I needed something tireless. I'd been using AI already, skeptically, cross-checking everything it produced. It could parse three hundred pages of legal doublespeak without needing a nap.

It was also a liar. It fabricated case law. Confidently. When confronted, it apologized politely and promised to do better — then did it again.

Which raised an uncomfortable question: if a machine can generate confident-sounding legal arguments built on invented precedent, how long had attorneys been doing the same thing manually — counting on exhaustion, limited access, and the practical impossibility of checking everything? AI doesn't lie because it's malicious. It lies because it's built to sound certain regardless of accuracy. The machine didn't corrupt the legal system. It learned from it. And then it handed me the tool to check. I recognized the method.

And occasionally, it was genuinely useful. It flagged a citation the Ryan Firm had filed — Osterberg v. Osterberg — offered to support the argument that notarization doesn't matter for foreclosure documents. The case was about private conveyances between parties who already had an agreement. Not foreclosure. Not forged notaries. They stripped the context, kept the quote, and hoped nobody read the actual opinion.

Same method. Different hardware.

When there's no evidence, you rely on interpretation. When interpretation fails, you rely on confidence. Judges don't like digging. They like momentum. My filings were denied for procedural defects. Their filings were indulged despite substantive emptiness. Procedure, it turns out, is flexible — depending on who needs it.

***

I thought hiring an attorney would fix this. I was wrong.

For trial, I hired an attorney. "Incompetent" doesn't quite cover it, but we'll keep things polite.

He had enormous confidence and minimal comprehension. He could sell sand in a desert. He just couldn't find the right form to file, the right argument to preserve, or the right moment to stop talking. He misunderstood the case. Missed critical arguments and objections. Mishandled evidence with a consistency that bordered on performance art. If there was a wrong procedural move available, he found it. Reliably.

***

Before trial, there's a required step called a "meet and confer"—a mandatory settlement negotiation before you can proceed to trial. The idea is to attempt settlement in good faith, though "good faith" in foreclosure litigation functions mostly as a costume. We scheduled ours at the offices of U.S. Bank's foreclosure counsel—the Ryan Firm—in Irvine, California.

Polished building. Marble floors. Ground zero for foreclosure mills.

I arrived with two attorneys on my side. The office door was locked. Not metaphorically. Physically. They wouldn't open it.

Instead, the meeting was relocated to a shared conference room elsewhere in the complex—neutral territory, apparently. Silly me for assuming I'd be allowed into the actual office. The crime scene was off-limits.

I had seen a photo of attorney Andrew Mace beforehand. I knew he was short. This detail mattered more than it should have.

I'm already five-foot-ten—Finnish Amazon, my mother used to say, though she meant it as a warning about fitting into conventional spaces. I'd stopped apologizing for my height around the same time I stopped apologizing for being right.

So I wore three-inch boots. When I shook his hand, I towered. Not aggressively. Just mathematically. It felt appropriate to say "You are just a itty pity thing."

I skipped the warm-up. No small talk. I went straight to the forged documents. Where do you stand in this issue?

"They are at best voidable, not void," he said.

I interrupted—not emotionally, just accurately.

"That's incorrect. OC Interior Services LLC v. Nationstar Mortgage LLC, 2017 case. A forged document is void ab initio. Legally equivalent to a blank sheet of paper. No force. No effect. It never existed."

There was a pause. A recalibration. Then the pivot. "But it's just robo-signing."

"No," I said. "Robo-signing is forgery with better branding. Still fraud. Still a felony." He shifted again. "This was a one-time clerical error."

Wrong again. I told him I had seventy-five additional documents with the same forged signatures. Same handwriting. Same names. Same defects. Pattern and practice. A machine, not a mistake.

"Well," he said carefully, "if you can provide that, you've given me something to take back to my client." Translation: I didn't know you had that.

What surprised me wasn't his reaction. It was mine. I was calm. Focused. Sharp. I knew the statutes. The deadlines. The case law. Not from law school—from necessity. Even my own attorney admitted afterward that I conducted myself like one.

I took that as both a compliment and an indictment.

***

A week later, my alarm company in Baja called. I was still in San Diego.

"Are you at your house?"

"No. Why?"

"Someone is in your living room."

I told them to send the police. I checked my security feed. All I saw was a hand reaching for the camera—and crushing it. Efficient. Final. Practiced.

The police report noted a broken window. Entry gained. The house otherwise untouched. No ransacking. No chaos. When I returned and looked closely, I saw what was gone.

Only one thing. My certified copies of the title documents — the paper trail that proved what had been done to my property and who had done it.

My dog's toy had been snapped clean in half—not chewed, not worn. Snapped. Neighbors mentioned a black Suburban parked nearby for hours.

This wasn't random. This wasn't theft. This was a message delivered without words.

Intimidation, maybe.

Coincidence, if you're feeling generous.

The system prefers that you keep asking yourself that question. Quietly. Alone. Until doubt does the work for them. I wasn't tired yet.

CHAPTER 22

Forgery Is a Strong Word

By the time the documents surfaced, I already knew the outcome wouldn't hinge on truth. That realization came early and stayed with me, like a warning label no one reads until it's too late.

I'd spent months investigating. Found the forgeries. Hired the experts. Compiled the evidence. Chapter 19 tells that story. The evidence was compelling. What happened when I presented it is here.

California Penal Code 470 defines forgery as the false signing, altering, or counterfeiting of documents, seals, or handwriting with intent to defraud. It sounds definitive. Criminal. Like a word that should end conversations. That assumption was my first mistake. I thought naming it would be enough.

Forgery is a word no one wants on the record. Judges resist it. Attorneys dilute it into safer terms — irregularities, discrepancies, clerical issues. Language designed to soften intent, blur responsibility, and make crimes sound like paperwork mishaps.

The theory is that mistakes happen. Here's the problem with that theory: forgery requires intent. Signatures don't accidentally appear on documents. Someone put them there. Deliberately.

The Geography Problem

There was another problem, more basic and harder to ignore. My property is in California. So why were title documents being created in Pennsylvania, Colorado, and wherever else was convenient that week? Why were critical declarations traveling thousands of miles while the house they governed stayed put? And none of them — not one — was signed under penalty of perjury as required by California law.

Apparently geography is optional in foreclosure.

California Code of Civil Procedure § 2015.5. I know that statute by heart now. I've cited it so many times it may as well be tattooed on my wrist. It's simple: written declarations used in California proceedings must be signed under penalty of perjury under California law. Plenty of case law reinforces it. Courts cite it routinely — when they feel like enforcing it.

Every one of these documents failed that test.

That single code section alone should have ended the case years ago.

It didn't. Which told me something important: the rules weren't unclear. They were just inconvenient. And inconvenient rules don't get enforced. They get ignored.

Why It Didn't Matter

A foreclosure rests on documents. If the documents are forged, the authority collapses — that's not radical, that's black-letter law. Strip away the theatrics and you're left with a simple equation: no valid signatures, no standing, no foreclosure. Forgery isn't a technical flaw. It's a structural failure.

And yet there it was — established cleanly, professionally, without drama — and still treated like an inconvenience instead of a disqualifier. I presented the evidence in court multiple times, in motions, in hearings, at trial. Judges read the expert report, reviewed the state records, heard the testimony, and then issued rulings that proceeded as if none of it existed. The court finds the evidence compelling. The testimony is uncontroverted. Motion denied. No explanation, no rebuttal, no engagement with the actual findings. Just acknowledgment without consequence.

The Legal Gymnastics

Opposing counsel developed a pattern to match. They never disputed the forgery directly — they couldn't, the evidence was too solid — so instead they argued around it. This is a technical issue that doesn't affect the validity of the foreclosure. The assignment may have procedural defects, but the underlying debt is still owed. The court should focus on the borrower's default, not on document irregularities. They weren't defending the documents. They were changing the subject — treating the legal authority to take someone's home as a technicality, forged signatures as procedural defects, and institutional crime as an irregularity.

I didn't understand yet that proving forgery and forcing a system to respond to it were two different ights. One is about facts. The other was about power.

Facts could be gathered, verified, and presented. Power decided which facts mattered, which evidence got weight, which crimes got prosecuted, and which got written off as mistakes.

The system had already done the math. I could prove forgery with expert witnesses and state certifications. But could I make them care?

That was the question. And for a long time, the answer was no.

The Weight of Knowing

There's a specific weight that comes with knowing you're right and watching the system pretend you're not. Not the weight of doubt — that would be easier. This is the weight of certainty. You stop asking if you're wrong. You start asking why it doesn't matter.

Knowing the documents are forged. Knowing the court knows. Knowing they're going to proceed anyway because admitting the truth would be too expensive, too disruptive, too inconvenient.

That weight doesn't make you question the evidence. It makes you question everything else — justice, procedure, the naive idea that truth matters simply by virtue of being true.

What holds is power. I didn't have it.

But I had something else: documentation, persistence, and an unwillingness to let forgery get softened into "document irregularities" just because calling it what it actually was made people uncomfortable.

Forgery is a strong word. The system prefers gentler language.

I was going to keep using the strong word. I'm still waiting for it to be strong enough.

CHAPTER 23

When Proof Meets Procedure

By the time forgery was established, I still believed something fundamental: that once facts were clear, the system would have to respond. I hadn't yet learned the distinction this chapter is about — the difference between being right and being permitted to matter. I didn't know those were separate things. This is the point where evidence stopped being evaluated and started being managed. Where documents didn't fail on substance but were neutralized on form. Where procedure became the preferred tool for avoiding conclusions the system couldn't afford to reach.

The Building With the Gun

The Substitution of Trustee told a strange story. It was recorded in 2017, requested by Fidelity National Title and LSI Title Agency — a company that no longer existed. I called the number. Disconnected. I called ServiceLink, the company that had absorbed LSI years earlier. The receptionist transferred me three times. Finally, someone in a back office told me LSI had been dissolved in 2011. "Then why is their name on a document recorded in 2017?" Silence. "I don't have that information." "Can I speak to someone who does?" "We don't have a public office."

I looked up the address anyway. Huge building, locked doors. I waited in the parking lot until I saw someone badge in, then slipped through behind them.

Inside was a lobby. No reception desk. Just a security guard behind a counter, watching me from the moment I entered.

"Can I help you?" "I'm looking for someone who can explain a document your company created." "Do you have an appointment?" "No." "You need a name." "I don't have one. I just need to understand—"

He stepped forward. His hand moved to his belt. Not aggressive. Practiced. "You need to leave." His hand was on his gun. This was a mortgage servicer. That disconnect stays with you longer than the fear.

I raised my hands and tried to explain I wasn't trying to cause trouble, I just needed to understand a recorded document bearing their company's name. A door behind the desk opened. Someone in business casual emerged, drawn by the commotion. I held up the document. "I'm just trying to verify this. If it's legitimate, there shouldn't be any problem answering a few questions."

The man — mid-forties, tired eyes — took the paper from my hand, glanced at it briefly. "I'll be right back." He disappeared. The guard didn't move. Didn't sit. Just stood there, hand still near his belt, watching me like I might bolt or detonate.

Forty-five minutes passed. Maybe longer. Time stretches differently under armed supervision.

Finally the door opened again. The man — Jeff, I'd later learn — returned and handed the document back. "I can't help you. I see you're in litigation." I tried to sound naïve, asked innocent questions. If the document was valid, what was the harm in explaining it? He listened. Didn't say much. After a long pause, he pulled a pen from his pocket, wrote something on a sticky note, then handed it to me quietly, close to his chest, out of the camera's line of sight. A case name. A number. Contact Zieve, Brodnax & Steele for the Trustee's Sale Guarantee. Then he turned and walked back through the door.

That afternoon, I subpoenaed the Trustee's Sale Guarantee.

ZBS Law was already a defendant in my case. But in early 2019 they had filed what is called a Nonmonetary Status — a procedural maneuver that allows a trustee to declare it has no financial interest in the outcome of a dispute and remove itself from active participation. I didn't fully understand what that meant at the time, and I failed to respond within the ten-day window the filing required. That silence was treated as consent. ZBS stepped out of the litigation and stayed out. My trial attorney was certain he could

Assignment of Deed of Trust, recorded 2017.

Signature attributed to Norman Edward Gottschalk, as Vice President of MERS. Notarized by Autumn R. Carnegie. Appendix B

This Instrument Prepared By:
VISIONET SYSTEMS INC.
After Recording Return To:
VISIONET SYSTEMS INC.
183 INDUSTRY DRIVE
PITTSBURGH, PA 15275
Voice: **1-(412) 927-0226**
Recording Requested By: Simplifile

DOC# 2017-0104809

Mar 07, 2017 09:04 AM
OFFICIAL RECORDS
Ernest J. Dronenburg, Jr.,
SAN DIEGO COUNTY RECORDER
FEES: $27.00

PAGES: 4

Tax Parcel ID: **291-121-23**

Assignment of Deed Of Trust

ORDER #: 186452
MIN #:100015305570199574 MERS PHONE #: 1-888-679-6377

For value received, MORTGAGE ELECTRONIC REGISTRATION SYSTEMS, INC., as nominee for CHEVY CHASE BANK, F.S.B., its successors and assigns, hereby grants, assigns, and transfers to: **U.S. Bank National Association, as Trustee relating to Chevy Chase Funding LLC Mortgage Backed Certificates Series 2007-2** all of its right, title and interest under that certain Deed of Trust dated March 15, 2007 executed by:

Borrower: LEENA HANNONEN, AN UNMARRIED WOMAN

To MORTGAGE ELECTRONIC REGISTRATION SYSTEMS, INC., as nominee for CHEVY CHASE BANK, F.S.B., its successors and assigns whose address is 1901 E Voorhees Street, Suite C, Danville, IL 61834, in the amount of: $483,750.00, recorded 03/21/2007 as Instrument No.: 2007-0191681 of the Official Records of San Diego County, California

Property Address: 3252 PINE HILLS ROAD, JULIAN, CALIFORNIA 92036
Legal Description: SEE EXHIBIT "A"

Effective date: 03/06/17

A notary public or other officer completing this certificate verifies only the identity of the individual who signed the document to which this certificate is attached, and not the truthfulness, accuracy, or validity of that document.

MORTGAGE ELECTRONIC REGISTRATION SYSTEMS, INC.

By: ______________________
NORMAN EDWARD GOTTSCHALK
VICE PRESIDENT

State of **PENNSYLVANIA**
County of **ALLEGHENY**

On 03/06/17 before me, Autumn R Carnegie the undersigned, a Notary Public in and for the county of ALLEGHENY in the State of Pennsylvania, personally appeared Norman Edward Gottschalk, Vice President personally known to me to be the person whose name is subscribed to the within instrument and acknowledged to me that he/she executed the same in his/her authorized capacity, and that for his/her signature on the instrument the person, or the entity upon behalf of which he/she acted, executed the instrument.

Autumn R Carnegie
My Commission Expires: **06/06/2020**

NOTARIAL SEAL
AUTUMN R CARNEGIE
Notary Public
FINDLEY TWP, ALLEGHENY COUNTY
My Commission Expires Jun 6, 2020

Signature on my document

Autumn R Carnegie
My Commission Expires: **06/06/2020**

Autumn R Carnegie's real signature

NOTARY SIGNATURE

Substitution of Trustee, recorded 2017.

Signature attributed Mark McCloskey, vice president of Speciliazed Loan Servicing, notarized by Agnes Bradshaw. Appendix C

DOC# 2017-0439136

Sep 25, 2017 04:33 PM
OFFICIAL RECORDS
Ernest J. Dronenburg, Jr.,
SAN DIEGO COUNTY RECORDER
FEES: $18.00

PAGES: 1

APN: 291-121-23-00
Recording Requested By
LSI Title Agency - FIS Default Solutions
Fidelity National Title

When recorded, mail to:
Zieve, Brodnax & Steele, LLP
30 Corporate Park, Suite 450
Irvine, CA 92606

TS No.: 17-48720

SUBSTITUTION OF TRUSTEE

WHEREAS, LEENA HANNONEN, AN UNMARRIED WOMAN was the original Trustor, and **CHEVY CHASE BANK, F.S.B.** was the original Trustee, and **Mortgage Electronic Registration Systems, Inc., as nominee for CHEVY CHASE BANK, F.S.B., its successors and assigns** was the original Beneficiary under that certain Deed of Trust dated **3/15/2007** and recorded on **3/21/2007**, under Instrument No. **2007-0191681** Official Records of **San Diego** County, **California**; and **WHEREAS, U.S. Bank National Association, as Trustee relating to Chevy Chase Funding LLC Mortgage Backed Certificates Series 2007-2** , the undersigned is the present Beneficiary under said Deed of Trust, and **WHEREAS** the undersigned desires to substitute a new Trustee under said Deed of Trust in the place and instead of said original Trustee or previously substituted Trustee;

NOW, THEREFORE, the undersigned hereby substitutes **Zieve, Brodnax & Steele, LLP,** whose address is **30 Corporate Park, Suite #450, Irvine, California 92606** as Successor Trustee under said Deed of Trust.

Whenever the context hereof so requires, the masculine gender includes the feminine and/or neuter, and the singular number includes the plural.

Dated: SEP 18 2017

U.S. Bank National Association, as Trustee relating to Chevy Chase Funding LLC Mortgage Backed Certificates Series 2007-2 by Specialized Loan Servicing LLC, its attorney-in-fact

By: Mark McCloskey
Its: Assistant Vice President

State of Colorado
County of Douglas

The foregoing instrument was acknowledgment before me this SEP 18 2017 by Mark McCloskey of Specialized Loan Servicing LLC, a Delaware Limited Liability Company, on behalf of the LLC.

(Notary's official Signature)

12/3/20
(Commission Expiration)

AGNES BRADSHAW
NOTARY PUBLIC
STATE OF COLORADO
NOTARY ID 20084040359
MY COMMISSION EXPIRES 12/03/2020

pull them back in. He never did. It was one more door that closed while I was still learning which doors existed.

***

Page five on the Trustee's Sale Guarantee said it plainly:

NOTE: PLEASE BE ADVISED THAT THIS COMPANY FINDS NO RECORDED SUBSTITUTION OF TRUSTEE, AFFECTING THE DEED OF TRUST THAT IS THE SUBJECT OF THIS GUARANTEE, EMPOWERING THE ASSURED HEREIN TO ACT IN THE PROCEEDINGS INITIATED BY THE RECORDATION OF SAID DOCUMENT.

This document is dated August 31, 2017. So they fabricated one.

Fidelity National Title — also mentioned on the document — later confirmed they had no record of requesting the document bearing their name. Checks and balances had left the building. Forgery wasn't an allegation. It was a workflow.

The Discovery They Refused to Produce

I didn't understand discovery when the case started. I thought evidence was something you gathered on your own — documents you obtained, experts you hired, testimony you recorded.

I didn't know that in civil litigation, you have the power to force the other side to produce documents, answer questions under oath, and admit or deny facts. It's how you prove standing, authority, chain of title. By the time I understood how it worked, the window had almost closed.

The Objections

Every discovery request I filed was met with the same response: objected to on several grounds. Interrogatories asking who owned the loan — objected. Requests for the original promissory note — objected. Demands for the assignment chain showing how MERS transferred the deed of trust to U.S. Bank — objected. The Ryan Firm, representing U.S. Bank, MERS, and Specialized Loan Servicing simultaneously, blocked every attempt to force them to produce the documents that would prove or disprove their authority to foreclose.

Here's what those objections actually looked like:

"Responding Party objects to this Request on the grounds that it is vague, ambiguous, overbroad, unduly burdensome, compound, and calls for a legal conclusion. Responding Party further objects on the grounds that the Request seeks information that is not relevant to the subject matter of this action and is not reasonably calculated to lead to the discovery of admissible evidence. Responding Party further objects on the grounds that the Request is argumentative and assumes facts not in evidence. Responding Party further objects on the grounds that the Request improperly seeks confidential and proprietary business information protected from disclosure. Responding Party further objects to the extent the Request seeks documents or information protected by the attorney-client privilege, attorney work product doctrine, or other applicable privileges. Subject to and without waiving the foregoing objections, Responding Party states: See objections."

Fourteen objections. Then: "See objections" where the answer should be. It looks like a response. It isn't. I wasn't asking for confidential business information. I was asking whether they had authority to foreclose. Questions any foreclosing party should be able to answer easily. Questions they refused to answer at all.

The "You Have No Evidence" Trap

I filed a motion to compel. Denied — not because my requests were improper, but because of formatting errors, service issues, technical mistakes. Hair-splitting dressed up as jurisprudence. Paper terrorism with a filing stamp.

But buried in the opposition was a remarkable admission. They quoted my own motion back at me — the part where I'd complained they objected to everything and produced nothing. Their response to that? That's exactly why your motion should be denied.

They blocked the evidence. Then punished me for not having it.

By the time I hired my trial attorney, discovery had closed. Too late to reopen it. Too late to fix what should have been fought for months earlier. The maze had walls on every side — and they'd built them one procedural objection at a time.

Then They Used It Against Me

On March 22, 2024, the Ryan Firm filed their trial brief — twenty-nine pages of aggressive legal argument designed to destroy my case before a jury heard a word.

"Plaintiff has sent out [no] discovery in this case which was not wholly objected to on several grounds. As a result, she will be wholly unavailable to meet this standard at trial."

Read that carefully. They admitted they'd objected to all my discovery requests. Then argued I had no evidence to support my claims. Of course I didn't. They refused to give it to me. And when I tried to compel them, the motion was denied on procedure.

This is how the trap works: the bank objects to all discovery, you file a motion to compel, the motion is denied on procedural grounds, discovery closes, you go to trial without the evidence they were sitting on, and then they stand up and tell the court you have nothing. The circularity is the point. It isn't a flaw in the system. It is the system.

We had expert handwriting analysis proving forgery. Notary testimony under oath. State records showing no notarizations occurred. What we didn't have were the internal bank records showing who created the Assignment, the MERS authorization policies, the original wet-ink promissory note, or the documents tracing actual ownership through securitization. Not because those documents didn't exist. Because U.S. Bank refused to produce them and the motion to compel was denied on formatting errors.

I went to trial with compelling evidence of forgery. It should have been enough. It wasn't. The problem was never proof. It was permission. That's when the rules stop feeling neutral.

Evidence didn't fail. It simply wasn't allowed to matter. Courts preserve order over truth — procedure shields the system when facts threaten it. This wasn't incompetence. It wasn't confusion. It was a choice. And once I understood that, the question was no longer whether I could prove forgery. It was whether any amount of proof would ever be enough.

March 24, 2024. Five days before trial.

I sat down to write an email I never imagined I'd have to write.

"Dear Duane, I don't mean to sound ungrateful, but I do have a concern on where we are at." That opening line—trying to be polite while panic rises—captures something about what it's like to need help from someone who isn't helping.

We'd missed the deadline for filing for a court reporter. Something I was entitled to as a fee waiver holder. Something basic. I'd sent him the form on Thursday. He'd promised to file it. By Friday, I filed it myself. On his behalf. Five days before trial.

The calls hadn't been made. Not to the San Diego County Recorder supervisor. Not to the Pennsylvania Secretary of State prosecutor who could authenticate the official letters proving the forgery. Not to the Pennsylvania county recorder. Not to Agnes, the notary who could testify to the fraud. The handwriting expert was still waiting for confirmation on the trial date.

The witnesses existed. The evidence existed. The preparation didn't.

"The two months that were to be for prepping me for being a witness have gone by with very little 'prep', my confidence level is nowhere near the level it should be."

Two months. Time that should have been spent getting me ready to testify, to present the documents, to withstand cross-examination. Instead: silence. Missed calls. Broken promises.

On Thursday the 21st, Richard and I were on standby for four hours, waiting for a call that never came. Friday, another five hours. Waiting to talk to the "dream team" that never materialized.

Meanwhile, my attorney was on a book tour in New York. Five years of my work. Five days before trial. And he was promoting a book.

"I know you have other cases and your book tour to New York was a priority, but this is crucial time after five years of my hard work, this case has potential to have a huge impact on so many people's lives, due to the dozens of additional documents I have discovered at the county recorder's offices." Evidence of systematic fraud that could affect tens of thousands of foreclosures.

And the attorney who was supposed to present it to the court was unreachable.

The Stress You Can't Delegate

There's a specific kind of stress that comes from hiring help and discovering you're still doing everything yourself—except now you have less control.

I couldn't file motions anymore. That was his job. But he wasn't filing them correctly. Or on time. Or at all. I couldn't contact witnesses directly.

That would undermine his authority as counsel. But he wasn't contacting them either.

I couldn't change strategy because I wasn't the attorney. But the strategy wasn't being executed. I existed in a terrible limbo: responsible for everything, empowered to do nothing.

The night I sent that email, my blood pressure spiked so high I thought I was having a stroke. My vision blurred. My hands shook. I sat in my car in a parking lot and forced myself to breathe slowly, methodically, until the world stopped spinning. This was supposed to be the relief. The help. Instead, it was another layer of helplessness.

By March 24, 2024, five days before trial, I had stopped hoping for justice. I was hoping for escape and a settlement offer of some kind will appear.

A settlement. Any settlement. Something that would end this without requiring the trial I no longer believed my attorney was prepared to handle.

Five years of work. Thousands of hours. Evidence that proved systematic forgery. Expert witnesses ready to testify.

And I was hoping someone would offer me a way out.

That's what institutional failure does. It makes you doubt the value of your own work. It makes you wish for less than you deserve because getting what you deserve requires trusting a system that has already failed you repeatedly.

I built the case. I found the evidence. I compiled the witnesses.

And in the final days before trial, I found myself begging my own attorney to do the basic work that would let any of it matter.

The trial happened. We'll get to that.

But this moment—five days before, sitting alone, sending emails that tried to sound grateful while documenting abandonment—this is part of the collateral damage too.

Discovering that even when you get help, you might still be alone.

CHAPTER 24

The Trial Begins, When Procedure Is the Defense

April 2, 2024. Department 69, San Diego Superior Court. Seven years of litigation distilled into four trial days. I'd spent those years gathering evidence, filing motions, representing myself when I had no attorney, learning California civil procedure from the ground up. Now I had counsel—Duane R. Folke, almost 50 years a lawyer—and we were finally here.

The courtroom settled. Judge Katherine Bacal took the bench. Two defense attorneys sat across from us: Andrew Mase and Matthew Aguirre. Behind them, the institutional weight of U.S. Bank, MERS and Specialized Loan Servicing.

The trial hadn't even started, and I already knew we were in trouble.

The Disaster Declaration

"Your Honor, in the 50 years I've been a lawyer, almost 50, I've never had a situation where my opposing counsel, who is supposed to be a trial lawyer, is supposed to get the case done and do it together. This has been a disaster."

Duane Folke stood before Judge Bacal, visibly frustrated. We were supposed to be selecting a jury. Instead, we were fighting about missing exhibits, incomplete notebooks, and jury instructions that should have been filed weeks ago.

The judge had asked a simple question: Did we have a joint set of jury instructions and a joint verdict form? We did not.

Defense had their proposed jury instructions. Exhibit lists that didn't match the trial readiness conference report. Numbers that kept changing—

was it Exhibit 27 or Exhibit 20? Was the Pooling and Servicing Agreement Number 19 or Number 26? We had... notebooks of certified documents that the judge didn't want.

"The nugget is I never got their exhibits per your order," Folke continued. "And when I finally got the exhibits per your order, Number 27 is not in here and the pooling service agreement, we still don't have. We never got a copy of."

I'd been watching their exhibit list carefully. The Pooling and Servicing Agreement—I knew it didn't exist. The securitization trust they claimed owned my loan had never been properly formed. When they listed it as Exhibit 27, I was excited. Finally, they'd have to produce the document that would prove their claim was fraudulent.

Oops. Exhibit withdrawn.

The complete audit, including the Bloomberg data and the affidavit sworn under penalty of perjury, is included in Appendix A— I'd encourage anyone who doubts the mechanics of what I've described to read it.

Gone from the list. Just like they deleted Mark McCloskey as a witness after they found out I had the notary who supposedly notarized his signature willing to testify that she did not. Evidence disappeared the moment it became dangerous.

The defense had withdrawn exhibits. Changed numbering. Failed to provide documents per court order. But this wasn't procedural chaos—this was evidence destruction disguised as administrative confusion.

And we hadn't even reached the critical issue yet.

The Ethics Violation That Got Buried

I watched Folke pull out a document—the Foreclosure Checklist Report, the one we'd been arguing about. Defense Exhibit 27. Or 20. Depending on which list you looked at.

"It's a forgery, your Honor," Folke said. "The person that we have—"

Judge Bacal cut him off. "I guess you have to prove that up."

"I agree, your Honor, but it has been proffered as that. And then there's another set of issues that happened. This particular witness, Agnes Bradshaw, was represented by counsel. And, unfortunately, it appears that Mr. Matthew Aguirre inappropriately spoke with a witness who was represented and tried to make that witness change their testimony."

There it was. Out in the open.

Matthew Aguirre—sitting at the defense table—had contacted Agnes Bradshaw, a Colorado notary whose forged signature appeared on multiple foreclosure documents. He'd contacted her while she was represented by attorney Lisa Foley. He'd tried to get her to change her testimony.

Agnes had saved the voicemail:

"Hi Ms. Bradshaw, this is Matthew Aguirre and I'm calling you because I am an attorney for Specialized Loan Servicing who is named in a complaint litigation by one Leena Hannonen and she recently told us that you were going to talk about how you didn't remember notarizing substitution of trustee on the loan and I was just wondering if maybe I could just shoot you over a document by email just to see if it would refresh your memory about this notarization in question if so be great can you call 858-336-xxxx again my name is Matthew and I will hear from you thank you bye..."

Read that again.

He wanted to "refresh her memory" by showing her the forged document. The document she'd already said she didn't sign.

This wasn't just an ethics violation. This was potential *witness tampering*. This was an attorney interfering with a represented witness in direct violation of Rule 4.2 of the California Rules of Professional Conduct.

Judge Bacal's response: "Well, that's a serious issue to be taken up with the state bar."

Folke tried again. "Well, no, I need to take it up with your Honor—"

"I mean, I know what the rules say, but I don't do anything without evidence, and I need to know where we are. So in this Court, because as far as I'm aware, Ms. Bradshaw was never represented by anybody here. The question of whether or not she was represented is between her, her counsel, and anyone else. I don't have her counsel."

"Well, I'm her counsel now, your Honor, but she was represented by Ms. Foley, and they knew that as of July of last—"

"And where's Ms. Foley? Well, hold on. Did you represent Ms. Bradshaw at the time of the contact?"

"No, I did not."

"Then I can't do anything now. And I'm not going to."

The exchange took less than two minutes. An ethics violation—documented, witnessed, material to the case—dismissed on procedural grounds.

I'd listed Agnes Bradshaw as a witness. Knowing defense counsel would try to contact her, I'd gotten her an attorney—Lisa Foley—and informed Matthew Aguirre and The Ryan Firm in writing that she was represented. Under Rule 4.2 of the California Rules of Professional Conduct, that should have ended any direct contact.

But when Folke raised it in court, the response was pure procedural dismissal: Folke wasn't representing Bradshaw at that moment, therefore the court couldn't address it.

Never mind that Aguirre knew she was represented when he made contact. Never mind that he'd violated the rule anyway. Never mind what he'd said to her or what he'd tried to get her to do.

The rules, apparently, don't apply to everyone equally.

No current attorney-client relationship at the moment of complaint = no jurisdiction = no remedy.

The Deposition That Wasn't

Hours later, after fighting through more exhibit confusion and procedural skirmishes, we reached Defense Motion in Limine Number 6: exclude Agnes Bradshaw's deposition transcript.

Judge Bacal read from the notebook. "I have a letter dated June 26, 2023, 'Attention to Rosty Gore, The Ryan Firm. Attention Robert Norum, ZBS Law,' regarding deposition of Colorado notary Agnes Bradshaw."

She read my letter aloud: "I have contacted Ms. Agnes Bradshaw today, which she has agreed to do a deposition, period. If you are interested in participating, please contact me as soon as possible, and I will provide the date and the Zoom link when available, period."

Then came the ruling.

"That is not a Notice of Deposition. A Notice of Deposition has the time and date of the deposition. It's not 'if you want to attend, we'll let you know then.' So the motion is granted as to the deposition transcript only." Folke confirmed: "Yes, your Honor."

"It has nothing to do with whether or not she will testify." "Yes, your Honor."

"But as to the transcript, it won't be allowed because the deposition was not noticed pursuant to the code."

I'd contacted Bradshaw. She'd agreed to be deposed. I'd notified defense counsel. I'd conducted the deposition. I had her testimony on record—testimony that would prove the systematic forgery, testimony that would show she never signed dozens of documents attributed to her.

But I hadn't included a specific date and time in the notice letter. I'd said "I will provide the date and the Zoom link when available." Wrong format. Wrong procedure. Deposition excluded.

The substance didn't matter. The evidence didn't matter. The fact that Bradshaw was willing to testify didn't matter. California Code of Civil Procedure mattered. And I hadn't followed it precisely.

Bradshaw could still testify live at trial. But we'd lost the deposition transcript—the controlled setting, the recorded testimony, the ability to impeach her if she changed her story under pressure. Another piece of evidence, procedurally neutralized.

What Damages Are Allowed

Defense Motion in Limine Number 7 sought to exclude evidence that I'd been stabbed after becoming homeless following the wrongful foreclosure.

Judge Bacal's tentative: grant as irrelevant. Folke argued proximate cause. He cited *Miles v. Deutsche Bank National Trust Company*, a California Court of Appeal case establishing that wrongful foreclosure allows recovery of all proximately caused damages.

"If you look to the very end, your Honor, if you go to the bottom... it talks about all damages proximately caused."

Judge Bacal pushed back. "Right. But how were you going to prove this was proximately caused by that?" "I'm going to be able to show that after my client was evicted, she was homeless as a direct result of being wrongfully evicted because they utilized a document that was forged and with that document, put her out. And then I have a lawyer that we have subpoenaed, his name is Zuberi. Hopefully, he will come. That's another issue I guess I should have brought up earlier, but—"

"Is he one of your designated experts?" "He's a witness to the fore—the wrongful—wrongful eviction that took place with my client." "Okay."

Folke pressed the legal standard. "And under the law, your Honor, with this case, it indicates that whatever is foreseeable. And you can take the Andrews approach or under Palsgraf or the other approach, but we still have an opportunity to present it to the jury."

Judge Bacal ruled: "The motion is granted. I find that it is tenuous at best that a stabbing was caused by a wrongful foreclosure. Certainly, a party who proves wrongful foreclosure is entitled to all damages that flow as the result, but I cannot find that this would have flown—be the result of that rather than an unfortunate incident that could have happened whether or not there was a foreclosure."

The chain of causation: Forged documents → wrongful foreclosure → illegal eviction → homelessness → stabbing while homeless.

Too tenuous. Too many links. Too difficult to prove.

The jury would never hear about it. They would never know that the foreclosure fraud didn't just take my property. It took my housing, my stability, my safety. They would never connect the institutional document forgery to the human consequences that followed.

Damages: limited to what the court deemed sufficiently proximate.

The Pattern Emerges

By the time we broke for jury selection, the framework was clear. We had expert testimony proving forgery. We had the forged documents themselves. We had Pennsylvania state records showing the notary never signed. We had Agnes Bradshaw willing to testify that her signature had been forged on thirty to forty documents.

And we had an ethics violation that couldn't be addressed because the procedural timing was wrong, a deposition excluded because the notice was short by three days, damages excluded because the causation chain was deemed too long, an attorney who declared the pretrial process "a disaster" in open court, and exhibits that were missing, renumbered, or withdrawn.

This wasn't incompetence. This was the system working exactly as designed. Every piece of evidence had to navigate a procedural maze. Every claim required perfect technical execution. Every error — no matter how minor, no matter how easily cured — became grounds for exclusion.

The institutions being sued for forgery? They took no depositions. They conducted no discovery on me. Their exhibits weren't in order. But they had two attorneys and the quiet confidence of parties who understood that procedure would carry them regardless.

We had an aging lawyer who couldn't manage the basic mechanics of trial preparation and a pro se plaintiff who'd learned civil procedure by living it.

The jury would hear what the system allowed them to hear. Evidence that made it past the procedural gatekeepers. Damages deemed sufficiently proximate. Claims that survived the motions in limine. Nothing more.

Voir Dire: The Final Setup

By 1:30 PM, we had our prospective jury panel. Forty-two people called for service. Judge Bacal explained the process, read the case summary, introduced the attorneys.

"The plaintiff has brought this matter, a wrongful foreclosure case..."

She read the witness list: "Beth Chrisman, Agnes Bradshaw, Sharon Guillent, Richard Mendez, Laura Ollier, Les Poppitt, Leena Hannonen."

The jurors raised no hands. They knew none of us. They knew nothing about foreclosure fraud or forged notary signatures or systematic document fabrication. They would learn only what survived the procedural filtering.

Duane Folke stood for plaintiff's voir dire. His questioning was brief, almost perfunctory.

"Are any of the jurors here homeowners or ever been homeowners?"

Nearly all hands went up.

"Has anybody ever had any problems with their mortgage in terms of maybe refinancing?" A few hands.

"Has anyone ever had circumstances where they—we had someone who was talking about being evicted or having evictions? Is anybody?"

More hands.

"Your Honor, that's all I need." Three questions. Three minutes. Done.

Defense attorney Andrew Mase was more strategic. He identified every juror who owned rental property. He asked specifically about bias against mortgage companies.

"I represent a few mortgage companies in this case. That would be U.S. Bank is one of them. Specialized Loan Servicing is my second client. And another company called 'Mortgage Electronic Registration Systems,' that's my other client. Without knowing anything else about the case, I just want to know, because I represent mortgage companies, I want to know, out of you 14, does anybody think that they're liable—they should be liable to the plaintiff without knowing anything else?"

Building the record. Establishing neutrality. Making sure no juror came in predisposed against banks.

By 3:50 PM, we had our jury. Twelve seated. Two alternates. The setup was complete.

Day Two: The Framing

April 3, 2024. 9:15 AM.

The jury returned. Judge Bacal gave preliminary instructions. Then: "At this time, we're going to hear the opening statements of both sides. Remember, what the parties say during their opening statements is not evidence."

Not evidence. Just promises of what the evidence would show.

Duane Folke stood. "Good morning, ladies and gentlemen."

The court had to stop him immediately. "Counsel, you need to speak up."

"Oh, I'm sorry. My mother used to always say I need to make—" He caught himself. "I'm sorry. Obviously, I'm very excited. I love trials. I'm a trial lawyer. I've been doing this almost 50 years. And I represent Leena Hannonen in a case of a lifetime."

He told them what we hoped to prove. "I have the opportunity to present to you evidence where we're going to be able to show that she was a victim of wrongful foreclosure and that she was a person who had the Homeowner's Bill of Rights violated. And as a result, she has some very serious injuries that happened but also lost her home."

Then came his central theme: "I think the most critical thing, if I don't get anything done in this trial, is to be able to show you just how easy it is to forge a document and then use it to take a person's home."

He described the Assignment of Deed of Trust, supposedly notarized by Autumn R. Carnegie in Pennsylvania. He promised testimony from Jeffrey Liebert, head of deeds for Allegheny County. He promised Beth Chrisman, the forensic document examiner who would prove the forgery. He promised Agnes Bradshaw herself, the Colorado notary whose signature had been forged on 30 to 40 documents.

"What that means is, is that after there's a forgery recorded in a chain of title, everything after it is a blank piece of paper." Void. Null. Legally nonexistent.

He told them my story. Finland. The American dream. A house in Julian purchased in 1999. Then tragedy: mother died, father died, brother died, divorce. Trips back to Finland. Financial strain. A refinance loan to consolidate everything.

And the strangest thing: "She was supposed to go to a meeting to sign all the documents, but the broker said, you don't have to show up. We'll just do it for you. We know who you are. Well, ladies and gentlemen, you can't do that."

Predatory lending. Document fraud. What Folke called "forgery roulette"—the mortgage version of Russian roulette.

He emphasized that I wasn't in default when this started. "Specialized Loan Servicing saying that they were the ones that were supposedly working with her on her mortgage. But she didn't know anything about a Specialized Loan Servicing company." Banks merged, servicers changed, and suddenly: "You've got to be three months behind before we can do anything. You've got to stop paying your mortgage."

The institutional trap. Stop paying so we can help you. Then foreclose because you stopped paying.

Folke's promised evidence: forged Assignment of Deed of Trust, forged Substitution of Trustee, expert analysis, notary testimony, Pennsylvania state records.

"The interesting thing about this case, other than all the forgeries that I just explained to you, is that the defendants have no defense, at least not one I've heard about."

Judge Bacal had to keep stopping him. "You need to slow down for the court reporter."

He apologized repeatedly. Too fast. Too excited. Jumping between points.

"So what we're hoping to do is show you that in this particular case, the defendants did not follow what's called the 'statutory scheme' with respect to mortgages and recording of mortgages..." Defense objected. "Argument." Sustained.

Folke tried to recover. "The evidence will show that there was a deed of trust that was a security instrument, that there was an assignment, that there was a substitution of attorney, that there was a declaration, a notice of default, a notice of trustee sale and a trustee's deed upon sale issued in this case, and that it cannot be valid because we have forgeries in this case."

He sat down. Maybe fifteen minutes total. Scattered. Disorganized. But the core message was clear: forged documents, stolen home.

The Defense Response

Andrew Mase stood for the defense. Calm. Professional. Methodical.

"Good morning, ladies and gentlemen of the jury, and thank you for being here. Thank you for dedicating your time to the jury service."

He introduced himself. He introduced his clients: U.S. Bank, the loan owner. Specialized Loan Servicing (SLS), the servicer. Mortgage Electronic Registration Systems (MERS).

Then he reframed the entire case in three sentences:

"Ladies and gentlemen of the jury, I'm going to move through this case, I wouldn't say rapidly but efficiently. And what I mean by that is this case is very simple. Ms. Hannonen in 2007, she received a mortgage loan. It's undisputed." Simple. A loan. Undisputed.

"The loan is for $483,750. It was a refinance. You're going to learn that it paid off two loans, and she also received about $121,000 in cash."

She got the money. She signed the documents. Contract law 101.

"In 2010, SLS, the loan servicer, began servicing her loan. SLS took Ms. Hannonen's payments for a time until she stopped making them, which occurred in August of 2012."

She stopped paying. That's when the problems started.

"From August of 2012, until the eventual foreclosure in 2018, a period of roughly six years, there were no payments made." Six years. No payments. The math was stark.

Mase walked the jury through SLS's attempts to help. Loan modification offered immediately in September 2012. "She applied, and she did not qualify." More communications from 2012 through 2017. More attempts to avert foreclosure. "But nothing could be done. The debt remained unpaid for a significant period of time, eventually leading to foreclosure."

He mentioned the prior 2012 lawsuit I'd filed against SLS. "You're going to hear that the month after Ms. Hannonen fell into default, September 2012, she sued SLS in a prior case in this courthouse." Folke objected. "Relevance." Overruled.

She admitted getting the loan. She lost the case. Dismissed.

"Over the next roughly five years—and I'm speaking about October of 2013, moving forward to 2018—there still were no payments being made on the loan."

"In November of 2017, after a significant default had developed, roughly $165,000 of payments, Specialized Loan Servicing and U.S. Bank had to do something, and they started the nonjudicial foreclosure."

They *had to* do something. After six years. After $165,000 in unpaid debt. Then Mase addressed my bankruptcy filing—the last-ditch attempt to stop the foreclosure sale.

"To avoid foreclosure, you're going to learn that Ms. Hannonen filed for bankruptcy. And in that filing, her petition and her schedules—" Folke objected again. "Relevancy."

"Overruled without prejudice," Judge Bacal said. "And I will remind the jurors what counsel says is not evidence. They're simply telling you what evidence—they expect the evidence will show."

Mase continued. "In her bankruptcy filing submitted to the bankruptcy court, which remained under the penalty of perjury, she stated that U.S. Bank had her loan. She stated that the value of her house was roughly $420,000, but that the debt, as she put forth in her bank schedules, was about $600,000, meaning, there's no equity in her house." No equity. Underwater. Nothing to save.

"You'll learn that U.S. Bank received an order from the bankruptcy court allowing it to foreclose during the pendency of the bankruptcy. That's called a 'motion for relief of stay.' Then in November of 2018, the property was ultimately foreclosed on and went to sale."

Legal. Proper. Authorized by the bankruptcy court itself.

Finally, Mase addressed the forgery allegations directly.

"On the issue of forgeries, which you're going to find out—and what you may have already heard from the plaintiff's opening statement is 'That's been forged.' The evidence is going to show and you'll hear variously that she received the loan. She entered into it voluntarily. She received this contract. She signed the note. She signed a deed of trust. And a contract runs both ways."

Both ways. She got the money. She owed the debt. "What the evidence will show is when someone doesn't perform the contract, there must be a remedy. And after six years of default, the remedy was a nonjudicial foreclosure."

Remedy. Not theft. Not fraud. Remedy.

He acknowledged the forgery claims but dismissed them as legally irrelevant. "The evidence will show that she admitted that in her prior 2012 lawsuit that she lost."

She admitted getting the loan before. She can't claim forgery now. The contrast was absolute.

Folke had promised to show systematic document forgery, institutional fraud, evidence suppression, and human devastation.

Mase promised to show a simple contract case: money borrowed, payments stopped, legal foreclosure followed.

One attorney spoke about forged notary signatures and void documents. The other spoke about $483,750 and six years of nonpayment. They were describing two entirely different cases.

The jury would have to decide which story the evidence actually told.

But the evidence they'd hear—the testimony they'd see, the documents they'd review, the expert analysis they'd evaluate—had already been filtered through Day One's procedural gauntlet.

The Aguirre ethics violation: buried. The deposition transcript: excluded. The homelessness and stabbing: irrelevant. The trial could begin.

CHAPTER 25

Proving Forgery Changes Nothing

The courtroom settled into an expectant silence. After months of procedural warfare, years of denied motions, and countless attempts by opposing counsel to prevent this moment, we were finally here. The evidence would speak.

"Your Honor, at this time, we would call Ms. Beth Chrisman to the stand, qualified document examiner."

The Expert Takes the Stand

Beth Chrisman didn't look like someone who could dismantle a foreclosure empire with a magnifying glass and eighteen years of experience. But that's exactly what she was about to do.

She stated her credentials with the practiced ease of someone who'd done this 180 times before: forensic document examiner, court-qualified in multiple states, certified after a two-year intensive program at the International School of Forensic Document Examination, three-year apprenticeship, 2,300 to 2,400 cases handled.

"And what does a forensic document examiner do?" my attorney asked.

"I examine documents that have been called into question. A handwriting expert is a subset of forensic document examination."

The judge interrupted with practical concerns: "It's not very good. It doesn't pull any closer to you, and if you get too close to it, it will distort. So the best thing you can do is speak a little louder and slower than usual, okay?"

But I wasn't worried about the microphone. I was watching the jury. They were leaning forward already.

The Foundation

We moved through her methodology, the scientific process that courts have accepted for decades. She explained the ACE method: Assessment, Comparison, Evaluation. The same framework forensic fingerprint experts use.

"No one person signs exactly the same way twice," she explained, "and no two people sign or write exactly the same way. So all other premises are based on those two basic premises."

She'd examined the questioned signature on my Assignment of Deed of Trust, the document that supposedly transferred my loan from one entity to another, signed by notary Autumn R. Carnegie. She'd compared it to four known, authenticated signatures from Pennsylvania state records.

Defense counsel objected to almost everything. The report was hearsay. The basis for her opinion was hearsay. The documents she relied on were hearsay. Judge Bacal sustained some objections, overruled others, gave limiting instructions. The legal fencing match played out in real-time. But underneath it all, the evidence was building.

The Dissimilarities

"When I did a comparison of the question signature to the known signatures, I found numerous distinct dissimilarities." She walked through them methodically, the way a surgeon might describe the anatomy of a failed operation:

The letter "A" in Autumn:

"The formation of the letter, the spacing of the letter was dissimilar in comparison to the known signatures. It was much more open. And the starting point of the A was almost completely inside of the A loop. In the known signatures, the starting point of the A almost met with the stem of the A."

The letter "U":

"In Autumn's known signatures, she actually does a formation of a Garland stroke that represents the letter U. And in the question signature, the Garland stroke is half missing."

The letter "T":

"The T formation in the question signature is looped. It looks like you're looking through the eye of a needle to sew. And the T bar is crossed very low on the T, almost to the baseline. In the known signature samples, the habit that we see is almost a retraced T. So there's no needle to look through, because the stroke follows itself up and down. And when she crosses the T, it's crossed to the middle to the top third of the T."

The middle initial "R":

"In the questioned signature, the person who wrote the letter 'R' started near the baseline and moved with a tiny stroke down to the baseline, then moved upward to form the stem, and then formed the entire letter 'R.' They do this in one pen stroke, with the pen never coming off the paper.

"In the known Autumn R. Carnegie signatures, Autumn's habit is to draw the stem of the R from the upper zone to the baseline, pick up her pen, and then go back on the paper. And she starts her R to the left of the stem and then makes the rest of the R formation in two distinct strokes that are visually even completely different. So, pictorially, the Rs do not match. And in configuration they do not match."

The last name:

"In the question signature, the person who signed the name of Autumn R. Carnegie writes what appears to be maybe a C and a maybe a G formation, because we have a lower loop. So it's two letters is what it appears to be.

"In the known signature samples, Autumn R. Carnegie actually legibly writes every letter. We can read her last name and pretty much figure out what her name is. We have a distinct formation of a C, an A, an R. She does not distinctly write an N, but then she goes into the G, the I, and the E."

She described Autumn's authentic signature formation as "very feminine," "big and bubbly", the kind of beautiful handwriting we all remembered from high school. The questioned signature? "Very angular, very small loop formation."

The Opinion

My attorney built to the critical moment: "Did you come to some kind of an opinion to a reasonable degree of scientific certainty in your area of expertise regarding this case?"

"Yes." "And what is your opinion?"

"My opinion is that the Autumn R. Carnegie of the known documents did not sign the questioned document."

She hadn't rendered a qualified opinion, one that leaves room for doubt or hedging. She'd found so many fundamental dissimilarities that her opinion was absolute.

The defense cross-examination tried to undermine her: You only examined one signature? "Yes."

You're not a legal expert? "No."

Do you know what an Assignment of Deed of Trust is? "Vaguely."

Were the exemplars original documents? "They were not."

The implication was clear: How could she be certain based on copies, not originals? How could one signature matter? But she'd already answered that question in her direct testimony: "In this case, it, to me, my opinion was not based on needing the originals. There was no need to request originals. Originals probably would not have been provided, because certified copy is as good as it's going to get with notaries."

And when pressed about whether she needed originals for this specific analysis: "In this case, there was no accusation of obliterations, alterations, retouching, or retracing. So you didn't need original documents for this case?" "In my opinion, no."

Beth Chrisman's testimony established one irrefutable fact: Autumn Carnegie did not sign the Assignment of Deed of Trust that transferred my loan to U.S. Bank. Someone forged a notary's signature on a document in the chain of title for my home. That should have been enough.

***

Notary

This was an industry insider who knew exactly how the mortgage system worked, and how it failed.

She'd started as a receptionist. Became a processor. Then a loan officer. Worked her way up to branch manager at Freedom Mortgage, running her own direct lending operation. Twenty-three years in the mortgage industry. Licensed in California and Colorado. She'd seen every angle of the business — origination, underwriting, sales, compliance.

Then came 2008. The market collapsed. Her company dissolved. Like so many others, she had to reinvent herself. She went back to school, studied phlebotomy, volunteered at health clinics, worked at Kroll Factual Data to understand how credit disputes affected mortgage applications, did tax preparation on the side.

And she became a notary. "After that, I got a job with SLS."

"And who is SLS?" "Specialized Loan Servicing."

The same company named as a defendant in my lawsuit. The loan servicer that had sent me threatening letters, filed false compliance declarations, and executed the foreclosure sale while I was fighting the fraud in court.

She'd worked there from November 2016 through 2019, eventually moving to the bankruptcy department. Her job: reviewing documents on dual screens, checking for data entry errors, preparing documents for executive signatures — vice presidents, senior vice presidents — and notarizing when required.

"Did you have any special training by Specialized Loan Services before you took on the role as a notary?"

"Yes. I was shadowing one of my coworker, how she does the documents, reviewing documents in our two screen and see what needs to be edited. And then we print it. We give it to one of the manager. And their titles are all different, either vice president, executive vice president. And then we give them the documents either to be notarized or not to be notarized."

She'd shadowed for two weeks. Then moved to scanning signed documents into the system, packaging them, sending them off — she couldn't quite remember where. "All I know is we have different labels of different documents — needs to go."

Then the detail that changed everything: "When I first got hired, I have to go upstairs and have them order my notary stamp and change my address on my notary in the state of Colorado address to SLS."

Her notary stamp wasn't delivered to her home. It was delivered to her work desk. At Specialized Loan Servicing.

Not every state requires notaries to maintain a journal. California, Pennsylvania, and Colorado do. Every notarized document must be logged sequentially — date, time, type of document, signer's name. It's a security measure, a paper trail, protection against exactly this kind of fraud. When I called Agnes

Bradshaw, she didn't deny it or deflect. She went straight to her book.

"Did you ever see a Substitution of Trustee that purportedly bore your name with a Mark McCloskey?" "Are you asking me if I am involved in her documentations?"

"I've signed a lot of documents, but in her case when she called me and asked me if you can please check your notary book, I told her I don't have September — the date that you mentioned — in my book."

Two days before trial, a foreclosure checklist appeared — Exhibit 27 — with initials that supposedly belonged to her. A document nobody had seen until that moment. No journal entry. No record. Just initials on a checklist that materialized at the last possible moment.

"That's not even my initial. My initial looks like an 'AM' and I don't initial that way. So that's not my initial."

She paused, then added: "But, you know, our supervisor would have a copy of our name stamp in their drawers. So if we forget to put our stamp on the document, she'll stamp it. But I would not — but that document is not my initial, that I could confirm."

The questioning continued. Had she seen other documents — mortgage documents, real estate documents — that bore her signature or stamp but weren't actually hers?

Defense counsel objected: Relevance. Speculation. Hearsay. Judge Bacal: "Overruled." "Does that mean I can answer?" "You can answer."

She took a breath. "It's not my signature."

We tried again: "In the course of your review of documents involving Leena Hannonen, did you find other documents — Substitutions of Trustees, documents of that nature — that had a notary seal and a signature that was not yours?"

Defense objected again: Asked and answered. Lacks foundation. "Overruled. It was not answered."

"Oh, yes." "How many?" "A lot."

"I mean, I don't know. I don't know how many. I know there is a few. More than two? More than three? More than four or five?"

She was trying to be precise, trying to give accurate testimony under oath. But the truth was overwhelming her.

"So I'm just really concerned. And I've been going through my brain about this, because the fact that I have to go upstairs — when I was hired, I have to go upstairs and have them order my notary stamp and change my address on my notary in the state of Colorado address to SLS. So, that, I'm pretty much blown away — because how do I know if they did not order two stamps? I have no clue. Because when I got the stamp, it was just delivered to my desk. It wasn't delivered to my home. It was delivered to my desk."

Her home address, according to the Colorado notary records, was now Specialized Loan Servicing's corporate office.

"So it looks like my home is Specialized Loan Servicing. So how do I know if they ordered one or two stamps?"

"And if you don't have it in your book, what does that mean?" "That means I did not sign."

My attorney asked directly: "In addition to that, were you provided some 30 to 40 documents where you noted that you did not sign or notarize those documents during your course of work with Leena Hannonen?" "Yes."

"So your testimony here today that you are giving this Court is that there was not one or two or three but as many as 30 to 40 documents that bore your signature and notary stamp that you did not execute?" "Right."

Defense moved to strike as nonresponsive.

But she wasn't done: "And let me add to something to that. Because there are, some of them are dated 7. I don't even write my 7 the way that they have the 7."

Even the handwritten dates on some documents didn't match her handwriting.

Judge Bacal had to intervene: "What you are directed to do is listen to the questions you're being asked, answer the questions you're being asked. Then when you're done answering, stop and wait for the next question."

But Agnes Bradshaw was visibly upset. "Yes. I'm, I'm, I'm heated right now. And I'm sorry for adding more things to it, because I want this thing to be cleared. I'm pretty upset at this point, so I'm turning red. I don't know if you guys can tell, but..."

Thirty to forty documents. Not an isolated incident. Not a single mistake. Not a "paperwork error." Systematic forgery.

The Ethical Violation

Later in her testimony, we established something else: She'd retained an attorney, Margaret Foley, on July 13, 2023. Not to sue anyone. Just to protect herself. Because "this is deeper than I thought it would be."

"Why did you hire an attorney?" "Because, I don't know. This is deeper than I thought it would be." "And when you say it was 'deeper' than you thought it would be, what do you mean by that?" "It's because there's a lot of signatures that are proven that is not my signature."

After she'd retained counsel, someone from the other side contacted her.

"Did you have an occasion to have an attorney contact you about this other than myself regarding this matter?" "Yes. Someone did contact me and I can't recall his name unless I look at my phone, because he left me a voicemail."

"And was his name Matthew Aguirre?" "It sounds very familiar, but, again, I have to look in my phone."

"And Mr. Aguirre is the attorney for Specialized Loan Services, U.S. Bank, and MERS. Did you know that?" "Yes. That's what he told me."

"And was it your understanding that he had the right to speak to you if you had an attorney?"

"No, I did not know that until, until Leena told me that I'm not supposed to speak to anybody because, without my lawyer. I said, 'Oh, I did not understand that part.'"

Matthew Aguirre, counsel for the defendants, had contacted a represented party directly. In California, Rule of Professional Conduct 4.2 prohibits exactly this: communicating with a person the lawyer knows to be represented by counsel without that counsel's permission.

The court sustained objections when I tried to pursue this line of questioning. Too prejudicial. Counsel testifying. But the jury heard it.

They heard that the defendants' own attorney had violated basic ethical rules trying to "verify" information from a witness who'd already retained counsel specifically to protect herself from this kind of contact.

The next day in court, my attorney did something spectacularly ill-advised.

Without warning. Without foundation. Without even pretending to understand evidence rules, he hit play on the voicemail. Just like that.

Judge Bacal's expression changed instantly. Not confusion. Not curiosity. Irritation. The kind reserved for breaches of decorum, not breaches of law.

"Turn it off," she snapped. "You can't do that. That is not how you present evidence."

She didn't ask what the recording was. She didn't ask why it existed. She didn't ask who left it or what it contained. "One more stunt like this," she continued, "and I will sanction you. We are moving on."

She cut him off mid-sentence. The voicemail was excluded.

What the voicemail contained—evidence of witness tampering—was never addressed. Not later, not indirectly, not on the record. It simply vanished. Playing a recording incorrectly? Sanction-worthy.

Attempting to interfere with a witness in an active case? Apparently administrative noise.

Another violation, another silence. The choreography continued. No one was confused. No one needed clarification. Everyone knew exactly what had just happened. The rules weren't being enforced. They were being curated.

And I was learning, in real time, which ones the court was willing to protect.

What the Notary Proved

Agnes Bradshaw testified under oath that she did not sign the September 18, 2017 Substitution of Trustee for my property, that the document was not in her notary journal, and that she had identified thirty to forty documents bearing her forged signature and stamp. She testified that her notary stamp had been ordered by and delivered directly to SLS's corporate office, and that she had no way of knowing whether SLS had ordered duplicate stamps. She also testified that after retaining counsel, the defendants' attorney had contacted her directly.

In any rational system, that testimony alone would have triggered criminal forgery charges, state bar complaints, banking regulatory action, title insurance claims, and referrals to the FBI.

Instead, defense counsel cross-examined her about whether she was a legal expert and whether she understood California's requirements for assignment validity. As if her legal expertise mattered when she was testifying about whether she had actually signed the documents. As if the technical requirements of notarization mattered when the notary herself was saying the signatures were fake.

The testimony was devastating. The trial continued anyway.

My Turn to Testify

April 4, 2024. After Beth Chrisman's expert analysis, it was my turn.

I raised my right hand. Stated my name. Spelled it for the record. H-a-n-n-o-n-e-n.

My testimony turned into a shitshow before I'd finished spelling my name. Then Judge Bacal stopped me before I could say a word.

"Ma'am, you can't say anything. You can't say anything. Hold on. You just have to wait for a question. This is a trial. It's not a conversation. In order for a witness to say something, they have to wait for a question."

I wasn't allowed to speak unless spoken to. Every answer subject to objection. Every sentence cut short if it went beyond what Folke had asked.

I'd asked him to prepare me for this. To rehearse. To go through the questions so I'd know what was coming. Never happened.

I'd arranged a projector for free so we could show the jury the forged signatures side-by-side—the Pennsylvania state records next to the Assignment, Agnes Bradshaw's real signature next to the Substitution. Visual proof that would take thirty seconds to understand.

Folke was supposed to pick it up two weeks before trial. He drove to LA from San Diego the day before to get it. We had no time to set it up. The projector sat unused. The jury never saw the side-by-side comparisons.

I had one shot to show twelve people what I'd spent years proving, and I was standing there unprepared, unrehearsed, alone in the most important moment of the case. Instead, they got this.

The Predatory Loan

Folke asked about the 2007 refinance. I explained: I'd met with a broker in Orange County to consolidate debt after my divorce and family deaths. We filled out the application. I assumed we'd meet again to sign in front of a notary.

Instead, I got the entire loan package in the mail. Already finalized. Already notarized. "I didn't know I could do that," I testified. The notary page showed I'd appeared before someone I'd never met.

Then I found the fees. A $25,000 broker fee—never disclosed, just added on. My income? Tripled on the application without my knowledge.

Defense kept objecting. "Nonresponsive." "Move to strike." Judge Bacal sustained most of them. I wasn't allowed to explain. Just answer the narrow question asked.

"Stop Paying Your Mortgage"

The critical moment came when Folke asked about Specialized Loan Servicing. In 2010, they took over servicing. I was current on my payments. Then in 2012, my payment went up. I called to ask about a loan modification—something I was told I could do after five years.

Their response? "You have to be three months past due before they even talk to me about the loan modification." I testified: "They told me to stop paying."

The jury heard it. SLS instructed a current borrower to go into default as a prerequisite for help. Defense would later call Laura Ollier, SLS's corporate representative, to dispute this. She'd testify that SLS never tells borrowers to stop paying. Judge Bacal would find her testimony "not credible."

But that would come later. For now, the jury just heard my account: I stopped paying because they told me to. Then they foreclosed because I stopped paying.

The Investigation

I explained how I discovered the forgery. My tenant got a call about foreclosure—I never did. So I went to the San Diego County Recorder's office and pulled the entire chain of title.

That's where I found the Assignment of Deed of Trust, supposedly signed by Autumn R. Carnegie in Pennsylvania.

I contacted the Pennsylvania Secretary of State. Got her oath and bond, her signature card. "Her real signature is totally different from what's on my document." I filed a complaint. They opened a case. I hired Beth Chrisman.

Then I found Agnes Bradshaw. The Substitution of Trustee bore her signature and Colorado notary seal. She'd never signed it. Thirty to forty other documents carried her forged signature.

I brought all of this to U.S. Bank, SLS, and MERS.

Folke asked: "Did they come to you and say, oh, we made a mistake?"

"Nope."

Did anyone try to fix the problem after I proved the documents were forged? "No." "No." "No." ZBS, the foreclosure trustee, ignored the evidence entirely. I told them about the forged notary signatures. They proceeded anyway.

Folke asked how that made me feel. "Betrayed. They are stealing my house with fraudulent documents, basically."

The Judge Helps the Defense

The judge didn't just rule on objections. She created them.

When Folke tried to show me a document, Judge Bacal stopped him: "I'm pausing you because I don't want you to do it in front of the jurors." Then she turned to defense counsel and asked: "Is there an objection?" Mase took the cue: "Objection. Relevance." Sustained.

A judge isn't supposed to prompt objections. She's supposed to wait for them. But here she was, actively preventing evidence from reaching the jury and coaching the defense on how to block it. Not neutral, not impartial. Protective.

The Eviction

Folke asked about the unlawful detainer—the eviction proceeding.

I tried to explain: My tenant locked me out. Called the sheriff. The sheriff showed up with a stack of papers and said I'd been evicted.

"I don't even know anything about it. I have no service, no notice, no nothing." The sheriff told me if I didn't leave my own property, I'd be arrested for trespassing.

I was later dismissed from the unlawful detainer case—no trial, no judgment, just dismissed. But by then I'd already lost access to the house.

Everything was inside. My artwork. My belongings from Finland—memories of my parents, my whole life there. My passport. Immigration papers. Files. All of it locked inside while ZBS proceeded with foreclosure based on forged documents I'd already proven were fraudulent.

I became homeless. Slept in my car with my dog. Spent nights on the street trying to figure out what had just happened.

Folke asked: "Isn't that dangerous? Were you afraid?" "I didn't feel very ladylike at that point. But, yes. This came as a surprise. This came out of nowhere. What are you supposed to do? You go home and there's a sheriff waiting for you." Everything I owned: gone. Forever.

Judge Bacal called lunch recess.

Day Two: More Evidence, More Fumbling

The next morning, I returned to the stand.

Judge Bacal reminded me I was still under oath. Defense counsel noted I'd brought documents with me. Both sides approached to inspect what I had. The questioning resumed.

The Companies That Didn't Exist

Folke asked about LSI Title Company—listed on the Substitution of Trustee as the entity that requested recording.

I explained: "I contacted LSI to ask under what authority are they requesting this document. Come to find out, LSI doesn't exist anymore. They were taken over by ServiceLink 6, 7 years prior."

So I went to ServiceLink's office in Irvine. "In the lobby, there's no receptionist. There's a security guard with a gun. He said, 'Ma'am, you can't be here.'"

Someone finally came down.

Told me they had no record of requesting the document. Said I needed to subpoena Zieve, Brodnax & Steele. A company that didn't exist had supposedly requested the document that gave ZBS the power to foreclose.

The IT Guy Who Was a Vice President

I testified about Visionet Systems—the Pittsburgh company that created the Assignment. Norman Edward Gottschalk signed it claiming to be a vice president at MERS. But I'd found him on Visionet's website. He wasn't a MERS vice president. He was Visionet's CTO—chief technical officer. IT department.

"How can you be two at the — if he's a vice president, why would he work for the IT department?"

The defendants could have called Gottschalk to explain. They could have put him on the stand and let him clarify his title, his authority, his signature. They didn't.

The Assignment also said MERS acted "as a nominee for Chevy Chase Bank."

Problem: "Chevy Chase Bank doesn't exist — 2017 — anymore. They were taken over by Capital One at 2009. Chevy Chase should not be mentioned in this document." Whoever created the 2017 Assignment was using a bank name that hadn't existed for eight years.

The Pattern

I'd found forty-two other assignments with the same forged Autumn Carnegie signature. Submitted them to the Pennsylvania Secretary of State.

Their first response: "One incident. No big deal. We're not going to prosecute." So I spent days at county recorder offices—San Diego, Orange County, LA—and compiled the evidence. Showed them the pattern. "I solved the pattern and the practice. This case is so much bigger than just me." The investigation was still pending.

Then between Carnegie and Bradshaw, I'd found sixty additional forged documents. Same companies. Same process. Different victims.

Defense kept objecting. "Irrelevant." "Lacks foundation." Judge Bacal sustained most of them.

The Safe Harbor Letter

Folke asked about the letter I'd sent The Ryan Firm in July 2023—more than a year before trial. I'd given them everything. The forged Assignment. The forged Substitution. Beth Chrisman's analysis. Agnes Bradshaw's information. "I was trying to work with them so we don't have to end up here at the trial. I gave them all the information, and I asked them to do their own investigation and counter what I had found."

Their response? "They do not want to litigate this prior to trial, that they will provide their own handwriting expert at the trial."

They never did their own investigation. They never produced their own expert. They just showed up and objected.

The People Who Never Signed Anything

Folke went through the list systematically.

Laura Ollier—SLS's corporate representative, sitting at counsel table. Had she signed my deed of trust? No. The Assignment? No. The Substitution? No. The declaration? No. Notice of default? No. Notice of sale? No. Trustee's deed? No. Had I ever talked to her? No. Had I ever met her before yesterday? No.

But she was here to testify for the defense.

The Subpoena Disaster

Then came the moment that exposed just how unprepared Folke was.

He tried to question me about attorney Nabeel Zuberi—the lawyer involved in my unlawful detainer. Folke had subpoenaed him.

Judge Bacal stopped him: "I'm pausing you because I don't want you to do it in front of the jurors. Is there an objection?"

She was prompting the defense to object. She was helping the defendant, a big NO NO. Mase took the cue: "Objection. Relevance." Sustained.

The jury left for morning break. Then the real disaster unfolded.

Judge Bacal asked for the original proof of service for the subpoena.

Folke: "I don't have the original, your Honor." Defense pointed out the problems: subpoena showed service on March 27 for appearance on April 3—less than the required notice period. Served by a non-registered process server. Witness fees box not checked.

Judge Bacal: "Witness fees are mandatory. You have to have that box checked one thing or the other. And it's not checked." Folke tried to argue the witness was an attorney, an officer of the court, should cooperate anyway.

The judge shut him down: "Before I order compelling on a subpoena, I need to see a good proof of service." A critical witness—someone who could testify about the wrongful eviction—gone because Folke hadn't properly served the subpoena or paid witness fees.

I'd asked him to prepare. To rehearse. To get the mechanics right. Never happened.

What I Lost

Folke asked about my losses.

My belongings: over $200,000. Art supplies, finished artwork, everything I'd brought from Finland—memories of my parents, my whole life there. Passport. Immigration papers. Gone forever.

The house: appraised at $600,000-$700,000. "Can you do math, ma'am?" "Yes." "What is 200,000 plus 700,000?" "It sounds like 900- to me. 900,000."

I was 63 years old. A senior. Homeless because of forged documents.

The Second Arrest

After the unlawful detainer trial—after U.S. Bank's attorney told me I could pick up my belongings once the tenant was out—I went to the house.

Empty. Everything gone.

Jason Lipovsky showed up—the realtor for REO properties. The same person who'd signed the stipulation at trial claiming to represent U.S. Bank as plaintiff. He wasn't the plaintiff. He was the realtor. He called the sheriff. Said I was trespassing on my own house.

"Six sheriffs show up against me. I must be a threat. They said that I'm trespassing and I have to leave or they can arrest me. I'm going to jail."

I told my friend to take my car and my dog. "It looks like I'm going to jail."

"They handcuffed me, roughed me up—two big gorillas roughed me up and cuffed me. And they said, 'Oh, no, your girlfriend is going to jail, and your dog is going to the pound.'"

San Diego County Sheriff's Department. In Julian. Nobody is touching my dog. I told them I'd leave. They let me go.

Everything I owned: stolen by someone. The tenant, SLS, U.S. Bank—I don't know who. Twenty years of life. All my stuff from Finland.

I filed a grand larceny report with the sheriff. Over $200,000. They wouldn't take it. Said it was civil, not criminal.

The Question I Wasn't Prepared For

Mase's cross-examination was efficient. Controlled. He wasn't trying to disprove the forgeries — he couldn't. He was trying to reframe the entire case around a simpler story.

You stopped paying. You filed bankruptcy to delay the inevitable. You stayed in the house for two years after foreclosure without paying rent. And now you want the house back but can't afford it.

That story doesn't require forged documents to be valid. It doesn't require standing, or beneficial interest, or chain of title. It just requires a jury to believe that a borrower who didn't pay is using a technicality to avoid the consequences. He was building that story question by question. And I walked right into it.

Near the end, he asked: "As you sit here today, do you have the ability to pay to the defendants the unpaid debt of what you said in your bankruptcy — over $600,000 — to get the house back?"

I answered: "I could get a loan." A loan.

I said it without thinking. Because that's how everyone talks about mortgages. That's the word everyone uses. That's what I thought I had taken out in 2007 when I sat across from a broker in a restaurant and signed a stack of documents.

I didn't know — not yet, not in that moment on the stand — that my own contract defined it differently.

Section "H" of my deed of trust, the document I'd been fighting over for years, says this: "Loan means the debt evidenced by the Note."

Not money received. Not funds transferred. Debt. Evidenced by a note.

The distinction matters more than it sounds.

When you say you received a loan, you're confirming their entire framework. You're saying: I got something. They're owed something. This is a straightforward creditor-debtor relationship, and whatever happens with the documents is beside the point.

But that's not what the contract says. The contract says the loan is the debt. Not the cause of the debt. Not the origin of the debt. The debt itself, evidenced by a promissory note.

And if the note was bundled into a closed trust in 2007, locked there permanently under IRS rules governing real estate mortgage investment conduits, and legally incapable of being transferred out after the trust's closing date — then every subsequent assignment was a legal impossibility. Not just fraudulent. Structurally impossible. The debt didn't move because the debt couldn't move.

Which means when Mase asked if I could pay $600,000 to "get the house back," the correct answer wasn't "I could get a loan."

The correct answer was a question.

"Could you define what you mean by loan? My contract defines loan as debt evidenced by a note. If the court's definition differs from the contractual language, I'd need to understand that before answering."

That answer puts the framework back in dispute. It signals to the jury — and to the record — that the language being used isn't neutral. It requires Mase to either accept the contract's own definition or explain why the court should use a different one.

I didn't know that answer in April 2024. I know it now.

What Folke Didn't Do

I had asked him. Directly. Months before trial. Prepare me. Rehearse the questions. Walk me through what cross-examination would look like so I'd know what was coming and how to answer without walking into traps. He waved it off.

The projector I'd arranged — the one that would have shown the jury the forged signatures side by side with the official records, a visual that would have taken thirty seconds to understand — sat unused at the back of the courtroom. He'd driven to Los Angeles from San Diego the night before to pick it up. There was no time to set it up. The jury never saw it.

The subpoena for Nabeel Zuberi, the attorney in my unlawful detainer case — a witness who could have testified about the wrongful eviction — was served too late. Wrong process server. Witness fees not checked. A critical witness gone because of procedural failures that a competent attorney handles in his sleep.

When Judge Bacal couldn't read his handwriting in the jury instruction crisis — the moment that might have changed everything — she sent us back into a supply closet. He snapped at me to be quiet. I wrote the law out neatly. It didn't matter. This was the attorney I'd trusted with five years of evidence.

The David v. Goliath group had taught me how to fight. How to file. How to stand up in court and make arguments that at least one judge, in at least one proceeding, would have to take seriously. They'd given me the tools to build a case that a jury would later understand well enough to ask exactly the right question.

What they couldn't do was fix an attorney who'd stopped preparing.

Or protect a client who walked onto a witness stand without knowing that the word loan — the word she'd been using for seventeen years to describe what happened to her — had a different, precise, contractual meaning that would have changed the answer to the most dangerous question she was asked.

"I could get a loan."

Three words. And the jury watched a plaintiff who'd proven systematic fraud confirm, in passing, the entire framework the defense had built their case on.

Nobody told me I couldn't say that.

Nobody told me I had to say anything else.

Nobody prepared me for the trap built into the question.

What I Know Now

The David v. Goliath group mapped this problem long before I understood it fully.

When you sign a mortgage document, you are not entering into a simple borrowing relationship with a local bank. You are becoming a unit of production in a global capital pipeline. The moment you signed, your note was destined for a closed trust. The lender knew it. The broker knew it. The rating agencies knew it. The only party who didn't know it was you.

And that pipeline requires specific language — language embedded in your contract — to function.

"Loan means the debt evidenced by the Note."

Not money. Debt. The distinction is not semantic. It is structural.

When someone asks "did you receive a loan?" they are asking you to confirm their framework. They are asking you to say yes, I received something, and therefore someone is legitimately owed something, and therefore the question of who owns the debt is a matter of paperwork rather than a matter of standing.

The correct response is to put the definition in dispute before you answer.

"That's a tricky question. Could the court define 'loan' for purposes of this question? My contract defines loan as debt evidenced by a note — not as a transfer of funds. If the court's definition differs from the contractual language, I need to understand that before I can answer accurately."

That response does several things at once. It signals to the jury that language matters. It forces the court to either accept the contract's own definition or explain why it won't. And it prevents the opposing party from slipping a framework past you inside a question that sounds simple.

I also know now what I didn't know in that courtroom: that the note was locked in a closed trust from the moment it was securitized. That the trust's governing documents — the Pooling and Servicing Agreement — prohibited new assets from entering after the closing date. That every subsequent assignment was not just fraudulent in execution but impossible in structure. The IT employee signing as a MERS vice president wasn't just unauthorized. He was creating a document that could not have any legal effect regardless of who signed it, because the entity it purported to act for had already been legally extinguished.

A forged assignment of a legally impossible transfer. That is what they used to take my home. I spent years proving the forgery. I didn't yet know I also had the structural impossibility. I know it now.

And everything in this course — every statute, every case, every objection — is built on this foundation: they had no right to be in that courtroom. Not because of a technicality. Because the chain of authority they claimed never legally existed.

The End

Folke tried to ask if there was anything I wanted to add to my testimony.

Defense objected. "Calls for a narrative." Sustained.

He tried again. Same objection. Same ruling.

The jury came back. Cross-examination would begin after the break.

The Defense Responds: "Business Records"

Defense called their witness: Laura Ann Ollier, Second Assistant Vice President of Specialized Loan Servicing. She worked from Florida. Remotely. Had been with SLS for ten years handling "default litigation."

She'd never met me. Never spoken to me. Never dealt directly with any customer "until court." But she had reviewed "business records."

The Contradiction

Folke asked about Agnes Bradshaw's testimony the day before—that she hadn't signed the documents, that they weren't in her notary journal, that even the initials on the foreclosure checklist weren't hers.

Ollier's response: "I heard her say that she didn't have entries in her personal logs, but they were entries in our business logs."

She claimed Agnes had accessed an "electronic notary log" with a password. That the checklist showed Agnes's signature.

Folke pressed: "Isn't it true that in 2018 you didn't have an electronic system for Ms. Bradshaw to sign into?" "That is not true."

"So you're disputing what she said?"

"I am disputing what she said. I accessed it." **She accessed it.**

From Florida. Reviewing records about a Colorado notary's personal actions. Years after the fact.

Agnes Bradshaw had testified under oath—directly, unambiguously—that she never signed those documents. That her notary journal had no record. That the initials weren't even hers.

Laura Ollier, sitting in Florida reviewing "business records," contradicted her.

Not because she was there. Not because she witnessed the notarization. Not because she had any firsthand knowledge.

Because the business records said so.

The SLS Policy

Folke asked about SLS's policy: "Are you aware—is it your company's policy that before you will even entertain a modification or any forbearance that the person that is the borrower has to be past due 90 days?" "That's not a company policy, no."

"So it's your testimony that SLS does not tell and did not tell Ms. Hannonen that she had to be 90 days past due before they would consider her modification?"

"I don't have any record of that call or anybody telling her that, no."

No record in the business records = didn't happen.

My testimony under oath about being told to stop paying? Irrelevant. Not in the business records.

Near the end of cross-examination, the mask slipped. Folke asked: "Do you understand that this is a wrongful foreclosure case?" Ollier: "No."

"So you don't understand it's a wrongful foreclosure case?" "No. She didn't pay for years, and that's not wrongful—that's a rightful foreclosure."

Judge Bacal had to intervene: "Hold on. Slow down."

But the institutional mindset was clear: Who cares about forged documents? She didn't pay. That's all that matters. Forged notary signatures? Irrelevant.

Documents bearing signatures that the notaries themselves say they never made? Doesn't matter. A Colorado notary testifying under oath that she didn't sign, contradicted by a Florida employee reviewing "business records"? Business records win. She didn't pay for years. Rightful foreclosure.

Verdict

The jury trial ran April 2–5, 2024. It covered one narrow issue: wrongful foreclosure. Not fraud. Not cancellation of instruments. Just that sliver.

After four days of testimony, exhibits, expert analysis, and a notary's emotional confession about systematic forgery, Judge Bacal read the jury instructions.

The only thing standing between me and a clean win was whether the jury would hear the law that governs forged documents. Spoiler: they didn't.

They filed out to deliberate at 9:01 AM on Friday, April 5, 2024.

By 10:18 AM, we had our first note from the jury.

CHAPTER 26

The Question That Should Have Ended the Case

The jury asked the only question that mattered. Juror Number 5's question told the real story: *"Is there really a law in California that states if there is a forgery by the notary on a legal document, the document is no longer valid?"*

They understood that something fundamental had been proven. They understood that the signatures were forged. They understood that this should matter.

Now they wanted to know: What does that mean legally?

The Scramble

While the jury was deliberating, the judge summoned us to clarify the answer.

She told us to work with the other side to come up with a proper supplemental instruction. Then she'd decide whether to give it. The court recessed.

During the recess, she did her own research.

My attorney and I were herded into a cramped side room — barely larger than a supply closet — and told to write the law so it could be given to the jury.

He scribbled on a yellow legal pad. His handwriting was gigantic. Five lines per page, the size of road signs, yet completely unreadable.

I leaned over and said, calmly, "Let me write it so it's legible."

"I KNOW HOW THIS IS DONE," he snapped. "SHUT UP."

Fine.

We handed the note to the judge. She squinted. "What is this? I can't read any of it."

Back into the closet we went.

This time, I wrote it. Neatly, clearly. Statute, case law, controlling authority. No drama. Just the law that should have ended the case.

The Law vs. The Defense

I cited *OC Interior Services LLC v. Nationstar Mortgage*: "A forged document is void ab initio. Legally equivalent to a blank sheet of paper."

Judge Bacal found *Wutzke v. Bill Reid Painting Service, 151 Cal.App.3d 36, a 1984* California appellate decision cited under OC Interiors. **The rule is simple: If the law is applied, the foreclosure cannot stand. If the foreclosure stands, the law was not applied.**

A forged deed is void. Everything flowing from a forged deed is void.

This was exactly what the jury wanted to know. But there was a complication.

Defense counsel immediately argued that *Wutzke* didn't apply. They had their own cases:

Osterberg v. Osterberg (1945): "In California the acknowledgment of a deed is not essential to its validity."

Lewis v. Booth (1935): "Irrespective of the question of the propriety of the notary's conduct, an acknowledgment was not essential to the valid assignment of the deed of trust."

Both cases say the same thing: notarization isn't essential to deed validity. True. But irrelevant.

Osterberg and Lewis address private conveyances between parties who already know each other and have actual agreement. If I sell you my house and we both sign but forget to notarize, the deed is still valid between us because we actually agreed.

But that's not what this case was about. This case was about nonjudicial foreclosure—a creature of statute that bypasses the courts entirely. No judge reviews the evidence. No jury weighs the facts. The process is purely administrative.

And that statutory scheme has one absolute requirement: the foreclosing party must prove its interest through the recorded chain of title.

The recorded chain of title is the entire basis for nonjudicial foreclosure. If that recording is based on forged notarization, the foreclosing party has no standing—regardless of whether some private agreement might be "valid" in the abstract.

The defense's cases were answering the wrong question. Their question: Is notarization required for deed validity between parties?

The actual question: Can a party foreclose based on a fraudulently recorded assignment?

The answer to their question: No. The answer to the actual question: Absolutely not.

Judge Bacal noted the tension. She ordered both sides to prepare legible proposed instructions answering the jury's question. She'd review them, hear argument, and decide how to respond.

"I am not yet going to answer the jurors' question. I am going to ask each of you to prepare a legible proposed instruction answering the jurors' notes. And after you've done that, I'll take you back up here." The court recessed at 10:56 AM.

Too Late

We were still working on proposed instructions when the court received another note.

The jury had reached a verdict.

We walked back toward the courtroom. The bailiff stopped us.

"The jury has reached a verdict."

But—but—the law.

Too late.

Judge Bacal read the situation immediately: "If you recall, I told the jurors that while they wait for any response to any note, they should continue to deliberate. They continued to deliberate. As a result, I am going to be taking the verdict."

The legal question that could have changed everything would go unanswered.

Judge Bacal thanked the jury, released them from their obligations, told them they were free to discuss the case or not discuss it as they chose.

They filed out. U.S. Bank won.

I stood. "They didn't get the law. The jury asked and—"

My attorney said nothing. The judge closed the case.

What the Verdict Meant

The verdict form was structured around three defendants: U.S. Bank, Specialized Loan Servicing, and MERS.

For each defendant, Question 1 asked: "Did [Defendant] cause a foreclosure sale of plaintiff's home under a power of sale in a deed of trust?"

If the jury answered "yes," they would proceed to Question 2, which asked about whether I paid all amounts due and whether the foreclosure was therefore wrongful.

But if they answered "no" to Question 1, they were instructed to skip Question 2 and move to the next defendant. The jury answered "No" to Question 1 for all three defendants.

Unanimously. 12-0. So no other questions were answered.

***

The jury didn't say the forgeries didn't matter. They didn't say the evidence was insufficient. They didn't say Agnes Bradshaw was lying about her own forged signature. They didn't say Beth Chrisman's expert analysis was flawed.

They said the defendants didn't "cause" the foreclosure sale. And technically, they were right.

The trustee—Zieve, Brodnax and Steele, LLP—conducted the actual foreclosure sale. They were the entity that advertised the property, stood on the courthouse steps, and sold my home to the highest bidder.

U.S. Bank, SLS, and MERS hadn't personally conducted the sale. They'd directed it, authorized it, provided the documentation for it, and benefited from it. But they hadn't technically "caused" it in the narrow sense the question asked.

The verdict form's structure—requiring the jury to answer whether defendants "caused" the sale before they could address whether the sale was wrongful—had created a procedural off-ramp. The jury took it.

The jury never got to answer their real question. They never got to decide: If a notary's signature is forged on a deed, is the deed void? They never got to apply Wutzke's holding that forged deeds are void and everything flowing from them is void.

The difference between an unnotarized deed and a deed with forged notarization isn't technical. It's the difference between an incomplete document and a fraudulent one. It's the difference between a mistake and a crime.

But the jury never got to make that determination.

The system made sure they didn't have to.

What Was Protected

The jury's verdict did not protect a legal principle. The principle itself was straightforward—clear enough that jurors asked about it directly during deliberations.

What the verdict ultimately protected was institutional practice.

If forged notary signatures void foreclosure documents, the consequences would not stop with one property in Julian. Every foreclosure supported by documents notarized by Autumn Carnegie during the relevant period would require review. Every foreclosure bearing Agnes Bradshaw's stamp while she was employed at SLS would warrant scrutiny. Loan servicers would be forced to audit their document production systems. Title insurers would confront claims for insuring properties transferred through forged instruments. Purchasers at foreclosure sales would face uncertainty about whether they acquired valid title at all.

The stakes extended far beyond a single homeowner's dispute. They implicated the reliability of an industry's document infrastructure—the paperwork upon which billions of dollars in property transfers depend.

Institutional immunity does not require disproving fraud. It only requires limiting what fraud is allowed to do.

The Cost of Proof

By then I had spent years fighting this case pro se. I hired a handwriting expert. I tracked down notaries across state lines. I obtained official records from Pennsylvania. I compiled evidence of systematic fraud. I survived dozens of procedural challenges designed to dismiss the case before evidence could be presented.

I made it to trial.

And I proved forgery. Unequivocally.

The jury believed the evidence. They asked the right question. The answer existed. The law was settled.

Once the verdict was accepted, everything shifted. The question wasn't whether the documents were forged anymore. The question became whether undoing the result was worth the disruption.

It wasn't.

From that moment on, the case stopped being about evidence and started being about containment. How much recognition could be given without triggering consequences. How much could be said on the record while ensuring nothing actually changed.

That's when I understood the hierarchy:

Truth sits below procedure.

Procedure sits below outcomes.

Outcomes sit below system preservation.

***

The jury did their job. They asked the right question. The answer existed. The law was settled. The system simply ran out the clock before the answer could reach the room.

The Pattern

This case is not an outlier. Homeowners who push foreclosure cases far enough to develop real evidence tend to encounter the same sequence. Expert testimony confirms forged signatures. Robo-signed documents surface by the thousands. Notaries admit they never witnessed the signatures they notarized.

Then the second phase begins. Cases resolve through settlements without admissions of wrongdoing. Foreclosures proceed despite documented fraud. Courts rule that technical defects do not invalidate sales. Procedural barriers prevent evidence from reaching juries. Verdicts may acknowledge irregularities yet provide no remedy.

The pattern is consistent. The system is not malfunctioning. It is operating as designed.

CHAPTER 27

The Part Where Forgery Is Proven and Nothing Happens

Five weeks later we returned for the bench trial. This is where the rest of the case lived.

Cancellation of instruments. Quiet title. Statutory violations. This was the part where forged documents are supposed to matter.

***

May 20, 2024. Department 69. Judge Katherine Bacal presiding.

I sat quietly while my attorney shuffled papers. The courtroom was small, institutional, fluorescent. The kind of space designed to make you feel like your problems are trivial.

But the evidence wasn't trivial. We'd spent three years building a case that should have been airtight. Should have been. Expert witnesses. State-certified documents. Notary testimony under oath. Side-by-side signature comparisons. Official records from two state governments.

The forgery was documented, uncontroverted, on the record.

And now, finally, the court would have to decide what that meant.

The Bench Trial — May 20, 2024

The judge had all of this evidence before her. Certified state records. Expert testimony. Notary testimony under oath. Document after document showing the same pattern.

The defense had no rebuttal. They didn't challenge Beth Chrisman's credentials or methodology. They didn't produce Carnegie or explain the three-week gap in her notarial activity. They didn't contradict Bradshaw's testimony.

They just... said nothing. Because what could they say?

"Your Honor, we'd like to introduce evidence that Pennsylvania state records are wrong"?

"We'd like to call Autumn Carnegie to testify that she actually did notarize this document, despite state records showing she performed zero notarial acts that month"?

"We'd like to impeach Agnes Bradshaw's testimony that she didn't sign the document with her signature on it"? They had nothing. So they stayed silent and hoped the court would move past it.

The Finding

The judge started with praise.

"As an initial matter, I wanted to put on the record my appreciation for the hard work that the plaintiff — self-represented for a long time — put into this case. I know she worked very hard to get us to where we are today."

She paused. Looked at me. *"In fact — and I mean this hopefully no disrespect seen — but I believe there's a Finnish word that describes much of what Ms. Hannonen has done. Sisu. S-I-S-U. I think it describes Ms. Hannonen to a tee."*

Sisu. She was right. That untranslatable Finnish grit. Stubborn persistence through impossible odds. The refusal to quit even when quitting would be easier. I'd earned that word. I'd lived it for six years. And in that moment, I thought maybe — just maybe — it would be enough.

The court has a special talent for praising you while pushing you off a cliff.

Then she kept talking. "This Court is sitting as a court of equity. **The Court finds by the appropriate burden of proof that both the assignment of deed and trust and the substitution of trustees were not signed or notarized by the parties who said they did.**"

Read that sentence again. The court found the documents were not signed or notarized by the parties who said they did. Not "may not have been." Not "appeared questionable." Were not.

"I find the plaintiff's evidence compelling."

She had before her Agnes Bradshaw's sworn testimony that she never notarized the Substitution, Beth Chrisman's handwriting analysis eliminating Carnegie as a signer, Pennsylvania Secretary of State records confirming Carnegie performed zero notarial acts during the relevant window with no journal entry to account for the document, and a complete absence of rebuttal evidence from the defense. That Pennsylvania certification arrived in a plain envelope — one page that dismantled their entire case. It's in Appendix D and E. (Available at www.leenadesign.com/mybook-pdf)

The forgery was proven. Uncontroverted. Admitted into the record by judicial finding.

Then she said this: "The question is: What do I do now?"

That question hung in the courtroom like smoke. Because the answer should have been obvious. Under California law, forged documents are void ab initio — void from inception, conveying no title, authorizing no action, incapable of supporting a foreclosure. The California Supreme Court said so in *Yvanova v. New Century Mortgage Corp. (2016).* The appellate court said so in *Wutzke v. Bill Reid Painting Service (1984).* The law was settled. The facts were proven. The defense was silent.

You void the documents. You cancel the instruments. You restore title to the homeowner. But Judge Bacal didn't say that. Instead, she deferred. She scheduled a hearing on my motion for judgment notwithstanding the verdict for June 14, 2024. The forgery finding would sit in the record — acknowledged, unresolved — for three more weeks.

What Never Got Raised

I had argued the clean hands doctrine in my briefs. The principle is straightforward: a party who comes to court with unclean hands is barred from the equitable relief they seek. U.S. Bank relied on forged documents. Their hands were not clean, that left the forgeries intact.

The Ryan Firm had been on notice of the forgeries since 2020. They had Beth Chrisman's expert report, the Pennsylvania County Recorder certification, Agnes Bradshaw's deposition, and four years of my filings citing the forgery evidence. Four years to withdraw the fraudulent documents. They filed motions instead.

That's not negligence. That's a choice. And under clean hands, it should have been disqualifying — the party relying on fraud to foreclose should not be permitted to ask a court of equity for help enforcing that foreclosure.

I raised it. The court didn't address it. A judge has the authority to raise legal issues on her own initiative, without waiting for a party to argue them — particularly in equity cases where the court is supposed to be doing justice rather than just scoring procedural points. Judge Bacal didn't do that here.

Because if clean hands were enforced, the foreclosure collapses. Title reverts. And the court has to explain why it took six years of litigation to arrive at what the evidence showed from the beginning.

Equity was invoked. It just wasn't enforced.

The Defense's Silence

What made the hearing extraordinary was not what the defense argued, but what it declined to argue. Andrew Mace, counsel for the defendants, did not challenge forensic examiner Beth Chrisman's credentials or methodology. He did not dispute the certified Pennsylvania records establishing a three-week gap in Autumn Carnegie's notarial activity. He did not produce Carnegie to testify, nor did he call Mark McCloskey to state that he signed the document in Agnes Bradshaw's presence. He offered no evidence that the signatures were genuine and presented no alternative explanation for how the documents came into existence.

He just stood there and let the court acknowledge forgery without offering a single word of defense. Because there was no defense. All you can do is stay quiet and hope the court moves on. And it did.

The Six-Month Gap

What happened between May and November wasn't justice delayed — it was procedural fumbling.

After Judge Bacal's May 20th finding, Folke filed a motion for judgment notwithstanding the verdict — a JNOV, which asks the judge to override the jury's decision and enter a different outcome in favor of the moving party. It was the correct motion. The execution was not.

A JNOV in this context had a specific and powerful argument available: a judge sitting in equity functions as a thirteenth juror. When she finds — as Judge Bacal explicitly did — that fraud has been committed, she is not merely permitted to act, she is obligated to. The jury's verdict doesn't protect a fraudulent foreclosure from equitable relief. The judge had already said the forgeries were uncontroverted. She had the authority and the duty to act on that finding regardless of what the jury decided on the narrow question of who "caused" the sale.

Folke didn't make that argument. The JNOV was denied. And once it was denied, Judge Bacal had her procedural exit — she'd ruled, the motion had failed, and she wasn't going back.

The deadlines for other post-trial motions ran out while the JNOV was pending. By the time everything expired we were into September. Then October.

Finally, in November, the court issued an Order to Show Cause on its own initiative — asking the defendants to explain why the court shouldn't reconsider its judgment on the equitable causes of action given the uncontroverted evidence of forgery. The hearing was set for November 22, 2024. Six months after Judge Bacal first said she found my evidence compelling, we were back in court to hear her say it again.

Both transcripts are in Appendix F. Read them and see for yourself how a court acknowledges forgery while allowing a foreclosure to stand.

The Order to Show Cause — November 22, 2024

This time, the judge was done deferring. "I am inclined—my tentative remains as what's set forth in the order to show cause, that I am going to reconsider, on the Court's own motion, amending the judgment on the equitable causes of action."

She laid out her reasoning: "At the end of the day, **I am not going to be relying on the exogenous fraud. I am going to be relying simply on the Court's equitable powers.** And I cited to the maxims of jurisprudence, which I can't remember another instance of having done that. But it seems to me, at this point in time, **I cannot allow to have occur what it appears to the Court to have occurred.**"

She continued: "I'm not disagreeing that a fraud on the deed of trust by way of the notary does not set aside the deed of trust. That's why I've left untouched the jury's verdict. On the other hand, **I cannot let stand what appeared to the Court to be uncontradicted evidence** having to do with the notary."

There it was again: **uncontradicted evidence.**

She'd found it in May. She was confirming it now in November. The forgery was a fact. On the record. Twice. But she still wasn't voiding the documents.

Instead, she was exercising "equitable powers" under maxims of jurisprudence—ancient principles of fairness that allow courts to do justice when strict application of the law produces unjust results. In other words: *The law says forged documents are void, but I'm not going to void them. I'm going to use equity instead.*

The Defense's Last Stand

Matthew Aguirre tried one more time. "Your Honor, even if true that a notary signature is forged, in and of itself doesn't invalidate the document."

The judge cut him off. "Mr. Aguirre, I know that. **I'm not finding the document invalidated. I'm finding uncontradicted—the forgery.** I note uncontradicted evidence. And in particular, as I noted previously, **I found the plaintiff's handwriting expert compelling.** I found other statements by defendant not credible, and I don't know what else I can do."

Aguirre pushed back: "There was uncontroverted evidence at trial that the plaintiff hadn't paid her mortgage since 2012. The intent of the parties was to foreclose on the property because of this monetary default of several years. **Regardless of how the notarization occurred on those documents, plaintiff was subject to foreclosure.**"

Translation: *Yeah, we forged the paperwork, but you owed the money anyway, so what's the problem?*

The judge didn't buy it.

"This Court cannot let stand what appears to be a forgery by a defendant. The Court cannot let stand something that occurred in front of this Court—again, uncontradicted, the plaintiff's testimony that somebody testified in this very courtroom as to a fact that was untrue. I'm not going to let that stand."

She was talking about the defense witnesses who'd testified under oath that the documents were legitimate—while the court now had certified proof they were forged. Perjury. On the record. In her courtroom. And she wasn't going to ignore it.

The Verdict Doesn't Matter

Aguirre tried to hide behind the jury verdict. He argued that the jury had found no wrongful foreclosure, so the forgery was irrelevant. The judge shut that down immediately.

"That's why this ruling today has nothing to do with the jury's verdict. I am not reconsidering the jury's verdict. I am not reconsidering the motion for new trial, which was denied. I am not reconsidering any of that. It is only the Court's conclusion on the equitable causes of action that were tried to the Court. Okay?"

She separated the claims cleanly: the jury had decided whether the defendants committed wrongful foreclosure under California's statutory scheme, while she, sitting as the bench trial judge, was deciding the equitable claims — including unjust enrichment. The forgery evidence applied to the equitable claims. And on those claims, she was ready to rule.

"What Would You Have the Court Do?"

Aguirre argued that even if there was forgery, the remedy was "vastly disproportionate" to the harm. The judge asked him directly: "What would you have the Court do?"

Aguirre answered honestly: "Truthfully, nothing, your Honor."

Pause on that.

The defense's position was: *Yes, we used forged documents. Yes, someone testified falsely in your courtroom. Yes, the evidence is uncontradicted. But you should do nothing about it.*

The judge responded: "In other words, the fact that somebody did something that I've just told and outlined, and you have your record of that, and it's in the Court's minutes, the Court should sit on its thumbs and do nothing?"

Aguirre tried to minimize it: "It had no effect on anything that occurred. It was **an irregularity in the foreclosure proceedings** that incurred no prejudice towards the plaintiff. The property would be subject to foreclosure regardless."

An *irregularity.*

Forged notary signatures on two foundational foreclosure documents. Certified by two state governments. Testified to under oath by the notary herself. Proven by forensic handwriting analysis. That's what systemic fraud looks like when it's sanitized for court.

The Tentative Ruling

The judge granted the relief requested in her own Order to Show Cause.

"The Court grants its order to show cause as reconsidering its judgment on the equitable causes of action. I will issue a ruling, or it will be an amended judgment, either confirming the prior judgment or setting you out further for closing argument on the effect of the new ruling."

She'd reconsider the judgment. She'd use her equitable powers. She'd acknowledge—again—that the evidence of forgery was uncontradicted and compelling.

But she still wouldn't void the documents.

Because voiding them would mean admitting what everyone in that courtroom already knew: **The foreclosure was built on fraud. The system let it happen. And no one with the power to stop it did.**

The Implication

By November, the record said everything it needed to say. Forgery found. Evidence uncontroverted. Two foundational foreclosure documents void under California law. The judge had said so twice, on the record, with no rebuttal from the defense.

If those documents were void, U.S. Bank never had standing to foreclose, the trustee's deed was invalid, the eviction was wrongful, and every ruling in the defendants' favor would have to be vacated.

The system couldn't afford that. So forgery became manageable. Not because the law was unclear. **Because enforcing the law would require admitting the system failed.**

All court exchanges quoted in this book are taken directly from official transcripts. The complete transcripts are available at leenadesign.com/my-book-pdf.

CHAPTER 28

Procedure, The Only Thing That Counts

This is where my attorney became a liability. I had been clear from the beginning: nothing gets filed without my approval. Every motion. Every brief. Every filing. He filed anyway.

August 28, 2024 — Judgment Entered

On August 28, 2024, judgment was entered. U.S. Bank won everything. I got nothing. Procedurally perfect. Substantively wrong.

November 1, 2024 — The Denials

The minute order denying my JNOV and new trial motions came down November 1. Two failures, both my attorney's.

On the JNOV, he'd proven the forgery but hadn't completed the legal formula. In California, wrongful foreclosure requires addressing tender — whether I'd offered to pay the debt or was legally excused from doing so. He never argued it. The judge cited my own trial testimony against me: I'd said I didn't have the money to pay off the loan and would need to get another loan. Without tender, wrongful foreclosure fails even with proven forgery. The bank forged the documents. Expert testimony proved it. State records confirmed the notary couldn't have signed them. And I lost because I couldn't pay off the loan those forged documents had no legal authority to enforce.

The new trial motion failed even more simply. California Code of Civil Procedure § 659 requires a formal notice of intent to move for new trial — designating the grounds, stating whether the motion will be based on affidavits or court minutes. He never filed it. The judge cited Kabran v. Sharp Memorial Hospital: failure to comply is jurisdictional. Meaning the content doesn't matter, the evidence doesn't matter, the merits don't matter. No notice, no jurisdiction. Motion denied.

The Lipovsky Problem

Buried in the November 1 order was something new. The judge acknowledged that Jason Lipovsky — the man who had appeared on behalf of U.S. Bank in the unlawful detainer proceeding and signed the stipulation that resulted in my eviction — had misrepresented his authority. He wasn't a bank representative. He was a realtor. He'd appeared in court claiming authority he didn't have, and the court had entered judgment based on that representation without knowing it was false.

The judge called it what it was: fraud on the court. She cited the court's inherent authority to set aside or amend a judgment to protect the integrity of the litigation process.

This mattered enormously. The unlawful detainer — the eviction proceeding that physically removed me from my home — rested entirely on the assumption that the foreclosure was valid. If the foreclosure was void, the eviction was void. If the eviction was void on its own additional grounds — fraud on the court by a party who had no authority to appear — the entire chain collapsed independent of the forgery question.

The Subpoenas

In preparation for the November 22 OSC hearing, I tried to develop that evidence. Three subpoenas. Three doors. All slammed shut.

I subpoenaed the county recorder to establish chain of custody for the forged assignments. Quashed. I subpoenaed the audio and video from outside the courtroom where the unlawful detainer stipulation was supposedly signed — trying to prove I was never there, that my attorney had signed without my presence or authority. Quashed. I subpoenaed Nabeel Zuberi, the attorney who had verified the unlawful detainer complaint instead of the actual plaintiff, a procedural violation that should have invalidated the entire eviction case. Quashed.

Every one of them. Overly broad. Burdensome. Irrelevant. The substance never got considered because the procedure killed it first.

If even one had been granted, I could have proven the unlawful detainer was based on fraud. If the UD was reversed, the foreclosure would have been nullified — not just challenged, nullified. Every door closed before I could walk through it.

You can have proven forgery, state-certified records, expert testimony, a notary under oath saying that's not my signature, and a judge who found it all compelling. And still lose because your attorney didn't file a one-page notice, didn't argue one element of the cause of action, and combined two motions that should have been separate.

Procedure isn't a safeguard against injustice. In the right hands, it's a weapon.

CHAPTER 29

The Court Blinks — Briefly

Then something unusual happened. On its own motion, the court set an Order to Show Cause. Not because my attorney asked. Because the record was bad enough that the optics needed management.

November 22, 2024 — The OSC Hearing

At the OSC, Judge Bacal ordered defendants to file an amended judgment awarding me Cancellation of Instruments and a violation of Business & Professions Code § 17200. The court quietly admitting there was a problem. The amended judgment was filed. No one told me.

My attorney received the notice and did nothing. He wanted to be done. He wanted to get paid. He did not want to oppose a vague, toothless judgment that listed no specific instruments to be canceled and attached no consequences. I found out five days later when it appeared on the Register of Actions. I filed an opposition within ten days, then a motion for clarification. Denied.

The Statement of Decision Window

Here's one I learned too late. After a recorded judgment, you have fifteen days to request a statement of decision. Without that request, the judge isn't required to explain their reasoning — the judgment can simply appear with no obligation to connect findings to law. I didn't know. I thought the trial itself was the forum, that once I'd presented evidence and shown forgery on the record the judge would be required to address it in writing. She wasn't.

Without that request, the court's reasoning remained invisible. The judgment arrived like weather — unexplained, immovable, immune to appeal on factual grounds. My attorney didn't file it and didn't explain the consequence.

That window closed. I fired him in April 2025. He was disbarred shortly after. He still tried to claim nearly a million dollars in fees for the case he'd lost. Almost funny.

The Amended Judgment — Victory Without Teeth

The judgment said I won on two causes of action: Cancellation of Instruments and violation of Business & Professions Code § 17200. The court awarded me the value of the property at the date of the foreclosure sale, offset by unpaid mortgage payments. Property value: $420,146. Unpaid mortgage payments: $629,002. Net award: zero.

"Cancellation of Instruments" turned out not to mean cancellation at all. The judge declined to cancel any specific documents. She relied instead on an "equitable remedy" — a gesture that looked like relief on paper and amounted to nothing in practice. The judgment said I won. It said the bank violated the law through fraudulent, forged documents. It said instruments should be canceled. But it didn't say which instruments. It didn't order the County Recorder to remove anything. It didn't restore my title. A finding without force. Justice without teeth. (Appendix G)

The Capital One Bombshell

Back in February 2023, I had received a letter directly from Capital One, N.A., successor to Chevy Chase Bank. My attorney hadn't used it at trial. But now, looking at a judgment that offset the property value against unpaid mortgage payments supposedly owed to U.S. Bank, the letter became critical.

Capital One wrote: "Capital One hereby agrees and acknowledges that it has no interest in or pursuant to the Deed of Trust dated March 21, 2007, recorded against the property located at 3252 Pine Hills Road, Julian, California." The original lender — the bank that supposedly originated the loan and had the right to foreclose — said it had no interest in the Deed of Trust. It had assigned the interest away and couldn't say who currently held it.

Nobody knows who owns this loan. The chain of title wasn't just compromised — it was nonexistent. And yet U.S. Bank claimed the right to foreclose based on forged documents purporting to transfer an interest Capital One said it no longer had. The fidelity bond should have paid the loan in full. So who exactly was authorized to collect the $629,002 in unpaid mortgage payments the court used to offset my award? This is precisely the question a statement of decision would have forced the court to answer. *(Appendix H contains the full Capital One letter.)*

The Fidelity Problem

In January 2023, I called Fidelity National Title Company. The forged Substitution of Trustee listed them as "Requested by." Sierra Straw at their San Diego office told me Fidelity hadn't requested it — usually the bank does. Nobody could say who created the document or why Fidelity's name was on it. Notarized by Agnes Bradshaw, who testified she never notarized it. Signed by someone without authority. Recorded as legitimate.

After the amended judgment was recorded, I sent a formal demand letter to Kevin McCalley, Title Operations Manager at Fidelity National Title, laying out the court's findings and demanding that Fidelity update title records, file a notice of cancellation with the County Recorder, and issue a corrected title report showing clear title in my name. (Appendix I)

McCalley refused. The judgment didn't list each document by recording number. It was ambiguous about whether title reverted to me. I'd need an expungement order with specific numbers before he'd do anything. He also noted my "litigious nature." When I pointed out that his company's name was on a forged document and his own employee had confirmed Fidelity hadn't requested it, his tone shifted. He didn't like being accused of forgery.

The catch-22 was airtight. I filed a motion asking the court to specify which documents were canceled. Denied — the ruling was considered sufficient. Without clarification, no expungement order. Without the expungement order, no County Recorder action. Without the Recorder, no clean title report. Without clean title, no sale, no refinance, no proof of ownership. The amended judgment sat in the public record saying I'd won on Cancellation of Instruments. Nothing moved.

The Phantom Chain of Title

Here is what we now know. Chevy Chase Bank ceased to exist in 2009. Capital One, which assumed Chevy Chase Bank, has no interest in the Deed of Trust, assigned it away, and can't say who holds it now. Fidelity National Title, named on the Substitution of Trustee, didn't request the document and has no record of it. Agnes Bradshaw, the notary on the Substitution, testified under oath she never notarized it. U.S. Bank claims ownership through forged documents transferring an interest nobody can prove exists. The court acknowledged uncontroverted forgery, awarded Cancellation of Instruments, refused to specify which instruments, and awarded zero dollars after offsets. The County Recorder won't remove documents without a court order specifying recording numbers. Title companies won't issue clean title without an expungement order. Nobody holds the beneficial interest. Nobody requested the Substitution of Trustee. Nobody notarized the documents legitimately. And the foreclosure stands.

April 22, 2025 — Recording the Judgment Myself

The court wouldn't clarify. The County Recorder wouldn't act. Title companies wouldn't move. So I recorded the amended judgment myself on April 22, 2025, as Document No. 2025-0103635, with a cover sheet stating exactly what the court's vague language wouldn't: "Plaintiff Leena Hannonen was awarded Cancellation of Instruments as pleaded in the Second Amended Complaint, and Violation of California Business and Professions Code § 17200 due to fraudulent, forged documents." If the court wouldn't say it clearly, I would.

June 23, 2025 — Title Insurance Claim

On June 23, 2025, Chicago Title Insurance Company sent an acknowledgment letter. They'd received my notice of claim and assigned it to Clinton Summers for investigation. As of January 30, 2026, that investigation is still pending.

The Distinction Judge Bacal Made

Judge Bacal stated on the record that she was not ignoring the forgery. She acknowledged it, found the evidence compelling and uncontroverted, then granted an equitable remedy that allowed U.S. Bank to retain title anyway. Under the color of law, forgery can be acknowledged, admired for its inconvenience, and politely set aside so the transaction may proceed. Title obtained by fraud remains intact, provided the fraud is too expensive to unwind. The acknowledgment itself was the theater. A judge who ignored the forgery could be appealed. A judge who found it compelling, uncontroverted, and ultimately irrelevant was bulletproof.

CHAPTER 30

Appeal: How Poor You're Allowed to Be

I filed a motion for reconsideration. Denied. I filed a motion to amend judgment. Denied. I filed a motion to clarify judgment. Denied. Every motion was procedurally correct. Every filing was timely. None of it mattered. The court had spoken. The machine was done with me. Except I wasn't done with it.

The Bank Appeals First

On January 7, 2025, defendants filed their own petition for writ of mandate — appealing the amended judgment that acknowledged forgery and granted me two causes of action. They won everything. And still they appealed, because even a toothless judgment that canceled nothing and penalized no one was too much to leave on the record.

Their petition ran 48 pages with 1,200 pages of exhibits. The core argument: Judge Bacal had exceeded her authority by amending her own judgment using equitable powers without identifying inadvertence, clerical error, or extrinsic fraud. They argued the notary forgeries were irrelevant to the foreclosure's validity, that I had no standing to challenge robo-signing, and that forged notary signatures don't void recorded documents.

Their most creative argument was that since I had introduced the Assignment and Substitution as exhibits, I was the one who had submitted fraudulent documents to the court. The smoking guns of fraud became, in their telling, evidence of my wrongdoing. The Court of Appeal denied the writ in less than 24 hours. Filed January 7. Denied January 8. One sentence, three justices, no analysis. That tells you something about the quality of their legal position.

My Appeal

On April 17, 2025, I filed my own notice of appeal on three grounds. First, the jury never received an answer to their written question about whether forgery voids a document under California law — a mandatory duty the court failed to fulfill under binding precedent.

Second, the amended judgment found forgery and awarded Cancellation of Instruments without specifying which instruments, leaving the cloud on title intact and the foreclosure standing.

Third, Judge Bacal acknowledged the forgery, acknowledged the controlling law — Yvanova and Wutzke — and then declined to apply it. The distinction she refused to make is the heart of the case. A voidable instrument can be ratified and is subject to limitations periods. A void instrument — one executed through forgery — never legally existed. You cannot run a clock on nothing. The signer never signed. The notary never notarized. The document never happened. Calling it voidable rather than void requires pretending that something occurred when the court's own findings prove it did not. Inferior courts are not permitted to overrule decisions of higher courts. That's not discretion. That's defiance.

The Transcript Fee Trap

That's when I learned appellate access is conditional. Not on merit. On money.

I'd already paid roughly $1,000 for trial transcripts. The Court of Appeal wanted an additional $3,500 deposit. I have a fee waiver. It covers filing fees. Not transcripts. Apparently there are tiers of poverty.

After months of stonewalling, someone admitted the actual cost was around $250. The rest would be refunded if unused.

As of December 11, 2025, the fees are covered. May 1, 2026 we are still waiting for the transcripts. Five months. The hearing was recorded. The court reporter was certified. The transcript exists. What takes five months is not production — it's automated reformatting. What takes five months is will. The appeal will take another year, maybe two. I'll keep showing up, keep filing, keep citing the law they claim to follow. Not because I think one ruling fixes this. Because every motion, every brief, every hearing adds another page to a record that can't be erased.

CHAPTER 31

The Expungement

For all those years, I had one weapon left: the lis pendens. A lis pendens is public notice. It tells the world that title to a property is in dispute. It warns buyers, lenders, realtors—anyone who might touch the chain of title—that there's a live legal claim. It doesn't stop a sale outright, but it makes the property radioactive. No title company will insure it. No buyer will touch it. I recorded mine early. It sat on the property like a legal land mine. And it worked.

Every time U.S. Bank tried to sell my house—through auction, through realtors, through private trustees—I sent them the evidence. The forged notary signatures. The expert reports. The court transcripts showing the notary's testimony. I attached copies of the criminal statutes. I explained, calmly and precisely, that proceeding with a sale based on forged documents would make them co-conspirators. Accessories after the fact. Liable.

They backed off. Every time. Realtors pulled listings. Auction houses canceled sales. Title companies refused to touch it. For years, the lis pendens held the line.

The only public record acknowledging that something here wasn't right. Then Judge Bacal expunged it. While my appeal was pending. While title was still in dispute. While the very issue being appealed—forgery, standing, chain of title—remained unresolved.

Let me say that again, slower, for anyone who missed it: the judge removed public notice of a title dispute while the title was actively being disputed in appellate court.

Under California law, a lis pendens cannot be expunged during a pending appeal unless the court finds, by clear and convincing evidence, that the underlying claim has no probable validity.

Clear and convincing evidence.

I had: Expert testimony confirming forgery. The notary's sworn statement that her signature was forged. Capital One's written disclaimer of any interest in the deed. The court's own findings that the evidence was "compelling" and "uncontradicted". An appeal actively challenging the very judgment the bank was trying to enforce. And the judge found no probable validity?

September 12, 2025 — The Expungement Hearing

Department 63 At 11:15 a.m., the hearing began.

Judge Bacal's voice came through the speaker, measured and bureaucratic.

"I do have a request for appointment of court reporter, which I'm signing. The matter is being reported." Appearances were entered. Matthew Aguirre for U.S. Bank—appearing remotely again, despite my objections. Me, in propria persona, standing at counsel table with all of evidence that was about to stop mattering.

The judge's tentative was already written. She was inclined to grant the motion to expunge.

"I would assume Moving Party would submit on the tentative, at least with regards to the Motion to Expunge," she said. Aguirre's video froze. His internet cut out. He called in by phone.

Even Zoom was trying to give me more time to make my case. The court wasn't interested.

When he reconnected, the judge posed her question about fees—whether my fee waiver (I'm a disabled senior on fixed income) should prevent the bank from collecting attorney's fees if the motion was granted. Then she turned to me.

"Ms. Hannonen, you might not [submit on the tentative]. So I'll hear from you."

The Criminal Record

Before this hearing, I had done what the court wouldn't.

I filed criminal complaints with the San Diego Police Department, the FBI's Internet Crime Complaint Center, the San Diego District Attorney, and the California Attorney General — all in September 2025, all documenting the same evidence the court had called compelling and uncontradicted. Every agency acknowledged receipt.

I submitted the notary's testimony. Beth Chrisman's handwriting analysis. The court's own findings from the November 22, 2024 hearing acknowledging forgery.

None opened an investigation. The standard response: "Referred to appropriate division for review." Which means: filed and forgotten.

I brought printed copies to the hearing. I had them ready to submit. Physical evidence that I had done exactly what Judge Bacal kept saying I should do—report it to the authorities.

The judge knew about the complaints. They were referenced in my opposition papers. She didn't want to see them. Because the point wasn't whether the forgery was real. The point was whether it had been officially recognized through prosecution. No prosecution = no crime. Even when the judge herself had found the forgery "uncontradicted."

The Arguments

I objected in the strongest possible terms. "The Court fundamentally misinterprets what the forged document is under California law. There's a huge misunderstanding on the legal effect of a forgery. The tentative treats the forged notary acknowledgement as a mere evidentiary flaw, continuing to regard the title document as valid. This is a clear error." The judge interrupted.

"But there's no evidence of a stolen seal, at least of which I'm aware." "Well, as long as the notary did not sign the document, somebody used her seal." "Okay."

"It's either a duplicated seal or it's a stolen seal. And since it's not in her notary journals, she did not sign it." "And I made that finding at trial." "Right. So it cannot be a valid document."

"But that's the problem," the judge said. "The fact that a notary—if the notary were not necessary, and it doesn't appear it was—the fact that it was not on the document doesn't affect the validity of the document itself."

There it was. The forgery doesn't matter. Because the notary wasn't necessary. Or so they said.

Except—it was necessary. Under California Government Code § 27287 and Civil Code § 1170, a real property instrument cannot be recorded without a duly acknowledged notarization. That's a statutory prerequisite.

I said this.

"The California law is clear: For a real property instrument to be recorded, it is a statutory prerequisite. It must be duly acknowledged pursuant to Government Code 27287 and Civil Code 1170." "The only reason the forged Assignment and Substitution were accepted for recordation was that the recorder's mandate is purely administrative. The recorder must record anything with the notary seal, either if it's real or a fraud." The judge pivoted.

"But, Ms. Hannonen, in part what you're arguing is the issues that were argued in either one trial or the other or both, and those are issues at this point for the Court of Appeal. The question now is what do I do with the state of things as they are?" In other words: that's not my problem anymore.

"You cannot expunge the lis pendens because we are in appeal, and this—" "And give me some authority that—"

"And this—" "If you could just give me some authority that the Court could not grant the Motion to Expunge because there is a pending appeal." "Because there's fraud. By Wutzke versus Bill Reid." "Okay."

I pressed further. "If we look at what's the difference between the notary forged signature and forged document, if a notary forged the signature, then that means the notary worked in error in forging the signature of the person who knowledgeably signed the document. And that's—we don't have that. This is a case where somebody utilized a notary's signature and committed a crime." The judge redirected again. "Again, that was a trial issue." "And now you're on appeal."

There was one more argument on the record that belongs in the appellate file.

Under California Code of Civil Procedure § 2015.5, every declaration relied upon in a judicial proceeding must be signed under penalty of perjury. The defendants' declaration of compliance — the document certifying that their foreclosure followed proper procedure — was not. The California Supreme Court confirmed this requirement in Sweetwater Union High School District v. Gilbane Building Company (2019), 6 Cal.5th 931, 943:

every declaration in a judicial proceeding must conform to § 2015.5 to be admissible.

Without a properly executed declaration of compliance, their foreclosure evidence is incompetent hearsay. Without competent evidence of compliance, title was never duly perfected — which is stated on the face of the trustee's deed itself. You cannot take judicial notice of a trustee's deed that certifies title perfection while its own supporting declaration fails the statutory requirement for admissibility.

I said this.

The court had another matter. That argument belongs on appeal.

There is a word for what the judge did by refusing to call the document void. The word is voidable. By declining to find the forged instrument void, the court implicitly treated it as voidable — defective, but capable of being ratified. That is the wrong category. Wutzke v. Bill Reid is explicit: a forged document is void ab initio. Not irregular. Not defective. Void. It never existed. You cannot ratify a felony. Penal Code § 470 makes falsifying a notary acknowledgment a crime. A crime cannot cure itself through recording. The county stamp does not transform forgery into a legal instrument. It just makes the forgery official. The judge who found the forgery compelling and uncontroverted did not have discretion to then treat it as voidable. Wutzke already answered that question. She was bound by it.

That is the heart of the appeal.

The Crime That Isn't a Crime

I brought up the criminal nature of what had occurred. "This is not irregularity. This is a forgery. It's a crime. It's a felony. And under—" The judge cut in. "And if, in fact, there were a proven crime, a felony, and you had evidence of that, I would consider it. But right now, we have your allegations, which are different, and as far as I'm aware, no crime has been charged."

"The notary testimony doesn't mean anything? The handwriting expert testimony—" "It meant something to me." "Right."

"If you recall, I made a finding based on that testimony; it's in the Court's order. It made—it didn't make something to me, but it's not the same as the finding—a legal finding that somebody has been convicted of a felony or even charged with one."

So. The court acknowledges forgery. The court finds the evidence compelling. The court refuses to forward it to the DA. And because no prosecutor has charged anyone yet, the forgery—acknowledged on the record—doesn't count.

The trap had a name, even if the court wouldn't use it: circular dependency. No DA will charge without a court referral. The court won't refer without a charge. The forgery sits in the middle — proven, acknowledged, entered into the court's own order — going nowhere.

I had done exactly what the court kept suggesting. Filed complaints with the San Diego Police Department, the FBI, the San Diego DA, the California Attorney General. Brought printed confirmations to the hearing. The agencies acknowledged receipt. None opened an investigation. So by the court's own logic, the forgery — found compelling, found uncontradicted — didn't exist.

Then came the retreat.

"It meant something to me," the judge said.

Then, immediately: "It didn't make something to me, but it's not the same as the finding — a legal finding that somebody has been convicted of a felony or even charged with one."

Read that twice. It meant something. Then it didn't. In the space of one sentence, a judge caught himself at the edge of his own logic and pulled back. The finding was real enough to put in an order. Not real enough to carry consequences. Compelling enough to acknowledge. Not compelling enough to act on.

The forgery existed in legal superposition — simultaneously proven and irrelevant, depending on which question was being answered.

That stumble — "It meant something to me... it didn't make something to me" — is the color of law made audible. A judge in real time, on the record, retreating from the implication of his own words.

"The Court needs to forward this to the DA for their investigation," I said. "There was fraud. It was obvious there was fraud. A forged notarized instrument is not defective. It is void. The instrument has no legal effect. *Bill Reid versus Wutzke* and the Penal Code 470 confirms that. The Penal Code 470 even lists that if anybody falsifies the acknowledgement of a notary public, that is a felony. That's a crime."

"Again, if I had evidence that somebody has been charged with a crime, convicted of a crime, or anything like that, the Court would consider it. I don't have that. And you certainly are free to make any reports to anyone you believe should be taking those steps. But that's different than what I have right now." Translation: I see the problem. I agree it's a problem. I'm not going to do anything about it.

"This is unreal," I said. "This document should be void because of the—but the Court said already on the record that there was forgery. Isn't that admitting that it's fraud?" "Okay." Just—okay.

Equity Stripping

I warned the court about what would happen next.

"If the Court allows the expungement, I'm going to give a notice to the Court over the equity of stripping." The judge didn't understand. "I'm sorry?"

"Equity stripping." "I don't understand—"

"They are trying to sell the house under—way under value. Distribute the equity, my equity."

"And you certainly have the right to take whatever steps you believe are the next steps you want to take." In other words: not my problem.

I put it on the record anyway. They'd list the property below market value, sell it quickly to a connected buyer, and pocket the difference—leaving me with nothing.

"If this Court permits expungement under these circumstances, it is, frankly, becoming a participant in the ongoing fraud against me, given the Court's own forgery evidence findings as noticed in the 18 U.S.C. Section 4, Misprision of Felony, and 241 and 242, deprivation of and conspiracy against their rights." "This places a duty to report, not conceal, felonies affecting property rights. Further, if expungement proceeds, I will file the notice of the equity."

The judge moved on to fees.

The Moving Goalposts

By this point in the hearing, the pattern had become visible.

Every time a substantive argument landed, the subject changed.

I cited Wutzke. That was a trial issue. I raised the pending appeal. The court asked for authority that an appeal bars expungement. I cited Penal

Code 470 and the notary testimony. The court required a criminal conviction. I named the criminal complaints I'd already filed. The court said that was different. I raised equity stripping. The court didn't understand the term. I cited Misprision of Felony and 18 U.S.C. § 4. The court moved to fees.

Each argument was acknowledged just enough to appear considered, then redirected while a different standard appeared in its place. Prove forgery. Done. Now prove it through a conviction. Get a conviction. But the court won't refer it. Report it to authorities. Done. But they didn't charge anyone. Show me a charge.

This is not a court failing to understand the arguments. I know what that looks like. This was a court that understood them and needed them not to land. You can't win a game where the rules change after every point.

The Vexatious Litigant Threat

Then Aguirre went further. He wanted me declared a *vexatious litigant.*

The statute allows a court to deem someone vexatious if they file multiple meritless motions. Once you're declared vexatious, you're prohibited from filing anything else in the case—and you can't file any new cases until you've cleared the status by court order. It's a legal muzzle.

Aguirre listed my attempts to stop the sale as evidence: "Five or six ex partes trying to stay the private sale of the property, the TRO, the unlawful detainer appeals, emergency writs to the Court of Appeal... they all talk about the fact that the lis pendens clouds title." As if that were improper.

That was the point of the lis pendens. To cloud title. Because title was in dispute.

He argued I was abusing the system by filing motions to protect my property. The judge looked at him. Then at me. "She believes in her case." That was it. Five words. A small bone tossed from the bench. But it mattered.

It meant: This woman isn't filing frivolous motions. She's fighting for her house. There's a difference.

The Fee Waiver Argument

The statute says that if a lis pendens is expunged, the moving party is entitled to attorney's fees—unless there are exceptional circumstances that make imposing fees unjust.

I'm a disabled senior. I'm on fixed income. I have a fee waiver. The bank argued that allowing fee waivers to excuse attorney's fees would "encourage litigants to get fee waivers and then make any motions they wanted." Translation: Poor people shouldn't be allowed to defend themselves because they can't afford the consequences.

Aguirre's argument was clear: make an example of me. Impose fees I can't pay. Send a message to anyone else thinking about fighting foreclosure fraud.

The judge sided with me—partially. "Having heard from both parties, I am going to confirm the tentative granting the Motion to Expunge, but I am not going to impose fees at this time."

She explained: "Although I did not find that her claim has probable validity, I think it supports her argument that imposing an order of fees, including the fact of her fee waivers, would be unjust. And so for that reason, I do not impose fees." Small mercy.

She didn't declare me vexatious. She didn't impose fees. But the lis pendens was gone. And without it, I had no protection.

At the end, I said it. 'My final note—' The judge interrupted. 'Well, both of you want a final note.' 'Yes. Remember the word "sisu"?' 'I do remember the word.' 'Yes. That's me. I'm not done.'

The judge explained to Aguirre: 'Just so you know, Mr. Aguirre, "sisu" means or—something along the lines of "intestinal fortitude"—and there's no doubt that Ms. Hannonen has that.'

Sisu—the Finnish concept of relentless endurance—was something I'd inherited but never named until this fight required it. She'd praised it when I was winning equitable claims—when the court's findings supported cancellation of instruments and acknowledgment of fraud.

Now she invoked it to explain why I didn't need the lis pendens. Why I could handle whatever came next. Why my 'intestinal fortitude' meant the court didn't have to protect me.

"The tentative order says here that the U.S. Bank has shown it is a party of interest in the real property. How did they prove that?"

The court's response: "You'll take that up on your next steps."

That question goes to the heart of the entire case — standing, chain of title, the forged assignment that was supposed to establish their interest. I caught a logical flaw in the tentative order itself, on the record, in the last sixty seconds of the hearing. The court's answer was effectively: not here, not now, not my problem.

Sisu had become the reason I didn't deserve relief. The hearing ended at 11:37 a.m. The lis pendens was expunged.

Minute Order

The minute order expunging the lis pendens is a masterpiece of circular logic. (Appendix J includes the minue order and the court transcript)

Judge Bacal wrote: "Hannonen has not met her burden... None of these arguments or evidence are convincing to show that the appellate court would more likely than not reverse this court's judgment awarding plaintiff the monetary value of property under the equitable causes of action." Read that carefully.

She awarded me the "monetary value" of my property—an award I never requested, never wanted, and which she has never actually paid—then used that phantom award as proof that I have no valid claim to the actual property.

So I won. Sort of. In theory. In a way that gives me nothing and costs me everything.

And because I won this thing I didn't ask for; I've lost standing to argue I should've won what I actually sued for. It's like being handed Monopoly money after someone steals your house, then being told you can't complain because technically you got paid.

The best part? She didn't request supplemental briefing. My reply brief—the one addressing the bank's motion—was filed exactly when she told me to file it. She decided not to read it. "Hannonen's supplemental briefing thus will not be considered." Not supplemental. Just my response. The thing you're supposed to file when someone asks a court to take away your last remaining protection. But why let facts get in the way of a clean ruling?

The Appeals

I filed an emergency motion for reconsideration. Denied. I filed a Writ of Mandate with the Court of Appeal, asking them to order the trial court to restore the lis pendens. The law was clear: you cannot expunge notice of a title dispute while the title is still being disputed.

The Court of Appeal denied it without explanation. Read and considered. That's all it said.

I filed a Writ of Supersedeas—an emergency request to stay enforcement of the trial court's judgment while my appeal was pending. Under California Rules of Court, a judgment cannot be enforced while an appeal challenging it is active. Denied. Read and considered.

I filed a Petition for Review with the California Supreme Court. I cited Yvanova. I cited Wutzke. I explained that the appellate court was allowing a foreclosure sale to proceed based on admittedly forged documents while my appeal of those exact forgeries was pending. Denied. Read and considered.

Three courts. Three denials. Zero explanations. Apparently "read and considered" is judicial shorthand for "we skimmed it and don't care."

How is that even possible?

How can an appellate court—whose entire job is to review errors of law—allow a trial judge to expunge a lis pendens before the appeal is over? The title is still in dispute. That's what an appeal is. The public has a right to notice. That's what a lis pendens does.

But the system had decided. The house could be sold. The appeal could continue—technically, ceremonially, like a wake for justice—but the property itself was fair game.

The courts had turned my appeal into performance art. I could keep filing. Keep arguing. Keep citing statutes that supposedly mattered. Just don't expect anyone to actually stop the sale.

The Expungement That Never Happened

The minute order was filed September 12, 2025.

Judge Bacal granted the motion to expunge the lis pendens. The order was clear. The appeals were denied. The bank had legal authority to remove the public notice and clear the path to sale.

And then... nothing. As of May 2026—eight months after the expungement was granted—the lis pendens remains on the public record. They haven't executed the order. I don't know why.

What Changed

The property was listed for a year. Then it went "off market" sometime in late 2025. Between the expungement order in September and now, two things happened:

December 15, 2025 — I sent formal notice to the realtor and the bank's attorney. I laid it out plainly: The appeal is pending. The trial court found "uncontradicted" evidence of forgery. Criminal complaints are on file with the FBI, the San Diego DA, and the Attorney General. The amended judgment acknowledged "fraudulent, forged documents."

Under California Civil Code §§ 1102 et seq., they are required to disclose these material facts to any prospective buyer. Failure to disclose exposes them—personally—to liability for misrepresentation, rescission, and damages if the sale proceeds and my appeal succeeds.

I demanded written confirmation that no sale would proceed without full disclosure and that they would provide details of any current offers. I cited *Peery v. Superior Court (1981)*: real property claims are protected during appeal. I made it clear: proceed at your own risk. (Appendix K)

December 23, 2025 — I sent the letter to Governor Newsom. Not because I thought he'd answer. Not because I believed in rescue. But because the system had finally made its position explicit:

Forgery can be proven, acknowledged, and ignored—and the courts will actively assist in the cover-up by erasing public notice while the victim is still fighting. I documented everything. The uncontroverted forgery. The trial court's acknowledgment followed by refusal to void the documents. The lis pendens expungement during a pending appeal. The appellate courts' denials without explanation. The violated precedents.

I cited the California Constitution. I requested investigation, oversight, legislative reform, and an emergency stay. By then I had years of proving fraud inside a system designed to ignore it, laid out in formal record. The letter remains unanswered. But it's logged. Public. Part of the record. (Appendix L)

The Waiting

I don't know which one worked. Maybe it was the formal notice—the explicit warning that selling this property with its documented history would create personal liability for everyone involved. Maybe it was the letter to the Governor—unanswered but creating another layer of public documentation. Maybe it was the criminal complaints filed with multiple agencies, sitting in their systems, making any sale a potential trigger for renewed scrutiny. Maybe it was the sheer volume of evidence now sitting in multiple jurisdictions—trial transcripts, appellate filings, state records, expert reports, notary testimony—making this house too legally radioactive to touch. Maybe it was the pending appeal itself, with the possibility (however remote) that an appellate court might actually read Wutzke and Yvanova and decide forged documents are supposed to be void.

Or maybe they're just waiting for a different moment. Waiting for the appeal to be denied. Waiting for me to run out of time or money or energy. Waiting for the public record to fade into bureaucratic obscurity. I don't know.

But I know this: they have legal authority to remove the lis pendens. The expungement was granted September 2025, months ago. They could execute it tomorrow and clear the way to sale. They haven't. The property remains off-market. The lis pendens remains on record. And for the first time in years, nothing is moving forward. Not reversed. Not corrected. Not resolved. Just... stopped.

The Story Continues

The appeal is still pending. The briefing is underway. The lis pendens—granted expungement but not executed—sits in legal limbo. Technically vulnerable. Functionally intact.

The house that was supposed to be sold years ago remains unsold. The foreclosure that was supposed to be final remains contested. And I'm still here.

Not because the system worked. Because something—I don't know what—made them stop.

For years of throwing everything I had at an immovable machine. Motions, evidence, statutes, precedents, criminal complaints, public records, formal notices, letters to governors.

Somewhere in that pile of documentation, something made them hesitate. Maybe it was the legal liability. Maybe it was the public exposure. Maybe it was the sheer stubbornness of one Finnish woman who refused to let forgery be called "irregularity."

Or maybe they're just regrouping. Waiting. Planning the next move.

But for the first time since 2018, I'm not the only one waiting to see what happens next.

CHAPTER 32

Court Is Theater

Early in the litigation, I filed a motion to compel discovery. The bank had refused to produce the original promissory note. Under the law they were required to. Without the note they couldn't prove standing. Without standing the case should have been dismissed. I cited controlling authority, attached exhibits, followed every procedural rule I could find.

I believed that mattered — that if you did the work carefully enough, someone would have to engage with it.

Judge Bacal didn't look at the exhibits. "The bank has already submitted a declaration stating they have complied with the requirements. The Trustee's Deed Upon Sale has been filed. All requirements have been complied with."

"Your Honor, a declaration not signed under penalty of perjury is legally defective. Under Kulshresha v. First Union Commercial Corp., it fails California Code of Civil Procedure section 2015.5—"

"I'm familiar with Kulshresha. Your motion is denied."

It happened quickly. Faster than the time it took to prepare it.

The bank's attorney smiled. Not cruelly. Professionally. The smile of someone who knows the ruling before the hearing begins. The law was clear. The defect undisputed. No one had sworn to anything. The court wasn't mistaken. It was choosing what to address. Stopping to enforce the statute would have required unwinding paperwork, questioning standing, reopening facts the system prefers settled.

That's the part you don't understand until you see it. The outcome isn't built in the hearing. It arrives with it. Deadlines. Formatting. Whether requests were grouped correctly. Whether notice had been given with the right number of days. The ruling moved through those issues in detail, acknowledged defects, overlooked some, enforced others, and stopped there.

The underlying question—whether the bank had to produce the note, whether the declaration met statutory requirements—was never addressed.

That's how it works. You don't lose because you're wrong. You lose because the system decides what it will consider, and what it won't.

The Declaration of Compliance drove the point home. California Civil Code § 2923.55 requires this document as a gatekeeper — without it, a foreclosure cannot legally proceed. It was signed by Ami McKernan, Second Assistant Vice President of Specialized Loan Servicing, with a neat checkmark next to the statement that the servicer had exercised due diligence to contact me, assess my financial situation, and explore alternatives to foreclosure. None of it happened. Not partially. Not imperfectly. Not at all.

The declaration was not signed under penalty of perjury. Which makes it hearsay — not evidence, not testimony, just a piece of paper asserting compliance while carefully avoiding any legal consequence for lying about it. Ami knew better. If she had signed under penalty of perjury, she would have been committing perjury. So she didn't. The document performs compliance without risking truth. And the court accepted it anyway.

Under California law that defect alone should have voided the foreclosure. It didn't. The box was checked. The system moved on.

My filings were rejected for formatting errors, wrong typefaces, exhibits attached incorrectly. Fatal procedural defects. The bank's declarations floated through without penalty of perjury clauses, signed by people who took great care not to swear to anything at all.

It wasn't subtle. That's what made it hard to ignore.

Precision was demanded of me. None was required of them.

Once you see it, you can't unsee it. And once I stopped mistaking the choreography for justice, I stopped playing my assigned role.

I needed to serve a subpoena on Nabeel Zuberi—the attorney who illegally verified the unlawful detainer complaint against me. Under California law, only a plaintiff can verify their own complaint. An attorney verifying on behalf of their client violates Code of Civil Procedure § 446. Zuberi had done it anyway.

His law firm, McCalla Raymer, occupies the 11th floor of an office building in Long Beach. Marble lobby. Harbor views. The kind of place that signals success. I arrived with a witness to serve the subpoena. Building security stopped us at the front desk.

"ID, please." They didn't just glance at my driver's license. They scanned it. Front and back. Into their system. "Who are you here to see?" "McCalla Raymer." "What's the reason for your visit?" I smiled politely. "Legal business." "I need a specific reason." None of your business, really. But I didn't say that. I just repeated: "Legal business with McCalla Raymer." After some back-and-forth, they let us into the elevator. We reached the 11th floor.

The receptionist sat behind a solid wall. She didn't open the door. She used the intercom. "Can I help you?"

"I'm here to serve a subpoena on Nabeel Zuberi." "We don't accept service here." I looked at the sign taped to the glass: *"Service is not accepted here. You can find out the name of our agent for service at the website of the California Secretary of State."*

I stared at the sign. This is a law firm. A firm whose entire business model involves serving legal documents on other people. And they won't accept service at their own office. "So I'm standing at your door," I said slowly, "but I can't serve you here?" "That's correct. You need to serve our agent." "And where is your agent?" "You can look it up on the Secretary of State website."

I looked at my witness. She looked at me. We were standing at the law firm's office. In Long Beach. Talking to a receptionist who wouldn't open the door. And I was being told I had to serve a company in Sacramento.

The Professional Process Server

Fine. I hired a professional process server. Process servers do this for a living. They know how to get past receptionists, building security, locked doors. The process server came back empty-handed.

"They wouldn't let me in," he said. "Same thing. Sign on the door. Agent for service in Sacramento." So I looked up the agent for service on the Secretary of State website.

It was a registered agent company. A P.O. box. A business whose sole purpose is to accept service on behalf of other businesses so those businesses never have to deal with unpleasant things like subpoenas. I served the agent in Sacramento. For a law firm in Long Beach. Where I'd been standing at their door. Make that make sense.

August 18, 2025 — Order to Show Cause, Department C-63

Judge Katherine Bacal had set an Order to Show Cause to determine whether the unlawful detainer judgment should be vacated due to fraud.

The question was simple: Did Jason Lipovsky have authority to sign the stipulation that ended my eviction case? The court had already acknowledged there was no written Power of Attorney. But he testified anyway.

Matthew Aguirre appeared for U.S. Bank. I objected immediately.

"I'm objecting to Mr. Aguirre being here because Nabeel Zuberi verified the UD complaint, and I subpoenaed him."

"I don't believe you have the power to issue subpoenas," the judge said. "Only a party can." "But the Court said last hearing that if I wanted anyone else to appear, I had to subpoena them." Pause.

"Okay," the court said. Just "okay." I explained that Zuberi had sent me an email stating he no longer represented U.S. Bank. "There is no association," I said. "Zuberi had no right to associate anyone in because he was no longer part of the case." "All right. But I don't have any statement—I don't have any evidence to that effect."

"There's an email in my exhibits," I said. "You have the binder that I sent out. It's all tabbed. Tab number 2." Silence. Then: "All right. Now I do." The email was acknowledged. Then ignored. Aguirre stayed. Zuberi never appeared. No substitution of counsel was ever filed.

Jason Lipovsky Takes the Stand

Jason Lipovsky was called. The court had already acknowledged there was no Power of Attorney. He testified anyway.

On cross, I stayed precise. "What documents did you show Mr. Coombs that you were authorized to sign the stipulation?" "I did not show him documents."

"Were you authorized to sign?" "Yes." "I don't see a contract authorizing litigation. I see one authorizing sale." "That's afield of this OSC," the court said.

I asked the question that mattered. "After signing the document, did you come inside and testify under penalty of perjury that you represented U.S. Bank—and under what authority?"

"No." Correct. Because he didn't come inside. He signed in the hallway. Outside the courtroom. Away from the record.

Robert Coombs Takes the Stand

Then Coombs testified. The judge asked him directly. "Did you have a written Power of Attorney from U.S. Bank?" No.

"Did you have written authorization from Jason Lipovsky?" No. The answers sat there. On the record. Unmoved.

I asked: "And who did you speak with to conclude that Mr. Lipovsky was the Bank's authorized representative?" "A representative from the attorney of record, Mr. Kyle Dillon."

"Kyle Dillon was not the attorney on record," I said. "Kyle Dillon is an office manager." The judge rephrased it as testimony rather than questioning.

"Was it your understanding that Mr. Dillon was employed by that law firm?" "Yes. It's my understanding he was not an attorney at that law firm, but he was in charge of the eviction department." So. An office manager, not an attorney. Authorized a stipulation, for a bank.

In a court proceeding, and this was considered—fine.

The Ruling

At the end, Judge Bacal spoke. "I've read and considered the filings. I am at this time going to discharge the order to show cause, the Court having concluded that there was no fraud on this court." Denied.

The court acknowledged: No written Power of Attorney existed. Authorization came from an office manager, not an attorney. The signature was obtained outside the courtroom, off the record. The verification of the complaint violated statutory requirements

And yet: "No fraud." Because fraud requires intent. And intent is hard to prove when institutions are involved.

CHAPTER 33

What I Would Tell Someone Starting This Fight

Eight hundred twenty-two docket entries. It doesn't feel like that while you're in it. It feels like one deadline at a time. One filing. One hearing you think might be the one where it finally makes sense. Sixty-four hearings. Seven years. If you're starting this fight, here's what I learned too late.

Learn the script — not how to be right, but how to speak in court. The phrasing, the procedures that act as gates, the codes and statutes you can use against them. Learn the court rules: the 15-day windows, the notice requirements, the format specifications that can get a filing rejected for the wrong font size. These aren't technicalities. They're the terrain. Most people don't realize that until it's too late. You can be right and still be excluded from the conversation if you don't know how to enter it properly. That's the part no one tells you at the beginning.

But here's where the case is actually won: discovery. This is not optional, not secondary. This is the entire fight.

Make them produce the original promissory note — not a copy, the original with wet-ink signatures. Make them verify who signed the assignment and under what authority. Make them prove chain of custody from origination through securitization to foreclosure. Make them identify every person who handled the documents and every entity that claimed ownership. Make them answer under oath, in writing, before trial begins. If it's not in discovery, it effectively doesn't exist. By the time you're standing in front of a judge, the record is already set.

File motions to compel when they refuse — and they will refuse, object to everything, claim documents don't exist. Force them to respond. Force them on the record. This is where most people lose without realizing it. They assume the hearing is where truth gets sorted out. It isn't. By then, the shape of the case has already been decided.

Discovery is where they're vulnerable. It's where contradictions become permanent, where standing falls apart, where they have to produce evidence or admit they don't have it. Or where they don't produce it—and nothing happens unless you force it to. Hold them accountable before the courtroom script begins — before a judge can wave away evidence as already litigated, before procedure replaces substance.

Two other things I learned the hard way: request a statement of decision within fifteen days after a bench trial, or the judge isn't required to explain their reasoning. And if you hire an attorney, watch them. If they stop preparing, fire them before they destroy your case with procedural errors you'll spend years trying to recover from.

Damage in litigation doesn't look dramatic when it happens. It looks like a missed deadline. A poorly framed motion. Something small that becomes irreversible. Waiting to see if it improves is how damage becomes permanent.

The case can be won at the beginning. But only if discovery is done correctly, and only if you understand that procedure isn't a safeguard. It's a weapon. I believed evidence was enough. That's what cost me. It isn't.

Learn to object. Not occasionally—consistently. If something is improper, incomplete, or unsupported, you say it. On the record. In the moment.

Most people hesitate. They don't want to interrupt. They assume the judge will catch it, or that it doesn't matter. It does. If you don't object, it's treated as accepted. Silence becomes agreement. Make sure you have a court reporter. Without one, the courtroom is effectively silent. What happens there exists only in memory, and memory doesn't win appeals.

Your mindset should be that you're building the record from day one. Not just for the hearing in front of you, but for the one that comes after it. Appeals don't reconsider feelings. They review transcripts. If it's not on the record, it didn't happen.

And the presence of a record changes behavior. People are more careful when they know their words are being preserved. Not perfect—but better. The room tightens. Things that might be said casually get said more precisely.

You're not just participating in the hearing. You're documenting it.

And if the judge starts asking questions that support the opposing side, pay attention. That's not neutral. That's intervention.

You object. Respectfully, clearly, on the record: "Your Honor, is the Court taking on the role of counsel?"

Because there are limits. Not flexible ones—structural ones.

A judge cannot testify. A judge cannot practice law from the bench. A judge cannot ask discovery questions on behalf of one party. These are not technicalities. They're boundaries.

The judge is the trier of fact—not the builder of the case. Their role is to evaluate what's presented, not to repair what's missing. Not to fill gaps. Not to guide one side toward a better argument.

And it doesn't always look dramatic when it happens. It can sound like a simple question. A clarification. Something that feels harmless in the moment. It isn't.

Because every question shapes the record. And when those questions only move in one direction, so does the outcome.

If you don't object, it becomes part of the process.

If you do object, it becomes part of the record.

That distinction matters later—when someone else is reading what happened instead of watching it.

CHAPTER 34

Collateral Damage

The case didn't just take time. It took things it never acknowledged touching.

Waiting erodes certainty. Slowly. Quietly. You don't notice it at first. You just stop sleeping well. Your body stays alert even when nothing is happening. Adrenaline becomes the background noise of your life.

My tolerance dropped to zero. Not figuratively. Zero.

Everything felt like an intrusion. Noise. Questions. Small talk. Any hint of bullshit. I snapped at things that didn't deserve it and people who didn't cause it. I wasn't looking for conflict, but I had no buffer left to absorb anything that wasn't strictly necessary.

Concentration disappeared. Entirely. I could read the same sentence ten times and retain none of it. Memory went with it—short-term, especially. New information wouldn't stick. Dates, names, instructions, conversations—gone almost immediately. I wrote everything down and still lost track. My brain wasn't broken; it was overloaded past capacity.

That's what prolonged stress does. It doesn't make you dramatic. It makes you unavailable.

***

My health paid early. High blood pressure. Muscles so tight they started cracking. My neck locked up, pulled my spine out of alignment, and sent pain shooting through my back hard enough that I ended up in the ER, afraid something was wrong with my kidneys. It wasn't. It was stress. Pure, unrelenting stress, stored in places no filing system reaches.

I gained weight from sitting and typing sixteen hours a day. From living in a chair. From existing in documents instead of rooms. Motion narrowed. Days flattened. The body keeps score whether you want it to or not.

Sleep became a negotiation. So did eating. So did joy.

The Erosion You Don't See Coming

There's a specific kind of exhaustion that comes from fighting institutional power while representing yourself. It's not the tiredness of hard work. It's the tiredness of being your own paralegal, your own researcher, your own strategist, your own support system—while also trying to remain a functional human being.

Every hearing required preparation that started days before. Reading case law. Drafting arguments. Anticipating objections. Printing exhibits. Organizing binders. Checking court rules for format requirements that could get your entire filing rejected for the wrong margins.

Then the hearing itself. Standing in front of a judge. Delivering arguments while opposing counsel—attorneys with decades of experience, with teams behind them—watched for any procedural misstep they could exploit.

Then the aftermath. Win or lose, there was always another deadline. Another motion. Another response due in 15 days, 10 days, sometimes 5.

The case never stopped moving. And I never stopped having to move with it. Sixteen-hour days became normal. Then eighteen. Sleep compressed into whatever hours the body would tolerate before the mind started running again—cycling through arguments, replaying hearings, second-guessing decisions, preparing for what was coming next.

I would wake at 3 AM with a realization: I'd cited the wrong subsection. Or I'd forgotten to include a critical exhibit. Or I'd missed a procedural nuance that might give them an opening.

The body adapted by not adapting. It stayed in fight mode. Cortisol became my baseline. My nervous system stopped distinguishing between actual threat and anticipated threat, so it treated everything as immediate.

When Your Own Attorney Becomes Another Obstacle

For five years, I fought pro se. I learned the rules, filed the motions, stood in court alone. I built the case piece by piece—discovered the additional forged documents, compiled the evidence, found the expert witnesses.

Then, finally, I found an attorney willing to take the case.

I thought that meant relief. Someone with credentials. Someone the court would listen to. Someone who could translate my evidence into the language judges actually hear.

It meant something else entirely. It meant watching everything I'd built start to crumble in slow motion while I had no power to stop it.

What the Mirror Showed

I stopped recognizing myself in phases.

First, physically. The weight came gradually, then all at once. Sitting, typing, eating whatever required the least effort. Fast food. Takeout. Things I could eat while reading case law, while drafting motions, while my attention remained split between the page and the deadline.

Movement became something I used to think about. Exercise was something other people had time for. My world shrank to the dimensions of my workspace—a desk, a chair, a laptop, stacks of paper that grew taller while my mobility grew smaller.

The neck pain started as tension. Tight shoulders. The kind of thing you tell yourself will go away once the stress passes. But stress doesn't pass when the case doesn't end. The tension became chronic. Muscles seized. My spine pulled out of alignment. One morning I woke up and couldn't turn my head. The pain radiated down my back, sharp and insistent, until I couldn't tell anymore if it was muscular or something worse.

The ER visit was surreal. Lying on a table while a doctor asked about my kidneys, my liver, anything that might explain pain that severe. Tests came back normal. Nothing wrong with my organs. "It's stress," the doctor said. As if that made it less real. As if stress isn't a thing the body stores when the mind has nowhere else to put it.

Then there was my face. I caught my reflection one day—really looked—and saw someone I didn't quite know. Older, harder, tired in a way that sleep wouldn't fix. Eyes that had seen too many courtrooms. A jaw that stayed clenched even when I told it to relax. I looked like someone in a fight. Because I was.

Relationships and the Slow Fade

Relationships didn't explode. They thinned. That's worse.

There's a specific loneliness that comes from being legally right and socially radioactive. People don't argue with you. They drift. The case is too long, too technical, too uncomfortable. Small talk keeps happening around you, and you're suddenly aware you don't know how to join in. For years, my vocabulary had been statutes and exhibits. Neither the case nor I belonged in casual conversation.

Friends stopped asking how the case was going. Not because they didn't care, but because the answer was always the same: ongoing. Complicated. Still fighting.

At some point, the question itself became a weight no one wanted to lift. I understood. I didn't blame them. The case consumed me, but it didn't have to consume everyone else. They had lives that moved forward. Jobs. Relationships. Plans that didn't hinge on court dates.

I lived in a different timeline. One measured in filings and hearings and procedural windows. One where victory wasn't about winning, but about surviving long enough to file the next motion. That's not a timeline other people can inhabit. So they stopped trying. And I stopped expecting them to.

The Conversation That Ended

I told someone I loved to go away. Not in anger. In triage.

The case took everything—time, energy, attention, hope. There was nothing left over. Not for romance. Not for the kind of presence a relationship deserves. I couldn't be the person he needed. I couldn't ask him to wait out a fight with no end date — not at his age, not with everything still ahead of him. He would have stayed. That's what hurt most.

But I couldn't ask him to live in the wreckage with me. To watch me disappear into filings and hearings and the endless procedural machinery. To accept that I would always be half-present, half-listening, half-available—because the other half belonged to a fight that wouldn't end. He had time I didn't have. I made the choice for both of us. It felt like mercy. It felt like failure. Litigation doesn't care who you are to each other. It only cares how much you can still give. And I had nothing left to give.

The Art That Survived

Art suffered, but it didn't disappear. It faded. It went quiet. Then it returned in flashes. Short, intense bursts when the pressure became unmanageable. Art stopped being about exploration and became about containment. A way to drain something before it poisoned everything else. The mosaics slowed. They require patience. Time to sit with color and pattern and let something emerge gradually. I didn't have that kind of time. I didn't have that kind of peace. But sometimes, late at night, after a particularly brutal hearing or a motion that got denied for reasons that made no sense, I would sit with glass and adhesive and let my hands do something that wasn't typing.

The work changed. Sharper edges. Darker tones. Less balance, more tension. It looked like what I was living. Art became evidence that I was still here. Still capable of making something that wasn't a legal argument. Still able to create, even if creation had become another form of survival.

I didn't share much of it. It wasn't for showing. It was for staying sane.

Rage as Discipline

Rage had to be managed. Not expressed. Contained. Anger is useful in small, controlled doses. Too much and it clouds judgment. Too little and you disappear. I learned how to hold it without letting it run me. That skill alone kept me in the game.

There were moments when the injustice was so clear, so documented, so undeniable—and the response was so dismissive—that rage would flood in like a physical force. I could feel it in my chest, in my jaw, in the way my hands wanted to slam things.

But you can't fight a system from a place of uncontrolled anger. The system is designed to absorb rage. To let you scream until you're hoarse, then calmly note your outburst on the record as evidence of instability. So I learned to transform it. Anger became fuel. I channeled it into research. Into drafting. Into finding the case law that proved them wrong, the statute they'd violated, the procedural rule they'd ignored.

I let rage sharpen my arguments instead of destroying my credibility. But it cost something to do that. To hold that much anger, that much injustice, and not let it escape in ways that would hurt me more than them. Some nights I would sit alone and let myself feel it fully. The unfairness. The contempt. The institutional indifference. I would let the anger fill the room until I couldn't breathe, and then I would breathe anyway, and the anger would settle back into something I could carry. This is what endurance looks like. Not the absence of breaking. The decision not to stay broken.

The Cost No One Sees

This is what the case took while pretending not to. It didn't just challenge facts. It tested endurance. It demanded a version of me that could absorb loss without folding, isolation without quitting, damage without surrender.

Those are numbers. They don't show the mornings I woke up and didn't want to keep going. They don't show the nights I sat with the overwhelming certainty that this would never end, that the system was designed to outlast me, that justice was a story we tell children and fools.

They don't show the moments I wanted to walk away. And they don't show the moments I chose not to. Because walking away would have meant accepting that everything they did was fine. That forgery doesn't matter. That evidence is optional. That institutional power gets to win simply by waiting for you to give up.

I couldn't accept that. Not because I'm brave. Because I'm stubborn. And because losing my home to fraud had cost me more than fighting cost.

What Remains

I didn't stay because it was easy. I stayed because leaving would have cost more—not financially, not strategically, but morally. If I walked away, I became complicit in my own erasure. I validated the idea that people like me—without institutional backing, without endless resources, without the right credentials—don't get to challenge the system. I refused that story.

Even when it hurt. Even when it isolated me. Even when my body paid the price, when my relationships paid, when my art paid. Even when my own attorney failed me, I stayed.

Waiting doesn't make you patient. It makes you durable. And durability, I learned, is its own kind of power—not the power to win easily or avoid damage, but the power to keep standing when the system expects you to fall.

That's what years of fighting taught me: not that justice is guaranteed, but that endurance is. Sometimes endurance becomes its own form of resistance. Sometimes refusing to disappear is the only victory available.

Sisu—that Finnish grit that refuses to yield—isn't about strength. It's about what you do when strength runs out and you keep going anyway.

What It Does to You Over Time

There's a point where it stops feeling temporary.

At the beginning, you tell yourself this will end. That there will be a hearing, a ruling, a moment where something resolves and you can go back to your life. That belief fades slowly. Not all at once. It erodes. You stop making plans too far ahead. You stop assuming anything will hold. Everything becomes conditional—on a ruling, on a deadline, on something you don't control. Your life reorganizes around uncertainty. People on the outside don't see that part. They see the case. The filings. The arguments. The outcome. They don't see the constant recalibration.

What you say yes to. What you stop committing to. What you quietly let go of because you don't have the capacity to carry it anymore. You become selective in ways you didn't intend. Not because you don't care—but because you can't afford distraction.

Everything gets filtered through one question: Does this help me survive this process? If the answer is no, it goes. And over time, that changes you.

Not dramatically. Not in ways people notice immediately. But steadily.

You get quieter. More precise. Less tolerant of things that don't matter. Less patient with things that pretend to matter.

You learn to conserve energy the way people conserve money during a crisis. Nothing wasted. Nothing unnecessary. That's the part the case never acknowledges. It measures filings. Deadlines. Outcomes. It doesn't measure what it takes to keep showing up.

What Survives

Not everything makes it through. Some things don't come back the way they were. Some relationships don't recover. Some parts of you don't return to their original shape. But something does survive. Clarity. Not the kind that feels good. The kind that removes illusion.

You stop assuming systems are neutral. You stop expecting fairness as a default. You stop believing that effort guarantees outcome.

And in that space—where expectation used to be—you get something else. Accuracy. You see what's actually happening, not what it's supposed to be. That's not comforting. But it's stable.

And stability, after years of uncertainty, is enough.

PART V

Art Under Pressure: *What the System Couldn't Break*

The wound is the place where the light enters you.
— Rumi

CHAPTER 35

What Litigation Does to an Artist

Art is a wound turned into light.
— Georges Braque

What art used to be. Before the fight, art was not survival. It was pleasure. It was curiosity. It was mine.

I stopped trying to make the paintings agreeable. I still negotiated with the viewer. I offered entry points. Beauty as an invitation. That impulse didn't disappear, but it lost authority. Truth outranked harmony. This wasn't anger. It was accuracy.

I didn't paint much then. My main medium was mosaic. Glass. Weighty. Slow. Precise. I had patience back then. I had space for it. My studio filled the entire basement of my house. At first it was one room. Then, during my divorce, I dug out the rest of it by hand. A shovel. Buckets. Dirt hauled out one load at a time. Blisters on my fingers. Sweat down my spine.

It was brutal. And it was healing. Every bucket carried something out with it—anger, sorrow, disbelief, longing, disappointment. Eventually relief. The kind that comes when you realize your life is yours again. I tiled the shower in mosaic. Installed a copper sink. Built a kitchenette. Added a sauna, naturally. Jewelry-making area. Sewing table. Sculpture space. Clay. Drawing. Painting. It wasn't a studio. It was a sanctuary. It was the first place that was fully, unquestionably mine.

I taught sculpture classes. Clay first. Then mosaic. We did life drawing. Nude models. Real bodies. Real presence. People talked. We told stories. We cried. Faces emerged from clay—portraits that started looking like lost relatives, old lovers, ghosts. There was grief in that room. And release.

One of my students was an attorney on sabbatical. She'd never touched clay. She took one class. Then another. Then another. Watching her left brain loosen—watching someone remember how to feel—felt like a victory.

I had a social life. An artist community. Gatherings where we talked about creation instead of case law. I had finally reached a point where I could afford to do what I wanted. That life is gone.

All the years later, I don't even know what people talk about anymore. If it isn't about litigation, I'm out of vocabulary.

The First Shift (When art stopped being joy and became oxygen)

The shift didn't happen all at once. In 2007, I refinanced. Consolidated debt. Trusted the professionals. Signed the documents. Believed the system worked the way it claimed to.

By 2012, I was in default. Because I was told to. By 2017, I was in litigation. And somewhere in that span, my art changed. And suddenly I had no studio. No office. No clients. No income.

Then everything accelerated. Foreclosure. Lockout. Litigation. Homelessness. Staying at friends' places. So thankful for my good friends.

Driving to court in San Diego every week. Sleeping on couches. Living out of my car. For four years, I made no art at all. None. I felt shriveled from the inside. Like something essential had collapsed inward. I needed an outlet—not to express myself, but to remember who I was. So I tested myself. To see if I still could.

My first painting was a bumblebee. A queen bee. It wasn't subtle. It wasn't ironic. It was a declaration. I am still here.

I am still sovereign. I kept that painting. I'll never sell it. It's proof I didn't lose myself completely. Art stopped being optional. I didn't paint because I wanted to. I painted because I had to.

Why Scale Became Necessary

Scale wasn't an aesthetic decision. It was a physiological one.

When your life collapses into documents, deadlines, and institutional language, your body starts shrinking without your permission. Shoulders pull inward. Breath gets shallow. Movements become economical. You live hunched—over files, over screens, over calendars that belong to someone else. Litigation compresses you.

Small work couldn't hold what I was carrying. It asked for restraint at the exact moment restraint was killing me. I didn't choose large canvases because I wanted impact. I chose them because my nervous system needed room. Thirty by forty inches was the minimum surface area required to move my arms fully again. To step back. To advance. To engage my whole body instead of just my wrists and eyes. Small work keeps things polite, large work makes demands.

In court, everything is reduced. Arguments are distilled into footnotes. Evidence is cropped to relevance. Your story is broken into admissible fragments and stripped of tone. You are told, repeatedly, that less is more. Say only what matters. Cut everything else.

But what matters to a system is not what matters to a body.

Large paintings let me exceed the margins. They let me exist outside the footnotes. They let me move faster than reason and slower than panic. They let me work at the scale of breath instead of procedure.

I didn't sketch. I didn't plan. Planning belongs to systems that still pretend they're neutral. I needed momentum. Large scale also removed the option of preciousness. You cannot fuss over a six-foot canvas. You cannot overthink when the surface refuses intimacy. There's no room for hesitation. If you stall, the painting dies. That urgency mirrored my life.

Litigation trains you to wait. For rulings. For filings. For continuances. For decisions made by people who are not living with the consequences. Large work interrupted that rhythm. It demanded action. It rewarded decisiveness. It punished avoidance. You show up or you don't. The canvas doesn't care why.

There's a myth that large art is about ego. Visibility. Dominance. That's gallery talk. In reality, scale is about containment. How much chaos a surface can hold without collapsing.

My life had exceeded the capacity of small things. I needed work that could absorb rage without turning decorative. Work that could survive impact. Work that could be brutalized and still stand. Large paintings don't ask permission to exist in a room. They change the room. They reassert presence. That mattered. When everything else was shrinking—my resources, my time, my certainty—I needed at least one place where expansion was still possible. Scale wasn't about being seen. It was about not disappearing.

The Crisis Cycle

I need to say this plainly: I am not superhuman. People love to say, you're so strong, you've got this. It's meant as encouragement. Sometimes it lands that way. Other times it is just another weight to carry — one more thing I am supposed to perform for someone else's comfort. Strength is exhausting. You cannot juggle sixteen balls forever without dropping one. Or yourself.

So eventually I crash. I burn out. I break. And when I break, I break completely.

The lights go out in my head. That is the only way I know how to describe it. Not sadness exactly, not frustration — a total eclipse. The exhaustion becomes so overwhelming that I cannot locate a single reason to continue. I lie in bed and I wonder: is this it. Is this the time I finally disappear for good. Is this where she goes and doesn't come back. I cry until my eyes are swollen shut and I cannot tell anymore whether I am grieving the case or the house or the years or just myself — the version of me that existed before all of this started. I cannot get up. I do not want to get up. I am an empty shell and I know it and for a day, sometimes two, I stop pretending otherwise.

No people. No talking. No performing resilience for anyone. I pull back hard and I let myself feel every bit of it — the defeat, the humiliation, the loneliness, the rage — because denying it only buries it deeper and it will find its way out eventually regardless. So I give it the room it demands. I feel sorry for myself. Completely. Without apology.

Friska stays. My four-legged constant companion, my one unconditional witness to all of it. She knows the signs before I do. When I am in that place her nose is in my face, warm and insistent, refusing to let me disappear entirely. She does not try to fix anything. She does not tell me I am strong. She just does not leave. In those days she is the only company I can bear.

And then — I cannot explain the mechanism, only the fact of it — something shifts.

It is not a decision exactly. More like a loosening. I get up. Not because I have found hope but because staying horizontal has stopped feeling like relief. I walk into my studio and I just stand there. Or I go to the beach and I sit and I stare at the water and I feel nothing yet, just numb, just the beginning of something that is not yet feeling but is at least movement in that direction. The studio calls again. It always calls again.

I pick up a brush. The first strokes are timid, tentative — like I have forgotten who I am, like I am introducing myself to my own hands. And then something breaks open. I need a large canvas, always large, nothing small will hold what is about to come out. Six-inch brush. Watery transparent paint. No pencil. No plan. No apology. Just motion.

Then my whole body. My hands. My fingers. Spatulas. Crumpled paper pressed into wet surface. Cheesecloth. Netting. Layers built on layers, texture accumulating like scar tissue over a wound that is still trying to close. I throw paint. I cry through it. I am not making something beautiful — I am making something honest, which is harder and more necessary. The painting that emerges is raw and chaotic and I do not care. It did its job. That is enough.

Native drums on in the background. Not Vivaldi — Vivaldi is too clean for this, too finished. I need something grounding, something with a pulse that matches what is moving through me. The beat does something to the body that the mind cannot do for itself.

Then I switch to my Finnish station on Spotify. My native words coming through the speakers, my language, my tribe — the sounds I grew up inside, the ones that live in the oldest part of me before the legal system, before California, before any of this. Finnish reminds me who I was before I became someone fighting. It reminds me what is real and what is noise. It reminds me that I come from people who endured winters that would break anyone, and did not break. Sisu is not a philosophy I adopted. It is something I was born into, something that lives in the language itself.

Somewhere in all of it — the paint, the drums, the Finnish words, the tears — clarity starts threading back in. I can feel it arriving. I am giving too much power to bullshit and to evil people and none of this is real, none of this is who I am. STOP. This is not who I am. I did not survive everything I survived to disappear on someone else's terms. I must claim my life back.

The thought arrives not as inspiration but as refusal. As the Finnish word that has no real English translation: enough. I am done being done.

After that — breath deepens. Energy returns. Life seeps back in around the edges, slow and quiet at first, then faster. I am always the first to tell other people: snap out of it, stop feeding the darkness, you are stronger than this. It turns out I have to practice what I preach. It turns out the advice I give everyone else is also the only advice that works on me.

I am not always sure I would still be here without the art. I say that plainly, without drama, because it is simply true. If this is what keeps the lights on — the large canvases, the six-inch brushes, the crumpled cheesecloth, the native drums — then it has earned its place at the center of my life and I will not apologize for treating it as essential, because it is.

People often tell me they can feel something in my paintings. That there is emotion in them, movement, a kind of aliveness they were not expecting. They ask how I do it. This is how. I pour the whole crisis into them — the collapse, the despair, the numb morning at the beach, the timid first brushstroke, the avalanche that follows. Every layer of texture is a layer of something that had to come out. The paintings are not decorative objects. They are evidence. They are the record of someone who went all the way down and found, at the bottom, a brush.

And then life continues. And I am ready to kick ass again.

The court is not allowed in my studio. You already stole years of my life. You don't get this space. I don't forgive. I get my remedy. Not quitting even when quitting would be easier. Not because you're strong, but because you're too stubborn to let them win.

And when the next collapse comes—and it will—I'll go back to the studio. I'll cry through another violent painting. Friska will stay close. And eventually, I'll come back. Recharged, not healed. Focused, not naïve.

Why Decoration Failed

Decoration assumes safety. It assumes a stable environment. A future intact enough to plan for. Walls that will still be yours next year. Viewers who want to feel comforted rather than challenged. Litigation dismantles all of that.

When your life is under active threat, decoration becomes dishonest. It starts to feel like lying with pigment. Making things pleasant while everything else is on fire requires a level of dissociation I no longer had access to. I didn't stop believing in beauty. I stopped believing in beauty without consequence.

Decorative art asks very little of the viewer. It's meant to harmonize. To recede. To reassure. Its highest achievement is blending in. But nothing about my life blended in anymore.

I was living inside conflict. Inside contradiction. Inside a system that smiled while doing damage. Polite surfaces masking aggressive outcomes.

There's a pressure—especially on women artists—to soften work. To make it livable. To make it fit above a sofa. To consider color palettes and moods and resale. Litigation strips that impulse out of you. You stop caring whether something is easy to live with. You start caring whether it's true.

I didn't want my work to calm people down. I wanted it to wake them up. Decoration avoids friction. My life was friction. I also couldn't afford inefficiency anymore. Every hour in the studio had to do something. I didn't need resolution, I needed discharge.

The paintings had to move energy, not manage it. Pain doesn't want embellishment, it wants witness. I wasn't interested in making work that people described as "nice." Nice is what systems say while denying you relief. Nice is the tone of rejection letters. Nice is procedural violence with a smile. My work stopped being nice.

And in that refusal, something sharpened. Color intensified. Movement accelerated. Composition became less about balance and more about force. These paintings don't decorate a space, they occupy it. They don't soothe. They confront. That doesn't make them angry work. It makes them honest work.

The Baja Studio — My Queendom

(The place where the system loses jurisdiction)

My studio in Baja is a three-car garage with heavy double doors. When I open them in the morning, it feels like opening my queendom.

I'm by the Sea of Cortez. The light changes constantly. Dolphins pass. Sometimes whales surface and breathe—deep, deliberate reminders that survival can be massive and calm at the same time.

The walls are covered. Paintings. Photography. Sculptures. Supplies everywhere. Acrylics for speed. Oils for depth. The smell of linseed and turpentine lingers. Grounding. Honest.

I listen to everything. Classical. Baroque. Jazz. Native flute. Finnish music. Audiobooks. Whatever the moment demands. Don't box me in.

I live off-grid. One hundred percent solar. Morning is studio time. When the light fades, the queendom closes. I move inside. Computer work. Or sit on the beach staring at the Milky Way.

This is where I survive.

Specific Paintings [2](Trauma leaves fingerprints)

Life Force Unleashed came after I was stabbed. It took a year before I could function again. When it came out, it wasn't gentle.

"If you are overcoming something so powerful it brought you to your knees—and you're ready to continue—this is for you." It sold to someone who understood. That mattered.

Petals of Passion came after the jury verdict. (All the paintings at www.leenadesign.com/mybook). Color returning. Fire rediscovered. Not flowers—rebirth. The moment the soul remembers itself.

Lumina Mare and **Lord of the Depths** came as a pair. Light and command. Jellyfish and octopus. Power without apology. Not décor. Statements.

She Lived Anyway is Frida—not as icon, but mirror. A woman who carried pain in her body and turned it into language. This portrait isn't about myth or martyrdom. It's about endurance. About making beauty while suffering. About refusing to disappear.

For anyone who has lived inside a broken system, a broken body, or a long fight that never asked permission. Frida didn't paint to be palatable. She painted to stay alive. She endured. So do I.

Why Art Became Evidence

At some point, I realized my paintings were doing what my legal filings couldn't: recording impact. Courts process format, not facts. If your truth doesn't arrive packaged correctly—in the right motion, with the right citations, within the right timeframe—it's treated as noise. Lived experience is inadmissible unless translated into approved language, stripped of emotion, reduced to elements that fit procedural templates. Apparently "Your Honor, this is destroying my life" doesn't have the same evidentiary weight as "Plaintiff submits pursuant to CCP Section..."

---

2 All the painting can be seen at *www.leenadesign.com/mybook-pdf*

Art doesn't ask permission to document. It doesn't need to be filed in triplicate or served on opposing counsel. Every painting I made during litigation became a timestamp, a record of state, a physiological log of what that week's ruling or that month's delay did to me. The system insisted nothing was happening—just routine procedural matters, standard discovery disputes. My body disagreed. The canvases disagreed. Turns out you can't demurrer a painting.

Evidence isn't just documents and certifications and expert reports. It's residue. These paintings carry residue—they show what sustained stress does to motion, color, density, rhythm. You can see escalation in the brushwork. Compression in the palette. Release when a small procedural victory created breathing room. They show when hope thinned to something barely visible and when it returned, not as optimism but as function, as the muscle memory of continuing when stopping would be easier.

Art became evidence because it survived when other records were neutralized. When filings were denied, when arguments were dismissed, when findings were acknowledged and then carefully set aside like interesting but inconvenient facts, the paintings kept going. They did something else the court refused to do: they connected cause and effect. You can trace events through the work—the palette shifts after certain hearings, the scale increases after denials, the aggression spikes after months of procedural delay. That's documentation the court can't strike from the record because it was never in the record to begin with.

No one cross-examines a painting. No one files a motion to exclude it as prejudicial. No one tells it to narrow its scope or limit its claims to those properly pleaded. No one argues it lacks foundation or constitutes hearsay. It stands. And because it stands, it testifies—without being sworn in, without facing hostile questioning, without having to explain why it didn't raise this issue earlier.

I didn't make these works to prove anything to a court. Courts, as I'd learned, weren't particularly interested in proof anyway—they were interested in procedure. I made the paintings to prove something to myself: that the system hadn't succeeded in flattening me into compliance, in reducing me to a case number, in erasing the person underneath the plaintiff. Each finished piece became evidence that pressure did not equal erasure, that I remained capable of creation even while fighting for survival. Take that, summary judgment.

They can challenge my filings. They can distort the record. They can pretend outcomes are neutral, that procedure is just process, that delay is nobody's fault, that finding forgery twice and doing nothing about it is somehow normal jurisprudence. But they cannot argue with what survived. They can't claim my paintings lack standing or were filed outside the statute of limitations. They can't dismiss them for failure to state a claim.

That's why art became evidence—not symbolic evidence or therapeutic expression (though my therapist would probably disagree), but functional evidence. Proof of endurance. Proof of continuity. Proof that something human remained active inside an inhuman process, and that it left marks they couldn't erase, redact, or declare moot.

The court got to control the legal record. I got to control everything else. Turns out that's not nothing.

The Cost

But I'd be lying if I said art didn't suffer. It did. Art didn't disappear. It was rationed. Galleries closed. Commissions lost. Exhibitions missed. Techniques abandoned. Communities gone. Studio time stolen in fifteen-minute increments between deadlines. My design business dried up. Clients don't wait when you disappear into court for months at a time. The ceramics business—gone. No kiln access when you're homeless.

Creativity didn't die. It went underground. And it came back sharper. Art stopped being about exploration. It became about survival. I stopped painting what people wanted to see and started painting what I needed to say, what I felt.

The work I make now is different. Not decorative. Not safe. Not meant to blend into a room. Large, physical strokes. Forceful. Urgent. Full of movement. These paintings demand attention instead of politely asking for it. They invite confrontation, conversation—witness.

Every painting I finish is proof I'm still here. Still functioning. Still capable of making something that didn't exist before. That's the one weapon they can't touch.

Wildfire Rising

One painting that came out of one of those collapses I called *Wildfire Rising.*[3] A horse surging forward through chaos. Mane wild. Eyes focused. Movement without permission.

I painted it during the fight—somewhere between hearings, between denials, between moments when I thought I couldn't keep going. The horse isn't asking if it's allowed to move. It's just going. The background is storm and fire—blues, reds, whites slashing across the canvas. The kind of chaos that should stop you. It doesn't stop the horse. I posted it online. It sold within hours. That mattered more than the money. It meant someone saw what I was feeling and wanted to keep it. It meant my art still had power even when everything else was falling apart.

It wasn't made to be pretty. It was made to survive. If you've been knocked to your knees by something overwhelming and you're standing up again—raw, shaky, but still standing—this is for you.

What Endurance Rewrites

Endurance is not a virtue. It's an adaptation. Endurance is what happens when retreat is no longer an option and stopping would cost more than continuing. You do not survive intact. You survive altered.

Prolonged pressure changes your assumptions first. I didn't lose faith in people. I lost faith in systems that claim neutrality while rewarding attrition. Trust stopped being automatic. Precision replaced optimism. Pattern recognition replaced hope. Litigation teaches you—repeatedly—that truth isn't persuasive on its own, that effort doesn't guarantee fairness, and that delay is a weapon. The process is the punishment. It corrodes your capacity to imagine an end.

Art absorbed that corrosion before I had language for it. The work changed because I did. What I could tolerate shifted. I stopped cushioning the impact. When pressure becomes constant, softness stops being functional.

This is where people misunderstand survival art. It's not about trauma or confession. It's about metabolism. If pressure doesn't move through the body—through motion, scale, resistance—it turns inward. It calcifies.

---

3 *www.leenadesign.com/mybook-pdf*

It breaks things that matter. The studio became the only place where cause and effect still made sense. You act. Something happens. Material responds honestly. That's restorative after years inside a system where nothing resolves.

The studio is non-negotiable. Not sacred—functional. Maintenance. Without it, endurance turns corrosive. People who haven't lived inside sustained pressure think recovery looks like rest. For some of us, stopping is dangerous. Stillness lets the noise catch up. Movement keeps the structure intact. That's the cost: you don't get to return to who you were before. There is no reset. Only substitution.

I became someone less surprised by cruelty and less impressed by authority. Someone more exacting with language, with line, with boundary. Someone who no longer confuses harmony with truth. The paintings are not gentler now. They are clearer. They do not ask to be liked. They ask to be witnessed. Endurance doesn't make you kinder. It makes you accurate.

And once accuracy outranks comfort, there is no going back. Art isn't escape. It's endurance. I return recharged, not healed. Focused, not naïve. Art puts me back together just enough to keep going.

You can't break me.

You tried.

You failed.

CHAPTER 36

Refusing to Disappear

I could have disappeared here. Many people do. The system counts on it. After years of litigation, after hearings that go nowhere, after motions denied on technicalities, after evidence acknowledged but never acted upon—most people stop fighting. Not because they're weak. Because they're human.

Exhaustion becomes a strategy. The institution's strategy. Wear you down, wait you out, let you fade quietly so no one has to explain anything. So the record stays clean. So the patterns stay hidden. I didn't vanish. I documented.

The Shift to Public Advocacy

After years of being told my evidence didn't matter—or worse, that it mattered but wouldn't change anything—I realized the courtroom wasn't the only venue that counted.

Maybe it wasn't even the most important one.

I turned to public advocacy. Not rallies. Not speeches. Not the kind of activism that requires a megaphone and a crowd. Documents.

I made a short video for YouTube and TikTok, walking people through court filings, notary signatures, recorded assignments. I showed the evidence the way the court refused to: visually, slowly, without euphemism.

I held up the signature comparisons. Side by side. Same name. Different handwriting. Filed in different counties, on different dates, notarized by people who—according to official state records—never notarized anything.

I showed transcripts where Judge Bacal acknowledged the forgery as compelling and uncontroverted, then granted an equitable remedy that offset to net zero. I won on paper. The bank kept the house. The words appeared in minute orders, followed by a remedy that gave me nothing. I named the players. The law firm. The attorneys. The servicers. The notaries whose names appeared on documents they never signed.

Fraud is easier to spot when you're allowed to actually look at it. This wasn't storytelling. It was translation. Taking the 822 docket entries, the 64 hearings, the thousands of pages of filings—and distilling them into something a person could see in five minutes and understand immediately.

They forged the documents. The court acknowledged it. Nothing happened.

No legalese. No procedural jargon. Just facts, displayed clearly enough that the absurdity became undeniable.

The Victory That Wasn't

On paper, it was a win.

Judge Bacal awarded me Cancellation of Instruments and a violation of Business & Professions Code § 17200. She called my evidence "compelling" and "uncontroverted."

But the judgment didn't specify which documents were canceled. It didn't unwind the foreclosure. It didn't restore my title. It didn't require anyone to fix anything. I won acknowledgment. I didn't get relief.

That contradiction—winning while losing, being right while getting nothing—is why I went public. If the courtroom couldn't hold the truth, I'd find venues that could. It's like training an algorithm on bad data. The system records the outcome, not the truth. Yes, there was fraud. No, we're not doing anything about it. Lesson learned: proceed as usual.

That contradiction—winning while losing, being right while getting nothing—is why I went public. A friend here in Baja, someone who'd absorbed the same story everyone absorbs, told me after reading the manuscript that he'd assumed I just hadn't paid my mortgage. Once he read it, he said: there's a lot more here than that. There is. But the simpler version had done its job for years. If the courtroom couldn't hold the truth, I'd find venues that could.

Leena.Artist.FightsBack

On my YouTube channel, Leena.artist.fightsback, I finally said what the courtroom wouldn't hold. That this wasn't just about my case.

That forged notary signatures aren't anomalies when you find dozens more with the same handwriting, filed across counties, across years, bearing the names of notaries who never worked for the companies listed, who never saw the documents, whose stamps were used without authorization. That procedure was being used to neutralize proof. To contain evidence. To let fraud exist on the record without requiring anyone to act on it.

That judges knew. Attorneys knew. Title companies knew. And the machine kept moving anyway. I showed people how to read a recorded assignment. How to spot the red flags: dates that don't align, notaries from the wrong state, corporate officers who don't exist, signatures that don't match.

I explained MERS. Robo-signing. Securitization. The things attorneys had been too afraid to say out loud in court. And I didn't soften it. I didn't say "alleged" fraud. I said fraud.

I didn't say "possible" forgery. I said forgery. Because I had the evidence. Expert testimony. State records. Admissions on the record from judges. At a certain point, hedging becomes complicity.

Art as Metabolization

My art became the backdrop for that truth. Every painting carried the residue of a hearing, a ruling, a letdown. The work got darker, sharper, more fragmented—but also more honest. Art didn't solve the injustice. It metabolized it. Took the rage, the grief, the exhaustion, and turned it into something that proved I was still capable of creation, even when the system was bent on erasure.

Refusing to disappear wasn't loud. It wasn't heroic. It was incremental. Showing up again. Posting another document. Answering another question in a Facebook group. Helping one more person understand what was done to them and what they could do about it.

Filing another motion even though the last ten got denied. Citing another statute even though the court ignored the previous ones. Presenting evidence again even though it had been excluded before. Not because I believed it would suddenly work. But because silence is agreement.

And I refused to agree.

The system expected me to exhaust. To give up. To accept that institutional power gets the final word simply by outlasting individual resistance. They expected me to disappear into the statistics. Another foreclosure. Another loss. Another person who couldn't afford to keep fighting.

Instead, I became visible. Not famous. Not viral. Just... documented. Every hearing. Every filing. Every piece of evidence. Every contradiction.

I made it public.

Say Less. Show More.

I learned something critical in those years of going public: people don't need to be convinced. They need to be shown. When you argue, people argue back. When you explain, people question your motives. But when you show them the documents—when you put two signatures side by side and ask "Does this look like the same person wrote both of these?"—they see it themselves.

The messages started coming in. Different states. Different banks. Different attorneys.

Same structures. Same forged signatures. Same missing chain of title. Same procedural runarounds. Same judges who acknowledged problems but issued no remedies.

"I thought it was just me." "I have the same notary on my assignment." "My attorney told me I couldn't win. I stopped fighting." "Can you look at my documents?" The reach wasn't wide enough. Not yet. But it was growing. A community formed through David v Goliath. Survivors. Homeowners. Pro se litigants who had been told their case was an "oops," a "clerical issue," a one-off mistake. It wasn't.

Once you say it out loud, clearly, without apology, it can't be unseen. Say less. Show more. Let the system indict itself. I didn't have to call it fraud. The documents did that. I didn't have to claim the judges were complicit. The minute orders did that—acknowledging evidence, then issuing rulings that ignored it. I didn't have to accuse the attorneys of lying. Their briefs contradicted themselves across filings. All I had to do was display it. Clearly. Repeatedly. And let people draw their own conclusions.

What Persistence Looks Like

They expected exhaustion. They got persistence. Not the heroic kind. The stubborn kind. The kind that shows up even when there's no guarantee it will matter. The kind that documents everything because documentation is its own form of resistance. The kind that refuses to let the narrative be written by the people who benefit from silence. I didn't vanish. I didn't settle quietly. I didn't accept that losing was inevitable just because winning was difficult.

I documented, I shared and helped others do the same. And that, it turns out, is much harder to erase than a single court case. Because court cases end.

But the record—the public record, the one you build yourself when the official one fails you—that stays. The videos stay. The documents stay. The community of people who learned to fight stays.

They can foreclose on a house. They can deny a motion. They can refuse to enforce their own findings. But they can't make the evidence disappear once it's been shown. They can't make the pattern invisible once it's been named. And they can't make me disappear. I'm still here, still documenting, still refusing.

What Refusing Looks Like

Refusing doesn't feel like strength when you're in it. It feels repetitive. Administrative. Sometimes pointless.

It looks like opening another document you don't want to read. Checking another signature you already know is wrong. Filing something you suspect will be ignored. It looks like doing it anyway.

There's no moment where it becomes clear that it's working. No signal that you've crossed from losing into winning. Most of the time, it feels exactly the same as it did when nothing was changing.

That's what makes people stop.

Not the opposition. The silence. The absence of response starts to feel like an answer. It isn't. It's just where the system expects you to end.

Refusing means you don't end there. It means you keep putting it on the record. Keep making it visible.

Keep showing what's there whether anyone acts on it or not.

Because once something is documented clearly enough, it stops being just your problem. It becomes part of the record.

And the record, unlike a ruling, doesn't expire.

CHAPTER 37

What Trust Means Now

November 22, 2024. Judge Bacal's courtroom. She said it out loud. On the record. "I cannot let stand what appears to be a forgery by a defendant. The Court cannot let stand something that occurred in front of this Court — again, uncontradicted, the plaintiff's testimony that somebody testified in this very courtroom as to a fact that was untrue. I'm not going to let that stand."

Then she asked the bank's attorney what she should do about it. Matthew Aguirre: "Truthfully, nothing, your Honor."

She issued an Order to Show Cause. Acknowledged the forgery was uncontradicted and compelling. Awarded me Cancellation of Instruments due to fraudulent, forged documents without specifying which instruments. Offset the property's value to net zero. I won. On paper. The bank kept the house. I should mention: I was also awarded a finding of Violation of Business and Professions Code. Let that sit for a moment. A California court, on the record, found that a defendant in my case had violated the Business and Professions Code. That is the formal legal language for these people broke the law. Said out loud. Entered into the record. Filed.

And then, nothing. No referral, no sanction, no consequence. Just a line item on a judgment that netted to zero. Winning a violation finding in California civil court is apparently like winning a participation ribbon. Proof that you showed up. Not proof that anyone has to do anything about it.

Nine months later, Jason Lipovsky testified he was authorized to sign a stipulation as U.S. Bank in the unlawful detainer case. He wasn't. He signed it in the hallway, outside the courtroom, with no written authority, no power of attorney. Judge Bacal acknowledged it from the bench. No POA. Lipovsky was signing for an entity he had no document tying him to. The judge said so out loud. Then she discharged the Order to Show Cause anyway. Whoop-ty-doo. In any other context, "no power of attorney" is the end of the conversation. In my case, it was a shrug. Bacal discharged the Order to Show Cause. No fraud. That's when I stopped believing good evidence alone would matter.

I grew up in Finland, where the basic social contract was assumed to hold. Deals made with a handshake stayed made. Your word carried weight because breaking it cost you something. You said what you meant, you did what you said, you stood behind it.

That wasn't naïve — it was infrastructure. I carried that assumption with me across the Atlantic and into every contract, every professional relationship, every institution I dealt with for forty years.

It didn't survive contact with this system.

The servicer told me to go ninety days delinquent to qualify for a loan modification. I did. They foreclosed. The tenant paid one month's rent, then worked with the bank to stay in the house for three years while I fought in court. My attorney stayed silent when I asked how to enforce the judgment, offered explanations to questions I didn't ask, and got disbarred. The realtor signed documents as the bank, testified under oath he was authorized, and listed my property for sale while my appeal was pending. The judge acknowledged uncontroverted forgery, called it compelling, then granted expungement so they could sell the property free of public notice.

Every single one knew better. Every single one had authority to stop it. Every single one proceeded anyway. No consequences. Anywhere. Ever.

What I lost wasn't faith in people. It was the assumption that credentials mean accountability. That a title, a robe, a seal on paper — that these things come attached to the person who issued them, that someone, somewhere, is willing to stand behind them.

They're not. Or not reliably. You have to find out which kind you're dealing with before you hand them anything you can't afford to lose.

That's not cynicism. It's calibration. I still extend good faith — but now I watch what people do with it. Silence counts.

CHAPTER 38

This Is Not Conspiracy Theory. It Is Fact.

Here's the keystone insight that made mass extraction possible: remove the injured party, and the Constitution never enters the room.

Article III of the U.S. Constitution requires a real case or controversy — an injured party who can swear, under penalty of perjury, that they suffered an actual loss. In my case, no one ever did. The debt had been sold, insured, paid against, fractionalized, monetized. No one raised their hand and said: "I lost money because Leena stopped paying." The only party who could demonstrate actual, documented loss was me — the homeowner who lost her home to a foreclosure built on documents no one could legitimately swear to.

Instead, proxies spoke for abstractions. Servicers enforced debts they didn't own. Trustees acted without authority. Attorneys filed declarations without proof of injury. Once you remove the injured party, due process felt reduced to paperwork. Courts stop resolving disputes between people and start facilitating transfers of property. Justice slows things down. So it was bypassed. This was not failure. It was design.

The Machine That Needed Your Mortgage

Before the forgery, before the closed trusts, before MERS and robo-signers and manufactured assignments — there was a problem that started not in your county recorder's office but in a boardroom in Beijing.

Somewhere around 2000, the world got very rich very fast. China was manufacturing everything. Saudi Arabia was pumping oil. Emerging economies were accumulating surpluses at a rate the financial system had never seen. Pension funds, sovereign wealth funds, insurance companies — all of them were sitting on mountains of capital that needed somewhere to go. Collectively they controlled roughly $70 trillion. Every dollar of it needed to earn a return.

For decades, that capital parked in safe places — Treasuries, municipal bonds, government-backed securities. Then Greenspan dropped the federal funds rate to one percent and the boring investments stopped paying. Seventy trillion dollars had nowhere to go. Wall Street had an answer. Your mortgage.

Millions of American homeowners were paying five, six, seven, eight percent interest on their loans. To a capital-starved investor pool, that looked like a river of money. The problem was the friction — individual mortgages were messy. Real people with job losses and divorces and medical emergencies. No institutional investor wanted that exposure. So Wall Street solved the friction problem by building a machine.

The machine worked like this: gather thousands of individual mortgages, bundle them into pools, slice the pools into tradeable securities, get the rating agencies to bless them as safe as Treasury bonds, and sell them to the $70 trillion pool of nervous money. Mortgage-backed securities — the instrument that connected a pension fund in Oslo to a school teacher in Stockton.

And the machine worked, until it ran out of raw material. By 2003, nearly everyone who qualified for a mortgage already had one. The machine had processed the easy supply. But $70 trillion doesn't slow down because the supply runs dry. It increases pressure until something gives. What gave was the standards.

First came stated income loans — you declared what you earned, no verification. Then stated income, stated asset loans — you declared both, nobody checked. Then NINA loans. No Income. No Assets. Half a million dollars, no job required. This was not recklessness. It was engineering. Because the banks originating these loans had no intention of holding them. They would own a mortgage for thirty, sixty days at most — just long enough to bundle it and sell it up the chain. The moment it left their hands, it became someone else's problem. They were not lending money. They were manufacturing product.

Washington Mutual embodied this perfectly. WaMu paid loan officers bonuses for volume, not quality. Executives were rewarded for pipeline flow regardless of what happened to the loans afterward. The machine needed volume. More loans meant more securities meant more fees at every link in the chain — the broker, the bundler, the investment bank, the rating agency. Everyone got paid at origination. Nobody got paid to care what happened in year three.

AIG insured the downside through credit default swaps that triggered at ninety days delinquent. The system was more profitable with failure than with performance. So they engineered failure.

The insurance had its own problem. If the note and mortgage were separated at closing — which MERS's involvement guaranteed — then AIG was insuring unsecured instruments. When they paid out, they had no claim to the property. They had insured a debt that no longer attached to anything real.

Your loan was not an isolated transaction between you and a bank. It was raw material. You were raw material. The moment you signed, you became a unit of production in a global capital pipeline that had no mechanism — and no incentive — to care whether the paperwork was real, the signatures were authentic, or the chain of title would hold up in a courtroom fifteen years later. The forgery on your documents did not happen despite the system. It happened because of it.

What They Didn't Tell Me: How Mortgage-Backed Securities Work

You sign a promissory note — your promise to pay — and a deed of trust, which is the security for that promise. You believe you're borrowing from a bank that expects you to pay them back. Within hours, your loan is sold, sometimes multiple times, until it lands in a securitized trust. That trust is governed by New York law and IRS tax rules. Once closed, it is legally static — no new assets, no substitutions, no modifications. The trust must remain frozen to preserve its tax status. Your individual loan becomes a microscopic slice of a billion-dollar pool. Certificates representing cash-flow rights are sold to pension funds, insurance companies, and institutional investors. Your monthly payment no longer goes to a bank that loaned you money. It is divided among investors who own certificates — not your debt.

And here is the problem that breaks the entire structure. The note and the deed of trust are separated. The note goes into the trust. The deed of trust stays behind in county records.

Legally, they cannot be separated — the deed of trust follows the note, always. California law is explicit. So is the *U.S. Supreme Court in Carpenter v. Longan.* And yet the system splits them on purpose, because if the deed followed the note into the closed trust as the law requires, no post-closing assignments would be possible. The trust can't take new assets. It's frozen. So the deed stays behind. And when foreclosure time comes, someone manufactures an assignment to make it look like the transfer happened legally. That is where the forgery enters.

When I signed the promissory note in 2007, I thought I was borrowing money. I was actually creating it. Under modern banking rules — confirmed in plain language by the Bank of England in 2014 — commercial banks do not lend out existing deposits. They create new deposits at the moment of origination, matched on the other side of the ledger by the borrower's signed note. My signature was the originating asset. Without it, no deposit. Without the deposit, no closing.

What happened next is the part nobody explained at closing. The note I signed was sold within days — to an aggregator, then to a sponsor, then into a securitized trust, then sliced into certificates and sold to pension funds and insurance companies. Credit default swaps were written against the certificates. The swaps were repackaged. By the time the chain settled, my single signature had generated fees and cash flows for a dozen entities I had never heard of and would never meet. One signature. Many revenue streams. That is the business model of American mortgage finance. The note is the asset. You are the source of the asset. The house is the collateral that makes the asset enforceable if the borrower stops feeding the machine.

MERS Hides Ownership

To avoid county recording fees and public transparency, the industry created MERS — Mortgage Electronic Registration Systems — a private database that acts as nominee for lenders. MERS is listed as beneficiary on millions of deeds of trust despite having no financial interest in the loan, no ownership of the note, and no right to payment. MERS exists to hide ownership changes inside a private database. When foreclosure time comes,

MERS or a MERS-appointed entity appears claiming authority — but they don't hold the note. The note is locked in a closed trust, legally unreachable. My deed of trust says the loan "may be sold multiple times." That line is a legal illusion dressed up as disclosure. Once a note enters a closed trust, it cannot be sold again. Any post-closing assignment violates trust law and tax rules. It is void. That conclusion had already been tested in court.

The question of what MERS could legally do had already been litigated. In Montgomery County Recorder of Deeds v. MERSCORP Inc., amicus briefs from the Public Interest Law Center, Community Legal Services, and the Legal Services Center of Harvard Law School argued that MERS violated state recording statutes, bypassed mandatory recording fees, and unlawfully severed mortgages from the notes they secure. The Pennsylvania Supreme Court ultimately ruled the county recorders lacked standing to pursue the claim. Not that MERS was right. Just that the recorders couldn't be the ones to say so. Nobody with standing ever did.

So who has the right to foreclose? Not the original lender — they sold the loan years ago. Not MERS — they're a placeholder with no financial interest. Not the servicer — they're a third-party contractor hired to collect payments. Not the trust — it's closed and cannot take new actions. Nobody has standing. So the industry manufactures the appearance of standing. Assignments are backdated. Substitutions of trustee are fabricated. Notarizations are forged. The foreclosure proceeds not because the authority is real, but because it looks real enough to keep property moving.

Why Forgery Became Structurally Necessary

Once you understand the closed trust problem, the forgery becomes inevitable. The note goes into the closed trust, frozen for tax purposes. The deed of trust stays behind in county records — an illegal separation, but done anyway. The trust cannot take new assets or execute new assignments. Years pass. The borrower defaults. Foreclosure time arrives. California law requires proof of ownership. The court requires a chain of title from origination to foreclosure. But the real chain is broken — the note is locked in a closed trust that can't act. So they create assignments after the fact, backdate them to make the timeline look legal, forge notary signatures to make them look authentic, and record them in county records to create the appearance of a valid transfer.

This is why the forgery exists. Not because someone made a mistake. Not because one bad actor cut corners. Because the trust structure makes legitimate assignment legally impossible while foreclosure requires documented assignment to proceed. The forgery bridges an unbridgeable gap.

My pattern forged documents aren't anomalies. They're the system working as designed. Agnes Bradshaw's signature appears on documents she never signed because someone needed a notary stamp on a substitution that couldn't legally exist. Autumn Carnegie's name appears during a window when Pennsylvania records show she performed zero notarial acts because her stamp was needed to legitimize a transfer the closed trust couldn't execute. The same signatures appear pixel-perfect across multiple documents because they're not signing documents — they're inserting images to create the appearance of authentication. They're not transferring ownership. They're manufacturing the appearance of ownership.

Courts allow it because stopping it would expose that the trust structure violates the law it claims to follow, invalidate millions of foreclosures built on the same impossible assignments, collapse the MBS market that pension funds depend on, and require admitting the system was designed to require fraud. I didn't just prove my foreclosure was forged. I proved the system proceeds even when legal requirements aren't met.

The Contract That Never Existed

A lawyer who practiced for forty years explained something that changed how I understood my case: there was no meeting of the minds.

Contract law goes back centuries. A contract requires two parties with a shared expectation — you borrow money, you pay it back, you own your house. But that's not what the banks were thinking. The evidence showed the banks knew most borrowers couldn't pay back the loans. They stopped verifying income. They stopped underwriting. They dispensed with due diligence entirely. Subsequent investigations, settlements, and sworn testimony documented what the numbers already showed: the machine was more profitable with failure than with performance.

This was not a side effect. It was the policy. As Neil Barofsky recounts in Bailout, Treasury Secretary Timothy Geithner described the federal housing program as designed to "foam the runway for the banks" — spreading foreclosures out over time not to save homeowners, but to distribute losses slowly enough that the banks could absorb them and recover. The homeowners were the foam.

And in documented cases — I am aware of more than twenty — servicers advised borrowers in default to stop making payments as a condition of loan modification review.

Or holding payments in escrow — refusing to apply them until the borrower was fully current on arrears. I learned this firsthand. I sent a partial payment once, thinking something was better than nothing. I was wrong. The payment sat in suspense, the default continued accumulating, and the clock kept running toward foreclosure.

Those borrowers were then foreclosed on for nonpayment. Why? Because WaMu, AIG, and the entire securitization machine made more money when borrowers defaulted than when they performed. Issue the loan, sell the note to Wall Street and get paid immediately, take out a credit default swap guaranteeing payment if the borrower defaults, wait for the default, collect the insurance payout recovering the full principal, then foreclose anyway and take the house. Double recovery. The trigger for the insurance payout was ninety days delinquent — which is why servicers told borrowers to stop paying.

When there's no shared expectation that the borrower will pay back the loan, there's no meeting of the minds. No meeting of the minds means no contract. No contract means no enforceable debt, no valid lien. But the foreclosure proceeds anyway.

Discovery: Where the Case Should Have Ended

I asked one simple question: do you own my note? They refused to answer.

I served twenty-six Requests for Admission. One of them asked U.S. Bank to admit that my deed of trust and note were not an asset for them. It was a yes-or-no question. Their response was thirteen objections: vague, ambiguous, overbroad, calculated to harass, calls for speculation, calls for a legal conclusion, attorney-client privilege, work product doctrine, not relevant, privacy, financial privacy. All twenty-six requests received the exact same thirteen objections, copy-pasted. When I filed a motion to compel answers, the court denied it on procedural defects. The bank was allowed to refuse to prove ownership. The foreclosure proceeded anyway. That is not adjudication. That is facilitation. The full discovery responses are in the Appendix M.

The Pension Fund Conflict

Here is the structural problem no one wants to name. When mortgages are converted into mortgage-backed securities and fractionalized into certificates, those certificates are sold to judicial pension funds, police pension funds, firefighters, county employees, and congressional retirement accounts. The people institutionally responsible for enforcing the law have a systemic financial interest in the market that the law would disrupt. This is not an accusation against any individual judge. It is a description of a structural conflict of interest that no disclosure requirement addresses and no recusal rule reaches. When the same asset class sits in the retirement accounts of the judiciary and the legislature, the incentive to treat forged mortgage documents as legally fatal — which would crack the MBS market and send those accounts into loss — runs directly against institutional self-preservation. No memo needs to be written. The structure does the work.

California's own Attorney General made the legal argument for me before I ever walked into court. In 2015, Kamala Harris filed an amicus brief in *Yvanova v. New Century Mortgage Corp.* arguing that borrowers have standing to challenge foreclosures based on void assignments — that a forged document cannot transfer what it never held. The California Supreme Court agreed. Harris's brief helped establish the very precedent Judge Bacal acknowledged and declined to enforce. Meanwhile, Harris's Mortgage Fraud Task Force received complaints from homeowners across the state documenting the same patterns I found — forged signatures, fabricated assignments, broken chains of title. The task force did not investigate. In 2011, Harris negotiated a $6.5 million settlement against Countrywide executives to fund foreclosure relief. The money went to state agencies. The homeowners it was supposed to help were never counted as beneficiaries. The law was written. The brief was filed. The precedent was set. None of it was enforced.

The federal government tried once to look directly at the problem. In 2011, under the Office of the Comptroller of the Currency, the National Foreclosure Review was launched. Homeowners who had already lost their homes were invited to submit paperwork for independent review. The reviewers assigned to examine the files were the lenders and servicers who had produced them. The conflict was not incidental. It was the structure. What the reviewers found was apparently so extensive that the review was shut down before it could reach conclusions. In place of findings, homeowners received payments. The standard range was $150 to $300. In the most egregious cases, the amount was described as slightly more. No one was given a list of the violations found in their file. The banks were protected from their own audit. The homeowners got less than a month's groceries for the largest financial loss of their lives, and were told the matter was resolved.

Judicial Impartiality — A Legal Fiction

This wasn't unique to my case.

Judicial conflicts of interest are presumed not to exist unless proven. And proving them requires access to financial disclosures that judges aren't required to provide unless directly asked—and sometimes not even then.

This wasn't new. The Linda Green robo-signing scandal had already shown what happens when institutional fraud is documented and acknowledged — one person goes to jail, the system absorbs the lesson, and continues.

DocX was the document mill at the center of that scandal. CBS's 60 Minutes documented it in detail — the assembly line of fabricated assignments, the signature forged by dozens of different hands, the notaries stamping documents they never witnessed. I had the footage. I tried to enter it into evidence at trial. The first judge said I could play it. When the moment came, she reversed herself and denied it.

A piece of evidence showing the exact fraud I was alleging — industrial-scale document fabrication by the same companies whose paperwork was in my chain of title — disappeared from the record on a judicial second thought. No explanation. No ruling on admissibility. Just: no.

That's not an oversight. That's a choice. (Appendix S)

Judge Robert C. Dales presided over a Ponzi scheme case in San Diego Superior Court. During the proceedings, it was discovered he had over $10 million personally invested in the very scheme before his court. He did not recuse himself.

Judge Katherine Jarbou ruled in favor of JPMorgan Chase in a foreclosure case—without holding a hearing. Later disclosures revealed she held approximately $800,000 in JPMorgan Chase stock. She did not recuse herself.

These weren't abstract conflicts. They were shareholders ruling on their own investments. No consequences. No reversals. Just the quiet understanding that some conflicts are tolerated if the machinery keeps running.

In 2020, a married couple in Washington State did what I did. They gathered their evidence. They named names. They filed a lawsuit alleging a conspiracy between state officials, judicial actors, and their mortgage holders.

The Attorney General of Washington filed a motion to stop them from litigating it. Not because the conspiracy was impossible. Because it was, in the AG's word, premature.

Zuchowski v. Ferguson is a procedural document. It does not resolve whether Washington State officials conspired with the mortgage industry. It resolves something more revealing: the Attorney General's determination that a court should never reach that question at all. Robert Ferguson — who would later run for governor on a record of holding power accountable — signed his name to a filing designed to ensure that accountability did not apply here.

Buried in the list of named state defendants is the Washington State Investment Board. The WSIB manages pension funds — teachers, state employees, public workers — and it invests heavily in mortgage-backed securities. The same instruments my property was funneled through. The same chain of assignments, transfers, and trust structures that required, at some point, a document no one could legitimately sign.

This is not coincidence. It is conflict.

A state that profits from mortgage-backed securities cannot be a disinterested adjudicator of mortgage-backed securities fraud. When the AG defends the Investment Board against allegations of conspiracy with mortgage holders, he is not defending abstract governance. He is defending a portfolio. The state is not the referee. The state is a stakeholder.

"Premature" is the procedural system's most elegant weapon. It neither denies the wrong nor corrects it. It simply ensures the clock keeps running while the evidence ages out of relevance. I heard versions of this across seven years and sixty-four court appearances. The language changes by jurisdiction. The function does not.

I was not an anomaly. I was a data point.

Placement note: This drops cleanly after your "shareholders ruling on their own investments" line, before any transition to the criminal referral section. It adds roughly 280 words — well within your "paragraphs, not pages" parameter.

The Pattern: Industrial-Scale Forgery

Once I proved forgery in my own case, I kept looking. I identified more than seventy-five forged instruments tied to the same notaries involved in my case — different homeowners, different properties, same notaries, same signatures. These weren't copied images. They were individually signed documents, executed again and again by the same people, falsely certifying events that never occurred. Separate from that set was a second pattern: identical signatures down to the pixel. Entire signature blocks duplicated with no variation — no pressure changes, no angle shift, no human inconsistency. These weren't signed. They were inserted.

Foreclosure doesn't happen case by case. It happens through mills. When fraud is built into the workflow, it doesn't stay small. It scales. The full list of forged documents by instrument number is in the Appendix N.

Courts as Throughput Machines

Courts are not neutral in this process. They are administrative systems funded by volume. Every filing generates revenue. Every foreclosure clears a docket. Stopping a foreclosure requires time, evidence, scrutiny, accountability. Letting it proceed requires none of that. Efficiency becomes the product. Cases that demand standing, proof, and an injured party threaten that efficiency. So they are contained.

The Rule That Was Already Written

What Judge Bacal did to me has a name in the law, and the name is old. In 1944 the United States Supreme Court decided *Hazel-Atlas Glass Co. v. Hartford-Empire Co.*, and held that fraud on the court unravels everything it touches — that equity will not aid the wrongdoer, and that no statute of limitations and no doctrine of laches can be used to let a party keep the benefit of a judgment procured by fraud. The principle goes back further still, to *United*

States v. Throckmorton in 1878. It is not a fringe theory. It is foundational. And in 2023, in *Tyler v. Hennepin County*, a unanimous Supreme Court held that when the government takes property to satisfy a debt, it cannot keep the surplus — taking more than what is owed is an unconstitutional taking under the Fifth Amendment.

Read those three cases together and the rule is simple: a court sitting in equity, having found forgery on the record, cannot then use its equitable discretion to deliver the forging party the same outcome it would have received with valid instruments. That is not equity. That is the inversion of equity. Bacal made the forgery findings — "compelling and uncontroverted" — and granted Cancellation of Instruments under Civil Code § 3412, the statutory remedy for exactly this situation. And then she offset the cancellation to net zero. The legal point won. The house was lost anyway. The party that produced the forged documents walked away with the same thing it would have walked away with if every signature had been real. Eighty years of Supreme Court law says a court is not allowed to do that. One did. That is not an aberration either. It is the same containment strategy, applied at the remedy stage.

The Receipt

In January 2025, a 1098 arrived in my mailbox. A standard IRS Mortgage Interest Statement. NewRez LLC doing business as Shellpoint Mortgage Servicing, Greenville, South Carolina. Tax year 2024. My name. My old address. Account number 1004688461. Origination date: March 15, 2007. Outstanding principal as of January 1, 2024: $490,371.69.

Read that number again. Four hundred ninety thousand, three hundred seventy-one dollars and sixty-nine cents. Reported to the Internal Revenue Service, under penalty of federal perjury, by a federally regulated mortgage servicer, as an active outstanding mortgage obligation on my house.

The property I no longer own. The property the trustee's deed transferred out of my name. The property the court found was taken using documents that were, and I quote the bench, compelling and uncontroverted evidence of forgery. The property whose underlying loan originated with a bank — Chevy Chase — whose corporate successor, Capital One, stated in writing that it had no interest in the Deed of Trust. The property whose foreclosure was built on an assignment into a securitized trust that had closed in 2007 and was, under its own governing law, legally incapable of accepting new assets in 2017. Shellpoint filed the 1098 anyway.

The line for mortgage interest received from the borrower was blank. Of course it was. I am not paying. I cannot pay. I do not own the house. There is no interest to receive. But the line for outstanding principal carries the full balance — $490,371.69 — as if the loan were live. Another line shows $2,696.50 in property taxes paid in 2024. Somebody is still paying the taxes. Somebody is still maintaining the asset. Somebody on a server in Greenville is still tracking this loan as a line item, year after year, long after the foreclosure, long after the judgment, long after the forgery findings were entered into the public record.

A note on the name. Throughout this book I have called the servicer Specialized Loan Servicing, because SLS is the entity I sued, the entity whose employee sat in depositions, and the entity whose name appears on seven years of filings. SLS still exists on paper, but its servicing operation was absorbed into NewRez/Shellpoint. Same portfolio. Same loan numbers. Same machine. New letterhead on the envelope.

This is standard practice in the mortgage servicing industry — servicers merge, rebrand, and transfer portfolios constantly, which is part of how accountability stays perpetually one corporate reorganization away. The 1098 for tax year 2024 came from Shellpoint because that is what SLS is called this week.

And if anyone wants to call my case an outlier, there is now a $4.65 million public record that says otherwise. In December 2025, the Attorney General of Massachusetts announced a settlement with Newrez — as successor by merger to SLS — resolving allegations that SLS had engaged in widespread unfair and deceptive servicing practices that put borrowers at unnecessary and unlawful risk of foreclosure, in violation of state mortgage servicing law, debt collection law, and the COVID-19 foreclosure moratorium. SLS's portfolio in Massachusetts alone included nearly twenty-four thousand properties. Twenty-four thousand. In one state.

The settlement included restitution to hundreds of homeowners who had been foreclosed on while subject to SLS's practices. I was not one of them — California is not Massachusetts, and my case remains on appeal. But the pattern I spent seven years proving in my own file has now been acknowledged, in writing, by a state Attorney General, against the exact same servicer, for the exact same kind of conduct. The pattern is the pattern. I was not imagining it. Massachusetts just confirmed the arithmetic. Settlement and my 1098 are in Appendix Q.

I am not the only one who noticed. In 2013, Sherry Hernandez was arrested in Washington, D.C., protesting outside Covington and Burling — one of seven older women standing in front of the law firm that had represented major servicers during the foreclosure crisis. In the years that followed, she documented dozens of homeowners who had been fraudulently foreclosed upon. Her forthcoming book, We Are Not Deadbeats, collects their stories. As a foundation for that work, she has published a record of settlements and supporting research establishing what the evidence already showed: it was the financial industry, not homeowners, that created this crisis. Our leaders knew. The record says so. It always did. The full record of settlements is in Appendix R

This is where the book stops being a story about my case and becomes something else.

Either the foreclosure extinguished the debt — in which case the 1098 is a false information return filed with the federal government by a regulated servicer. Or the debt was never extinguished — in which case the trustee's deed transferred nothing, the foreclosure was void, the eviction was wrongful, and I still own the house. Both cannot be true. One of them has to give. Neither has.

The 1098 is the thing no cover story survives. It is not my argument. It is not my interpretation. It is the servicer's own sworn statement to the IRS, arriving every January, year after year, on pre-printed federal forms. It is a receipt from the machine itself, confirming that the machine is still running on a loan a California judge already flagged as built on forgery.

I have kept every one of them. They are the paper trail of a system that cannot stop running because stopping would require admitting what the 1098 already says: the loan is still an active asset on somebody's books. Whose books? On what authority? Serviced for which investor? Paid from which account? Under what power? Those are the questions an accounting claim is made for. Those are the questions the closed trust cannot answer without unraveling. Those are the questions nobody has been willing to put to the servicer under oath. So the 1098 sits in the file. Every year, another one. Another receipt. Another admission in writing, filed under federal penalty, that the machine is still running.

You wanted proof it was designed this way? Here it is. On IRS letterhead. Signed by Shellpoint.

What This Means

When enforcement no longer requires proof of ownership, consent stops being the foundation of the transaction. It becomes decoration. Once courts allowed foreclosure without proof of loss, standing became cosmetic, due process became procedural, and property became inventory.

Robo-signing, backdated assignments, lost note affidavits, boilerplate objections, discovery obstruction — none of these are aberrations. They are the administrative residue of a system that reorganized itself around fraud rather than stopping it.

I put the 1098 in front of a federal court. In May 2025, I filed a Rule 59(e) motion in the Southern District of California asking the court to alter or amend a dismissal in my case against Mark McCloskey and The Ryan Firm — the attorneys who had spent years defending the forged documents. I attached two additional forged Substitutions of Trustee from North Carolina and South Carolina, both bearing McCloskey's signature and Bradshaw's forged notary stamp, recorded in states where neither of them had any business being.

The Ryan Firm's opposition did not deny the 1098 was real, or the North Carolina document, or the South Carolina document. It did not explain how Shellpoint, a mortgage servicer, came to report $490,371.69 in outstanding principal on a property that had already been foreclosed, on a loan whose underlying documents had been found forged. It did none of those things, because doing any of them would have required engaging with the substance. Instead, the opposition called the evidence "entirely speculative" and "irrelevant," cited the procedural rule that a motion to dismiss tests only the sufficiency of the complaint and not the evidence, and moved on.

Eleven lines. That was their entire response to a federal information return issued in my name on a loan they were defending as valid.

The court denied my motion. The 1098 went back in the file. The machine kept running. Psychotherapist Karin Huffer named what this does to people: *legal abuse syndrome.* The trauma of being unheard, dismissed, and methodically exhausted inside a system that was never designed to hear you. This is what containment looks like from inside the courtroom. Not an argument. A shrug.

Outcome subject to ongoing appeal in the Ninth Circuit, Case No. 25-7322. The defendants filed their answering brief on April 13, 2026. I read it carefully. It is, in its own way, the most useful document in the file.

Not because it defeats my argument. Because it explains the architecture.

They opened not with a legal argument but with a description of my motives. They called my complaints to the State Bar, the Department of Justice, and local police a campaign of retribution. They did not open with a denial of the forgery findings. They did not open with a defense of the documents. They opened by explaining why I shouldn't be taken seriously. After seven years of litigation, that was apparently the strongest ground they had.

The brief devotes considerable space to a doctrine I had never seen named so plainly. Citing *Kimbro v. Kimbro from 1926* and *Osterberg v. Osterberg from 1945,* the defendants argue that a notary acknowledgment is "merely evidentiary in character, not a requirement" — that the absence of a valid notary signature cannot void a document, cannot affect the authority of the trustee, and cannot give a borrower standing to challenge the instrument. They state, without apparent concern, that there is no case in California where a document was found void due only to a forged notary signature. They are probably right. That is not a concession. That is the mechanism.

Once a forged substitution of trustee is recorded, Civil Code § 2934a creates a conclusive presumption of the substituted trustee's authority to act. The forgery launders itself on recording. The county stamp does the work the real signature was supposed to do. After that, the doctrine says: too late. The instrument is presumed valid. Standing to challenge it belongs to the beneficiary, not the borrower — and the beneficiary has already been paid.

This is the exit ramp the system built for itself, written into law before the MBS machine existed, now doing work its authors never imagined. The forgery is not a defect that breaks the chain. It is a defect the chain was designed to survive.

The second doctrine in the brief is the one that protects the attorneys. California Civil Code § 47(b) creates an absolute litigation privilege for communications made in judicial proceedings. The defendants' brief quotes *Morales v. Coop. of Am. Physicians* directly: the privilege is absolute, "even if the result is inequitable." Any doubt as to whether it applies is resolved in favor of applying it. The only tort claim that can arise from litigation conduct, under California Supreme Court precedent the brief cites, is malicious prosecution. Everything else is covered. An attorney who files a document in court — even a document the court has already found to rest on forged instruments — cannot be held liable for filing it. The privilege does not ask whether the document is legitimate. It asks only whether the filing was made in a judicial proceeding. It was. That is enough.

Three separate legal doctrines. The closed trust structure prevents legitimate post-closing assignment, making forgery necessary to proceed. The recorded instrument presumption launders the forgery on filing, stripping the borrower of standing to challenge it. The litigation privilege protects every attorney who deploys the forged instrument in court. Each doctrine does one job. Together they form a complete circuit — from origination to foreclosure to courtroom — with no point at which accountability can enter.

The defendants wrote this in a federal appellate response, under their names, filed in the public record. They did not describe it as a problem. They described it as the law. They are not wrong. That is the part that should stay with you.

Documented. Repeatable. Scalable.

CHAPTER 39
EPILOGUE

Still at the Helm

I didn't set out to write this book. I set out to save my home. I just refused to disappear. And once you see the system clearly, holding course isn't courage. It's navigation. Because once the architecture is visible, the question stops being how did this happen to me and becomes: how many times has this already happened — and to whom?

The prologue opened with me at eleven, steering a ship I had no business commanding. The epilogue closes with me at 65, still steering — through waters I never expected to navigate. The book covers seven years. The fight is now in its ninth.

The Case Isn't Over

I lost the house. The foreclosure went through. The stipulation was signed in 2020. The tenant left. U.S. Bank has title. But they haven't been able to sell it. Not because a court stopped them. Not because the law required it. Because every time they try, I send what I've come to think of as my "fuck you letters" — formal notices explaining, in exquisite legal detail, that proceeding with a sale based on forged documents will make them personally liable as defendants in the federal case. I've sent the evidence. The forged signatures. The notary testimony. The expert reports. The criminal complaints on file with the FBI and the San Diego District Attorney. And every time, they stop. Not justice. But something.

As of April 2026, my appeal is pending before the California Court of Appeal, Fourth Appellate District. Most recently the property was listed by Jason Lipovsky — the realtor who signed documents as U.S. Bank, who testified under oath he was authorized when he wasn't, who appeared in court claiming authority he couldn't prove.

The House

I haven't lived in the house since April 2019. The house has sat empty for almost five years. I know what's happening inside only from the real estate listing photos: the house has been stripped. The pellet stove gone. The wood-burning fireplace ripped out. Even the benches from the sauna. Who steals sauna benches? People who know no one is watching. People who know the house is in limbo and nobody is coming. Stupid, petty theft — but theft nonetheless. And I can't go near it to stop them, because if I step foot on my own property, I'll be arrested for trespassing.

Then on February 16, 2026, something shifted. Zillow returned the listing to me. The property Jason Lipovsky had been controlling for two years is no longer his to manage. The listing now shows my name. I don't own the house. Title is still with U.S. Bank. I can't sell it. But I can control the listing. There is a photograph of a sculpture I made for my driveway entrance — a little head peeking out of a box with one hand showing, genuinely unsettling. I used to keep a spotlight on it at night. There is a sign underneath that reads: House Not For Sale. House Is In Litigation. (Appendix O). And Lipovsky is out.

I feel lighter. Something worked. It's a strange feeling after years of pressure — like walking out of a storm and not trusting the quiet. I still expect the next hit. I just don't see it yet.

The Agencies

On February 17, 2026, I finally received a response from the San Diego District Attorney's Real Estate Fraud Unit. They'd had my case since 2022, Case #2022RE0346. Their letter began: "We're sorry that you had to go through this ordeal, but glad that the civil judge awarded you the value of the property due to the bank's misconduct."

The judge awarded me Cancellation of Instruments, offset to net zero. I got nothing. I lost the house. U.S. Bank has title. They didn't even read my case.

Six weeks after I responded with additional documentation, another door closed. They couldn't prove charges beyond a reasonable doubt. The evidence was outside the state. Finding the individual who committed the offenses would be difficult. That is not to suggest that this office condones any of the conduct described. Case closed. Never mind that the forgeries spanned three states. That I'd documented a pattern across multiple properties. The crime wasn't where the signature was forged. The crime was using forged documents to foreclose on a house sitting fifteen miles from their office. The system protects itself.

The Federal Case

My federal case against Mark McCloskey and the Ryan Firm is pending at the Appeals Court. McCloskey allegedly signed the substitution of trustee in front of Agnes Bradshaw — the Colorado notary who testified under oath she never notarized his signature, and never signed the document herself. The Ryan Firm couldn't find McCloskey when I tried to subpoena him for trial. When I started looking, it took ten minutes to get him on the phone. So I sued him, and added the Ryan Firm and each of their attorneys individually as defendants after they stepped in to defend him. I've filed my opening brief. They filed a response. I'm filing a reply. Now we wait.

The state court appeal could reverse Judge Bacal's ruling and send it back for a new trial. Bacal has already said she'll comply with whatever the appellate court decides. So there's still a chance. Not a guarantee. Not even a probability. Just a chance. And that's enough to keep going.

What I Know

I don't know how this ends. I know what the law says. I know what the evidence proves. I know the courts acknowledged forgery and ruled for the bank anyway. I also know I haven't stopped fighting — not because I think I'll win, but because silence feels like complicity. Because exposure matters even when correction doesn't follow. Because someone needs to document what happens when you prove the system is broken and the system shrugs. Because others need to know they should fight their foreclosures too.

The banks win when people give up, when homeowners believe the system is too big, too complex, too rigged to challenge. The banks lose when people document everything, subpoena notaries, demand original wet-ink signatures, and refuse to disappear quietly.

The Art Came Back

I didn't set out to become a litigator. I came to America to make art. To build things. To live quietly in the mountains and paint horses that don't ask permission to move forward. The system had other plans. To move forward — whether I did or not.

At first painting was survival — a way to stay intact while the courtroom tried to grind me down. Force of Will came during the darkest stretch — a black horse surging through storm water, hooves churning, mane wild. Not rage. Resolve. Then, briefly, when a ruling looked like it might go my way, something broke open. Color exploded. Joy returned.

I'm writing now too. I didn't know I could do this. It's not just documentation anymore. It's creation. Not a comfortable one — this story is not comfortable. But mine. You can take my house. You can ignore my evidence. You can expunge my lis pendens and try to sell the property while my appeal is pending. But you cannot take my ability to see clearly, to document accurately, and to create beauty in defiance of systems designed to erase me. That part is mine.

This Book

This book was not written to win any awards for elegant prose. It was written because the story needed to exist in public.

It is not legal advice. It's not a manual for winning. It's a manual for not disappearing. For staying visible when the process is designed to exhaust you into silence. For learning the language of the law so precisely that ignorance can no longer be used as a weapon against you. For turning survival into competence, and competence into resistance.

If you're reading this because your modification was denied after you followed instructions to stop paying — you're not alone. If you're reading this because you found forged signatures on your foreclosure documents and no one will help you — you're not crazy. If you're reading this because you proved fraud in court and the judge ruled for the bank anyway — you're not imagining it. The system is working exactly as designed. And the only thing that disrupts it is people who refuse to go quietly.

Still at the Helm

At eleven, my father didn't teach me to avoid storms. He taught me to read them. I've been reading the water ever since.

This case isn't over. The appeal is pending. The evidence is on the record. And the record doesn't expire. Somewhere between a courtroom in San Diego and a county recorder's office full of forged signatures, this stopped being just my story. Seventy-five documented forgeries across multiple counties. A judge's own words — "compelling and uncontroverted" — preserved in a transcript that isn't going anywhere. A pattern so clear that the only reason it hasn't been prosecuted is that no one with authority has been forced to look at it long enough. That's starting to change. Not because the system decided to look — but because I refused to look away.

What's documented here isn't a closed chapter in American housing policy. It's an open wound. The trusts are still closed. The documents are still forged. The system that required fabricated signatures to function in 2008 has never been dismantled — it was settled, fined, and allowed to continue. History doesn't get made by the people who win. It gets made by the people who refuse to let the record be sealed.

The strangest part is what it gave me. A stabbing cured my fear of public speaking. Seven years of litigation taught me to read a room, a statute, and a lie — in that order. The difficult chapters turned out to be the useful ones. Bullshit doesn't survive proximity to real loss. It just moves out of the way.

Seven years at a desk also gave me a pimple on my butt. Nobody puts that in memoirs. Consider it a public service.

For the record, I'm very much alive, in excellent spirits, and not suicidal. If that changes unexpectedly — it wasn't me. Check the documents.

GLOSSARY OF LEGAL TERMS

This glossary defines terms as they function in my case and in foreclosure litigation generally. These are not comprehensive legal definitions—they're working explanations for readers navigating this book.

Assignment of Deed of Trust — A document that transfers ownership of a mortgage (or deed of trust) from one party to another. In theory, this is how banks sell mortgages to investors or transfer them between servicers. In practice, assignments are often fabricated after the fact to create the appearance of a valid chain of title.

Automatic Stay — When you file for bankruptcy, all collection activity must immediately stop. This is the "automatic stay"—creditors can't call you, sue you, garnish wages, or foreclose. They must ask the bankruptcy court for permission first by filing a motion for relief from stay. The stay is supposed to give debtors breathing room.

Bankruptcy Chapter 7 — Liquidation bankruptcy. The trustee sells your non-exempt assets to pay creditors, and most unsecured debts are discharged. If you have no assets (a "no-asset case"), there's nothing to sell and creditors get nothing. Most consumer bankruptcies are Chapter 7. I filed Chapter 7 to stop foreclosure and force the bank to prove they owned my mortgage.

Beneficiary — In a deed of trust (the mortgage equivalent used in California and other states), the beneficiary is the lender—the party who loaned you money and has the right to foreclose if you don't pay. In securitized mortgages, the beneficiary is supposed to be the trust that holds the loan.

Beneficial Interest — The legal right to collect payments on a loan and to foreclose if those payments stop. In a properly documented mortgage, it belongs to whoever holds the note. In a securitized mortgage, it belongs to a closed trust — which means it belongs to no one anyone can name.

Chain of Title — The documented history of ownership transfers for a property or a mortgage. A valid chain of title shows an unbroken line from the original lender to the current owner. If any link is missing or forged, the chain is broken and the current claimant may not have legal standing to foreclose.

Clean Hands Doctrine — An equitable principle that says a party seeking relief from the court must not have acted unfairly or dishonestly in the matter at issue. If you come to court with "unclean hands," the court can deny your claim regardless of its merit. Apparently clean hands are only checked on one side of the courtroom.

Color of Law — Action that looks legal because it's performed by people in robes inside buildings with marble floors, but isn't actually authorized by any statute when you read the statute carefully.

Deed of Trust — California's version of a mortgage. You (the borrower/trustor) give a deed to a neutral third party (the trustee), who holds it on behalf of the lender (the beneficiary). If you default, the trustee can sell the property without going to court—this is called non-judicial foreclosure.

Discovery — The pre-trial process where parties exchange evidence. You can request documents, ask written questions (interrogatories), and take depositions (recorded testimony under oath). Banks routinely obstruct discovery by claiming documents are "lost" or protected by attorney-client privilege.

Endorsement (of a Note) — A signature on the back of a promissory note transferring ownership to another party—like endorsing a check. For a mortgage to be enforceable, the note must be endorsed to the party trying to foreclose. My note was never properly endorsed. The bank claimed to have it but couldn't produce a valid endorsement chain.

Equitable Remedy — A court-ordered solution based on fairness rather than strict legal rules. Sounds reasonable until you see it work. Judge Bacal granted me Cancellation of Instruments — an equitable remedy — but didn't specify which instruments. An equitable remedy that changes nothing is a footnote dressed up as justice. A judge who grants one and then says on the record she can't remember ever granting one before has admitted two things at once: the facts left her no other option, and the machinery she works inside doesn't usually let the facts get that far.

Foreclosure Mill — A law firm whose entire business model is processing foreclosures at industrial scale for mortgage servicers. Volume over accuracy. Templates over advocacy. The same handful of motions filed against thousands of homeowners who can't afford to fight back.

Forgery — Creating or altering a document with intent to defraud. In foreclosure cases, forgery usually involves fabricating assignments, forging notary signatures, or backdating documents to create a false chain of title.

Hearsay — An out-of-court statement offered to prove the truth of what it asserts. Generally inadmissible, except for the seventeen exceptions that swallow the rule. When a homeowner offers a document, it's hearsay. When a bank offers the same kind of document, it's a business record.

Judicial Notice — A court's acceptance of certain facts as true without requiring formal proof—usually public records or widely known facts.

Lis Pendens — Latin for "suit pending." A lis pendens is a public notice recorded against a property's title warning that the property is subject to litigation. It clouds the title and prevents the property from being sold until the lawsuit is resolved.

Meeting of the Minds — The contract law principle that a binding agreement requires both parties to share the same understanding of what they're agreeing to. When you signed a mortgage believing you were borrowing money from a bank that expected to be paid back, and the bank was originating a unit of inventory for a securitized trust, betting on default, and collecting insurance when you stopped paying — there was no meeting of the minds.

MERS (Mortgage Electronic Registration Systems) — A private database created by banks in the 1990s to track mortgages electronically without recording assignments at county recorders' offices. MERS claims to act as "nominee" for lenders, holding legal title while the lender keeps the beneficial interest. In practice, MERS has no financial interest in the loans and no authority to foreclose or assign mortgages. Courts have ruled both ways on whether MERS has standing.

Mootness — A legal doctrine that says courts won't decide issues that are no longer "live"—where a ruling would have no practical effect. In my case, the appellate court ruled my appeal was "moot" because the property had already been foreclosed at a trustee's sale—even though I was still living in the house, still fighting the foreclosure, and the sale had never been finalized.

Motion in Limine — A pre-trial motion asking the court to exclude certain evidence before the jury hears it. Used by defense counsel to keep the most damaging facts out of the courtroom on procedural grounds.

Motion for Relief from Stay — In bankruptcy, a secured creditor (like a mortgage holder) files this motion asking the court to lift the automatic stay so they can foreclose. To win, they must show either: (1) they're not adequately protected (you're not making payments and the property is losing value), or (2) you have no equity in the property and it's not necessary for reorganization.

Nominee — A party who holds legal title to something on behalf of someone else, without holding any beneficial interest in it. MERS calls itself a nominee. Nominees are not supposed to exercise rights of ownership, like foreclosing on people's homes. MERS does it anyway.

Notice of Default (NOD) — The first formal step in California's non-judicial foreclosure process. The lender records a Notice of Default with the county, notifying you that you're behind on payments and have 90 days to cure the default before they can proceed to foreclosure sale.

Notary Public — An official authorized by the state to witness signatures and verify identities. Notaries keep journals documenting every notarization. By law title transfer documents must be notarized to be recorded at the County Recorder's Office.

Power of Sale — A clause in a deed of trust that lets the lender, or a substituted trustee, sell the property without going to court if the borrower defaults. In California, this is the entire mechanism of nonjudicial foreclosure: no judge, no jury, no evidence, no testimony. An administrative process and a sale on the courthouse steps.

Proof of Claim — In bankruptcy, a form that creditors file to register their claims and participate in distribution of the estate. The 2017 amendments to Bankruptcy Rule 3002 require secured creditors to file a proof of claim "for the claim or interest to be allowed." The bank in my case didn't file one.

Pro Se / In Pro Per — Representing yourself in court without an attorney. "Pro se" is Latin for "for oneself." Courts claim to hold pro se litigants to the same standards as lawyers, but in practice, judges often dismiss pro se arguments as incompetent or procedurally defective even when the substance is correct.

Promissory Note —The IOU—the document where you promise to repay the loan. The note is separate from the mortgage/deed of trust. Whoever holds the note has the right to collect payment. Whoever holds the mortgage has the right to foreclose if you don't pay. Under the law, the mortgage follows the note—you can't split them. In securitized mortgages, banks often can't produce the original note or prove valid endorsement.

Res Judicata — Latin for "a matter judged." Once a court has ruled on an issue, you can't relitigate the same issue in another court—it's considered settled. Banks use res judicata to prevent borrowers from raising forgery or standing issues in multiple cases, even when new evidence emerges.

Robo-signing — A cute name for felony-scale document fraud. Mortgage industry employees signed thousands of foreclosure documents per day without reading them, and often without legal authority to sign at all. Notary stamps were applied with the same care. Banks called it a paperwork problem. Homeowners called it the reason they lost their houses. The 2012 National Mortgage Settlement called it $25 billion. Nobody called it a crime.

Securitization — The process of pooling mortgages and selling them to investors as mortgage-backed securities (MBS). Your mortgage gets bundled with thousands of others, transferred to a trust, and sliced into bonds. In theory, this is documented through proper assignments and endorsements. Securitization broke the chain of title for millions of mortgages.

Standing — The legal right to bring a lawsuit. A party must show both that it owns the claim and that it was actually injured by the conduct it's suing about. To foreclose, a bank must prove it holds the mortgage and note through the original documents or a valid chain of assignments, and that it suffered a real loss when the borrower defaulted. Without both, it lacks standing and the case should be dismissed. In theory, a bedrock constitutional principle. In foreclosure cases, courts let entities with no documentable injury foreclose on borrowers anyway, as long as the paperwork looks plausible.

Statute of Limitations — Statute of Limitations — The deadline for bringing a lawsuit. In California, the statute of limitations for fraud is three years, but it does not begin to run until the fraud is discovered or reasonably should have been discovered. For written contracts, it is four years. Banks argued I waited too long to challenge the foreclosure — even though the forgery wasn't discoverable until I subpoenaed the notaries. The discovery rule exists precisely for this situation. Courts rarely apply it in foreclosure cases. A forged document is void ab initio — legally equivalent to blank paper from the moment of creation. California courts have held that a void instrument can be challenged at any time, with no statute of limitations. The banks' limitations arguments assume the forged documents were valid instruments subject to ratification. They were not.

Stipulation — An agreement between parties in a lawsuit.

Substitution of Trustee — In a deed of trust, the trustee is the neutral party who holds title and can conduct foreclosure sales. The lender can replace the trustee by recording a Substitution of Trustee. This is often the first step before foreclosure—the bank substitutes in a new trustee (usually a foreclosure mill law firm) who will do the actual sale.

Summary Judgment — A ruling without a trial. If there are no disputed facts, the judge can decide the case based on written arguments alone. Banks routinely seek summary judgment in foreclosure cases, arguing the facts are simple: you borrowed money, you didn't pay, they can foreclose. Borrowers lose at summary judgment because judges won't consider evidence of forgery or standing issues—they rule on procedure instead.

Trustee (in Bankruptcy) — An official appointed to manage your bankruptcy case. In Chapter 7, the trustee's job is to collect and sell your non-exempt assets to pay creditors. In a no-asset case, the trustee reviews your paperwork, conducts a meeting of creditors, and closes the case. The trustee doesn't represent you—they represent the bankruptcy estate.

Trustee's Deed Upon Sale — The document recorded after a nonjudicial foreclosure sale that transfers title from the former homeowner to whoever bought the property at auction. Generated by the same trustee who conducted the sale, recorded by the same county that recorded the original assignments, and treated by everyone downstream as conclusive proof of ownership.

Unlawful Detainer (UD) — California's eviction proceeding. After foreclosure, the new owner (usually the bank) files an unlawful detainer action to evict the former homeowner. UD cases are fast—you typically have five days to respond.

Vexatious Litigant — A legal designation for someone who files repetitive, frivolous lawsuits. Once declared vexatious, you need court permission to file any new case. It's a tool to silence pro se litigants who refuse to give up. Banks threatened to have me declared vexatious because I kept filing appeals and motions.

A Note on the Appendices

The documents that prove what happened to my home exist. They are not summaries or interpretations—they are certified records, court transcripts, state government certifications, and official correspondence. Where I cite them in the text, they are real.

In the interest of keeping this book readable, I have included only the most essential documents in print: the Assignment of Deed of Trust, the Substitution of Trustee, and the signature comparisons that form the core of the forgery evidence. These appear in the chapters where they are most relevant.

The complete appendix package—all court transcripts, judicial orders, discovery records, institutional responses, state certifications, and supporting documentation—is available as a free PDF download at:

www.leenadesign.com/mybook-pdf

The appendices are organized to match the references in this book. If a chapter directs you to Appendix D, you will find it there in full, with context.

Nothing has been redacted. Nothing has been softened. If you want to verify what you've read, you can. The evidence speaks for itself. It always has.

Appendix B — Substitution of Trustee
Appendix C — Assignment of Deed of Trust and
Signature Comparisons

If You're Going to Fight This

Most people shouldn't. That's not discouragement. It's reality.

This system is complex by design. It rewards precision, timing, and persistence—and it punishes mistakes. Small ones become permanent ones.

This book explains what happened. Fighting it is something else.

If you decide to go further—if you want to understand how to:

- pull and analyze your complete chain of title

- identify forged or defective documents
- use discovery to force answers onto the record
- build a case that can survive inside the system

I've laid that out separately.
David vs. Goliath: How to Fight the Mortgage Machine
This is not theory. It's the process I learned—mostly the hard way.
You can find it here: www.davidvgoliathcourse.com

If you do this, do it carefully.
The system doesn't correct your mistakes.

www.ingramcontent.com/pod-product-compliance
Lightning Source LLC
LaVergne TN
LVHW091027080826
845145LV00002B/377